FORMULA ONE 2022

Published in 2022 by Welbeck

An Imprint of Welbeck Non-Fiction Limited, part of Welbeck Publishing Group.

Based in London and Sydney.

www.welbeckpublishing.com

A CIP catalogue record for this book is available from the British Library

ISBN 9781787399112

Editor: Ross Hamilton
Design: Luke Griffin, Russell Knowles
Picture Research: Paul Langan
Production: Rachel Burgess

Printed in the United Kingdom

10 9 8 7 6 5 4 3 2 1

Above: Lewis Hamilton and Max Verstappen leave the other 18 drivers in their spray as they power away in last year's race at Imola.

FORMULA ONE 2022

TEAMS | DRIVERS | TRACKS | RECORDS

BRUCE JONES

WELBECK

⟫ CONTENTS

Right: Max Verstappen celebrates his maiden World Championship victory after the climactic Abu Dhabi GP.

A splash of colour as cars from Ferrari, McLaren, Williams Alfa Romeo and Red Bull sit in parc ferme at last year's British GP at Silverstone.

» ANALYSIS OF THE 2022 SEASON

Any season with a new set of technical regulations presents the possibility of the World Championship running to a new order. This year, the cars will have a new shape that offers more chance of overtaking. Expect Mercedes and Red Bull Racing still to be at the front, but perhaps McLaren, Ferrari or another team will take a step up to join them.

The new technical regulations (*see* Talking Point on page 58) ought to shake the F1 pot, as major changes always do. Yet, unlike the 1960s, 1970s and 1980s when designers had fewer parameters restricting their genius, quantum leaps are not expected. The top teams will likely be the top teams again, but those that diverted the attention of their designers to the new-shaped cars earlier last year, perhaps to the detriment of their 2021 challenge, ought to have found some advantage to help ease their teams up the order.

Red Bull Racing is sticking with its line-up of Max Verstappen and Sergio Perez and will continue to be focused on the Dutchman. It knows though that if it's serious about winning the constructors' title

for the first time since 2013, it will need to offer support to Perez too.

Lewis Hamilton stays on for a 10th season with Mercedes and will be trying again to land a record eighth F1 title. He will face a different situation, though, as he has a new team-mate in George Russell, a driver thought capable of giving him his first challenge from within the camp since Nico Rosberg rose up and toppled him in 2016. It will be interesting to watch the intra-team dynamics.

Pressure on Ferrari to find form is growing by the year after its poor showing in 2020 when it ranked sixth. Last year was better, but the *tifosi* won't be happy if British teams continue to better their beloved red cars. In Charles Leclerc and Carlos Sainz Jr, it has

a duo capable of winning if their machinery is competitive, with the Spaniard notably worthy of taking a first victory.

Daniel Ricciardo returned McLaren to winning ways last year, but the team watched its form drop away and will be praying that its first car built to this year's new rules will offer him and Lando Norris the chance to get back up onto the podium again.

Alpine appeared to be gathering form through the course of last year as Fernando Alonso got back up to speed after his sojourn in the World Endurance Championship, and Esteban Ocon famously gave the team its first win in years. However, that form evaporated and questions remain over whether it will be at the front of the midfield this year or further back.

Scuderia AlphaTauri's form has improved year on year and Pierre Gasly continues to be one of F1's unheralded stars, especially in qualifying. His Japanese sidekick, Yuki Tsunoda, can also be quick and the question will be how he settles down in 2022 with a year's F1 experience under his belt.

Last year was notable for the return of the Aston Martin name to F1 for the first time since 1960. However, despite looking striking in their metallic green livery, the cars were not what owner Lawrence

Stroll would have wanted, the team dropping from its 2020 ranking of fourth to eighth. There were flashes of glory courtesy of Sebastian Vettel, but disappointments too. He and Lance Stroll will be praying that investment in the team – with a huge expansion of its Silverstone base – will turn into consistently good results.

Williams has one major change as it gears up to its second season under new ownership: it has lost George Russell to Mercedes. This year, Nicholas Latifi will be partnered by a driver back from a year in the F1 wilderness, as Alex Albon returns after a year racing in the DTM after being dropped by Red Bull Racing.

Alfa Romeo has completely revamped its driver line-up. Kimi Raikkonen retired after stretching his record tally of F1 starts to 352 grands prix, while Antonio Giovinazzi has been dropped to make way for China's first F1 racer, Guanyu Zhou. The team will be led by Valtteri Bottas, freed from Mercedes to race again for Frederic Vasseur who was his team chief on his way up to F1.

Haas F1 is sticking by last year's rookies Mick Schumacher and Nikita Mazepin. A year of F1 experience will have helped them, but both would undeniably have improved more had they had an experienced driver from whom to learn.

MERCEDES-AMG PETRONAS

Mercedes won an eighth consecutive constructors' title in 2021, though in notably less dominant fashion than in years past. However, its season-long battle with Red Bull Racing will have honed its skills further and made it even more ready to win again in 2022.

Lewis Hamilton had a real fight on his hands last year against Red Bull Racing, but the tables might have turned with the new technical rules.

Those with long memories will recall Mercedes' first foray into F1. This was in the mid-1950s when F1 was still finding its feet. And the impact was instant, with victory first time, at the French GP, for Juan Manuel Fangio, and this forced their rivals to raise their game. No one should have been surprised. Mercedes had taken racing to new heights in its previous spell on the grand prix scene before World War Two and the World Championship.

However, after 1¾ seasons in F1, with two titles for Fangio, it was over, Mercedes withdrawing following the horrendous death tally of spectators after one of Mercedes' works cars flew off the track at the 1955 Le Mans 24 Hours.

The Mercedes name didn't hit F1 again, as a team at least, until 2010. The manufacturer had supplied engines to F1 teams from 1994, first with Sauber and then, most successfully, with McLaren as Mika Häkkinen landed the 1998 and 1999 drivers' titles. However, returning in its own right in 2010 was different and even the returning Michael Schumacher couldn't take on the dominant team of the day: Red Bull Racing. Mercedes didn't start afresh and build its own team. Instead, it saved time and money by lending its name to the team that had started life as BAR in 1999, changed its

KEY PERSONNEL & 2021 ROUND-UP

ANDREW SHOVLIN

The race engineer who gets to instruct Lewis Hamilton about race strategy graduated with a PhD in vehicle dynamics from Leeds University in 1998 and went straight into F1 with BAR in 1999. Once there, Andrew rose through the ranks to be a race engineer in the now Brawn team's year of years, 2009 when their car found a technical loophole and Jenson Button blitzed the opposition. When the team morphed into Mercedes in 2010, he performed the same role for Michael Schumacher when he became trackside engineering director.

FIGHTING BACK FROM A MID-SEASON SLUMP

A one-three finish at the opening race might have heralded another season of winning at will, but 2021 was different as not all the teams wanted to focus their development budget on the current car, as many had one eye focused on the all-new 2022 car. Mercedes was one such team and Red Bull Racing's mid-season advance was largely due to that. But then its car suited the faster circuits and it wrapped up the constructors' title but not the drivers'.

2021 DRIVERS & RESULTS

Driver	Nationality	Races	Wins	Pts	Pos
Lewis Hamilton	British	22	8	387.5	2nd
Valtteri Bottas	Finnish	22	1	226	3rd

FOR THE RECORD

Country of origin:	**England**
Team base:	**Brackley, England**
Telephone:	**(44) 01280 844000**
Website:	**www.mercedes-amg-f1.com**
Active in Formula One:	
	As BAR 1999-2005, Honda Racing 2006-08, Brawn GP 2009, Mercedes 2010 on
Grands Prix contested:	**425**
Wins:	**124**
Pole positions:	**136**
Fastest laps:	**94**

name to Honda Racing in 2006 – with Button taking an unlikely win in the 2006 Hungarian GP – and then to Brawn GP at the start of 2009 after Honda pulled out.

Then, with largely the same personnel who found a technical advantage in 2009 and were surprise world champions, the team was rebadged as Mercedes for 2010 and its cars painted silver to echo the two previous generations of silver arrows. Claiming a fifth-sixth finish in the season-opener in Bahrain was a good start and a pair of early-season third places scored by Nico Rosberg helped the team to rank fourth behind Red Bull, McLaren and Ferrari. There were no quantum leaps in performance, but Rosberg, rather than seven-time world champion Michael Schumacher, landed the first win as Mercedes at the 2012 Chinese GP. It signalled a changing of the guard.

But the driver who would propel the third generation silver arrows into sure-fire winners was Lewis Hamilton who arrived in place of Schumacher for 2013 and outscored Rosberg to help Mercedes rank second. He then began a purple patch that lasts to this day as he won the 2014 world title in a year in which he landed 11 of the incredible 16 wins from 19 starts achieved by the team. Hamilton added the next one too, when Mercedes again won 16 from 19, before Rosberg grabbed the 2016 title through sheer determination to always operate at 100% as he and Hamilton won all but two of the 21 races.

However, Rosberg then shocked the team by retiring and this opened the door at the 11th hour for Valtteri Bottas to join for 2017. For five years he has very much been kept in the supporting role as Hamilton added the next four titles and the Mercedes road show flattened all before it. Not even Ferrari in its Schumacher years could match seven titles in a row, with the supporting constructors' titles added for good measure.

Technical director Paddy Lowe joined from McLaren to become technical director in 2013 and he helped the team continue in its sweet spot under three-time F1 champion Niki Lauda and Toto Wolff who took over the team reins

THE TEAM

Head of Mercedes-Benz Motorsport:	**Toto Wolff**
Technical director:	**James Allison**
MD, Mercedes-AMG High Performance powertrains:	**Hywel Thomas**
Director of digital engineering:	**Geoff Willis**
Technology director:	**Mike Elliott**
Engineering director:	**John Owen**
Performance director:	**Loic Serra**
Sporting director:	**Ron Meadows**
Chief race engineer:	**Andrew Shovlin**
Chief track engineer:	**Simon Cole**
Test driver:	**Stoffel Vandoorne**
Chassis:	**Mercedes F1 W13**
Engine:	**Mercedes V6**
Tyres:	**Pirelli**

after Brawn's departure. After Lowe was coaxed to Williams, James Allison took the top technical post in 2017 and he remains to this day, having spent most of last year with considerable focus on the new car for the 2022 regulations.

Hamilton goes over the data with principal Toto Wolff as they seek to identify any advantage.

"We have been in a constructive dialogue with the FIA and Formula 1 to create clarity for the future so that all competitors know the rules under which they are racing and how they will be enforced."

Toto Wolff

LEWIS HAMILTON

There is a new playing field for 2022 as F1's new technical rules are embraced. Expect Mercedes to be right on the pace, which is something that will be essential if Lewis is to be able to take aim at a record eighth F1 title.

Lewis not only has to take on Verstappen in 2022 but a new team-mate as well: Russell.

From prodigy in radio-controlled car racing via a searing career in kart racing to F1 World Champion, Lewis has always made it look so easy, with titles always seeming to be a matter of when rather than if.

His first karting title came when he won the British cadet title and further success encouraged him to ask McLaren chief Ron Dennis at an awards dinner whether he might back his career. Famously, Dennis did, and this not only eased the financial strain but meant Lewis was being watched.

After winning the World Kart Cup and European Formula A series in 2000, Lewis finished third in the British series of Formula Renault in 2002, then won it in 2003.

Lewis scorched to 15 wins for ASM to claim the 2005 Formula 3 title by a huge margin. GP2 was next and five wins helped Lewis pip Nelson Piquet Jr to the crown.

McLaren offered him his F1 break and Lewis was on the pace from the very first race. A winner by the sixth round, he looked to be heading for the title, but was pipped by Ferrari's Kimi Raikkonen, ending up second with team-mate Fernando Alonso.

At the second time of asking, Lewis got the job done, recovering from a tricky situation to claim a position on the final lap of the year to deny Felipe Massa.

Try as he might, he had no answer to Brawn GP in 2009 and then Red Bull Racing for the next four years. But a move to Mercedes in 2013 gave Lewis his second title in 2014 and his third in 2015. Beaten by team-mate Nico Rosberg in 2016, Lewis then rattled off four titles in a row, smashing records by going past 100 F1 wins.

BATTLING FROM START TO FINISH

There have been several years in Lewis' remarkable run to F1 titles where he doesn't appear to have had to break sweat, his Mercedes the best in the field and his performance better than that of his team-mate, firstly Nico Rosberg and then Valtteri Bottas. Last season was definitely not one of those, as Red Bull Racing was Mercedes' equal and, although he took three wins and a second from the first four rounds, it was clear from the off that he had a race on his hands. Some circuits suited Red Bull, others suited Mercedes, and so there was a novel scenario as Lewis sometimes had to rely on advice from the pitwall as much as his own speed and gut instinct. Sometimes, this wasn't enough, and Max Verstappen was able to beat him. This is why he made such a robust move to try to take the lead at the start of the British GP, firing Verstappen off, and why Verstappen didn't back out of it at Monza.

TRACK NOTES

Nationality:	**BRITISH**
Born:	**7 JANUARY 1985,**
	STEVENAGE, ENGLAND
Website:	**www.lewishamilton.com**
Teams:	**McLAREN 2007-12,**
	MERCEDES 2013-22

CAREER RECORD

First Grand Prix: **2007 AUSTRALIAN GP**

Grand Prix starts: **288**

Grand Prix wins: **103**
2007 Canadian GP, United States GP, Hungarian GP, Japanese GP, 2008 Australian GP, Monaco GP, British GP, German GP, Chinese GP, 2009 Hungarian GP, Singapore GP, 2010 Turkish GP, Canadian GP, Belgian GP, 2011 Chinese GP, German GP, Abu Dhabi GP, 2012 Canadian GP, Hungarian GP, Italian GP, United States GP, 2013 Hungarian GP, 2014 Malaysian GP, Bahrain GP, Chinese GP, Spanish GP, British GP, Italian GP, Singapore GP, Japanese GP, Russian GP, United States GP, Abu Dhabi GP, 2015 Australian GP, Chinese GP, Bahrain GP, Canadian GP, British GP, Belgian GP, Italian GP, Japanese GP, Russian GP, United States GP, 2016 Monaco GP, Canadian GP, Austrian GP, British GP, Hungarian GP, German GP, United States GP, Mexican GP, Brazilian GP, Abu Dhabi GP, 2017 Chinese GP, Spanish GP, Canadian GP, British GP, Belgian GP, Italian GP, Singapore GP, Japanese GP, United States GP, 2018 Azerbaijan GP, Spanish GP, French GP, German GP, Hungarian GP, Italian GP, Singapore GP, Russian GP, Japanese GP, Brazilian GP, Abu Dhabi GP, 2019 Bahrain GP, Chinese GP, Spanish GP, Monaco GP, Canadian GP, French GP, British GP, Hungarian GP, Russian GP, Mexican GP, Abu Dhabi GP, 2020 Styrian GP, Hungarian GP, British GP, Spanish GP, Belgian GP, Tuscan GP, Eifel GP, Portuguese GP, Emilia Romagna GP, Turkish GP, Bahrain GP, 2021 Bahrain GP, Portuguese GP, Spanish GP, British GP, Russian GP, Sao Paolo GP, Qatar GP, Saudi Arabian GP

Poles:	**103**
Fastest laps:	**59**
Points:	**4165.5**

Honours: 2008, 2014, 2015, 2017, 2018, 2019 & 2020 F1 WORLD CHAMPION, 2007, 2016 & 2021 F1 RUNNER-UP, 2006 GP2 CHAMPION, 2005 EUROPEAN F3 CHAMPION, 2003 BRITISH FORMULA RENAULT CHAMPION, 2000 WORLD KART CUP & EUROPEAN FORMULA A KART CHAMPION, 1999 ITALIAN INTERCON A CHAMPION, 1995 BRITISH CADET KART CHAMPION

GEORGE RUSSELL

A series of classy drives in his three years with Williams, and none better than taking second in Belgium last year, landed George his break with Mercedes and it's going to be enthralling to see how he takes on Lewis Hamilton.

After three years with tail-end Williams, George will be going for wins with Mercedes.

A star in kart racing, George was European KF3 champion in 2012 at the age of 14 and used that reputation to move into single-seater racing two years later when he stormed the BRDC F4 series and also impressed by winning in one of four guest outings in European Formula Renault and these results plus demonstrating an unusual level of maturity landed him the coveted McLaren Autosport BRDC award.

In 2015, George advanced to European F3 and was sixth overall in his rookie season with Carlin, as well as coming second in the F3 Masters invitation race. Back for another go at the title in 2016, George was disappointed to rank only third as Lance Stroll took the crown. However, he decided to try GP3 instead and won that title at a canter. Then, at the end of the year, he had some F1 testing team with Mercedes and impressed all who witnessed his runs, showing how wise Mercedes had been in getting him onto its books.

So, it was time for a crack at F2 in 2018 and George took to this last level below F1 like a duck to water. Driving for ART Grand Prix, he won seven times, an incredible return for a rookie season at this level, and this left him well clear of fellow British challengers Lando Norris and Alex Albon. Further F1 tests showed that he was more than ready to move up to the World Championship, with Mercedes-powered Williams selected as the place for him to learn his craft while waiting for a place, possibly, with Mercedes in the years ahead.

The 2019 season was all about learning the ropes, peaking with 11th in the German GP, and in 2020 there were further good runs in a car that wasn't good enough for points.

Then, Lewis Hamilton was unwell in the lead-up to the penultimate round and George was given a run by Mercedes in the Sakhir GP, showing enough pace to beat Valtteri Bottas, only to be denied what would have been a remarkable win by a mix-up in the pits and a puncture just as he caught leader Sergio Perez, leaving him to finish ninth.

REWARDED WITH SECOND AT SPA

Having arrived in F1 potentially as the best new talent since Max Verstappen, it will have been frustrating for George to have had to spend three years with a team stuck at the tail of the grid. Still, George's performances through 2021 were excellent. And none was better than his qualifying run in diabolically wet conditions at Spa-Francorchamps. He was a stunning second fastest and then was rewarded with the points for that finishing position too as the race was almost immediately called off. This was a huge fillip for the team as it rebuilds under new management. Strong qualifying runs were key to George hanging on to land the odd point in races in the second half of the season as his FW43B didn't have equal pace across a grand prix. In all, George was in the points four times. The one low point was his accident at Imola with the driver he is replacing at Mercedes this year, Valtteri Bottas, when he tried to pass him.

TRACK NOTES

Nationality:	**BRITISH**
Born:	**15 FEBRUARY 1998,**
	KING'S LYNN, ENGLAND
Website:	**www.georgerussellracing.com**
Teams:	**WILLIAMS 2019-21,**
	MERCEDES 2022

CAREER RECORD

First Grand Prix:	**2019 AUSTRALIAN GP**
Grand Prix starts:	**60**
Grand Prix wins:	**0**
(best result: 2nd 2021 Belgian GP)	
Poles:	**0**
Fastest laps:	**1**
Points:	**19**
Honours:	**2018 FORMULA**

2 CHAMPION, 2017 GP3 CHAMPION, 2015 F3 MASTERS RUNNER-UP, 2014 BRITISH F4 CHAMPION & McLAREN AUTOSPORT YOUNG DRIVER AWARD, 2012 EUROPEAN KF3 KART CHAMPION

⏵⏵ RED BULL RACING

For the first season since 2013, Red Bull Racing was able to fight consistently at the front of the field, with Max Verstappen taking on Lewis Hamilton's Mercedes for the title. The big question is whether the team can do this again with the new-style car.

Taking a first Monaco win last year will have felt worth more than 25 points for Max Verstappen. Be sure he will lead the team attack again.

With 17 years in the World Championship behind it, some might imagine that Red Bull Racing entered F1 in its own right in 2005, but it had already been competing in F1 for eight years before that, spending its first three years of existence as Stewart GP before being rebranded and repainted to spend the next five years as Jaguar Racing.

The team has been based in Milton Keynes for all of that time, using a base that started life years before when the team was set up by three-time World Champion Jackie Stewart and his elder son Paul. They ran a team first in F3 and then in F3000, which was then the final stepping stone into F1. Jackie used his fabled contacts book to draw in the backing and their Ford-engined cars were fairly competitive from the outset, with Rubens Barrichello taking second in Monaco in their first year in F1, 1997. Two years later, the team claimed its only win, with Johnny Herbert first home in a wet/

dry race at the Nurburgring to help the team rank fourth overall.

Then the team was sold to Ford which branded it Jaguar Racing but interference from the automotive manufacturer prevented the team making the sharp decisions required to be competitive in F1. Both Eddie Irvine and Mark Webber

KEY PERSONNEL & 2021 ROUND-UP

PAUL MONAGHAN
Chief engineer of Red Bull Racing's car engineering division, Paul used his degree in mechanical engineering to land a job with McLaren in 1990. After acquiring experience as a data engineer, he moved on to Benetton in 2000, where he became Jenson Button's race engineer before working with Fernando Alonso as he took his first F1 win. After a brief spell at Jordan, Paul joined Red Bull Racing in 2005 and liked it so much that he has stayed on.

TAKING THE BATTLE TO MERCEDES
After seven years in which Mercedes dominated F1, the 2021 campaign was different as Red Bull Racing provided a truly serious challenge. This was clear from the opening round when Verstappen qualified on pole and would have beaten Hamilton but for a slip-up. Victory next time out at Imola showed that this was no flash in the pan. The battle grew ever more intense and was, of course, settled in Verstappen's favour on the last lap of the last race.

2021 DRIVERS & RESULTS

Driver	Nationality	Races	Wins	Pts	Pos
Max Verstappen	Dutch	22	10	395.5	1st
Sergio Perez	Mexican	22	1	190	4th

FOR THE RECORD

Country of origin:	**England**
Team base:	**Milton Keynes, England**
Telephone:	**(44) 01908 279700**
Website:	**www.redbullracing.com**
Active in Formula One:	**As Stewart GP 1997-99, Jaguar Racing 2000-04, Red Bull Racing 2005 on**
Grands Prix contested:	**460**
Wins:	**75**
Pole positions:	**71**
Fastest laps:	**76**

went well when the car was good, but it was an opportunity wasted.

Seeing an opportunity to take the team off Ford's hands, Red Bull founder Dietrich Mateschitz bought the team and renamed it as Red Bull Racing for 2005. Having backed a large number of drivers through the junior single-seater categories, it then picked the best of these and discarded the rest, but few really shone in the way that talent spotter Helmut Marko might have liked. They had a decent yardstick in David Coulthard, who had won grands prix with Williams and McLaren, and took the return of Webber to the fold for a driver to match him.

What Coulthard did next was massive in helping the team to shift up through the gears: he attracted Adrian Newey across from McLaren and soon F1's leading designer made the team truly competitive. With Webber going well but Sebastian Vettel going even better, they pushed Brawn GP hard in 2009 and then the German and the team claimed both the drivers' and constructors' titles in 2010. They enjoyed the experience so much that

they repeated the feat across each of the next three seasons as they won 41 grands prix between 2010 and 2013.

In time, Mercedes used its considerable financial clout to mount a serious challenge and Lewis Hamilton guided it to a new level, leaving Red Bull Racing to fall back into the pack despite the best efforts of Daniel Ricciardo who still managed to rank third behind the Mercedes drivers in both 2014 and 2016.

Red Bull Racing never fell far, and was always at the head of the challengers, even through the years when team chief Christian Horner expressed a lack of confidence in the engines that the team was using, feeling that they were not competitive compared to the Mercedes and even Ferrari engines used by their leading rivals.

In 2016, the team felt that Daniil Kvyat wasn't shaping up and replaced him with Max Verstappen and the result was remarkable as he won on his debut in Spain. By 2018, he was outscoring Ricciardo and the team has rotated around him ever since.

THE TEAM

Chairman:	**Dietrich Mateschitz**
Team principal:	**Christian Horner**
Chief technical officer:	**Adrian Newey**
Technical director:	**Pierre Waché**
Chief engineering officer:	**Rob Marshall**
Chief engineer, car engineering:	**Paul Monaghan**
Chief engineer, technology & analysis:	**Guillaume Cattelani**
Head of performance engineering:	**Ben Waterhouse**
Team manager:	**Jonathan Wheatley**
Chief engineer:	**Guillaume Roquelin**
Test driver:	**tba**
Chassis:	**Red Bull RB17**
Engine:	**Honda V6**
Tyres:	**Pirelli**

Changing to Honda power in 2019 appeared to improve matters a little as Verstappen began to press Hamilton harder, but the team's inability to run a decent second car continued to hinder its tally in the constructors' championship.

Sebastian Vettel's win in Abu Dhabi in 2010 was when Red Bull landed its first F1 title.

"The championship came down to the last lap and it was a great strategy call by the team to make that pitstop onto the set of softs and then it was down to Max to make it happen, which he did in typical Max style."

Christian Horner

MAX VERSTAPPEN

Last year was a turning point in Max's career, as he took on Lewis Hamilton on equal terms and not only recorded 10 wins but was able, somehow, to win the final round and so become world champion at 24.

Max grabbed last year's opportunities with both hands as he won race after race.

As the son of two racers – F1 racer father Jos and karting star mother, Sophie Kumpen – Max was always going to have a competition career. And he was good, from his first karting title at eight – in the Belgian Rotax Minimax series – right through to the world and European titles he won in 2013.

Then came car racing. With his obvious ability, Max didn't bother with Formula 4 or Formula Renault and went straight into Formula 3. He was more than ready for it, becoming a race winner in the sixth race of the European series. He didn't stop at that, going on to finish the season more strongly even than champion Esteban Ocon, being denied the title only because he retired from five of the early-season races.

Then the family said that Max wanted to advance to F1 in 2015. Sure, at 17. But they were serious and Scuderia Toro Rosso signed him as F1's youngest ever debutant. Many wondered whether he could possibly be ready for the sport's top level, but they weren't left wondering for long as Max came seventh on his second outing and bagged a couple of fourths as he outperformed team-mate Carlos Sainz Jr.

Back for more in 2016, Max's career took a leap as he got to swap drives with Red Bull Racing's Daniil Kvyat after the opening four rounds when the Russian driver was dropped to Toro Rosso. Max promptly won the Spanish GP. Having ranked fifth overall to team-mate Daniel Ricciardo's third, Max pushed the Australian harder in 2017, winning in Malaysia and Mexico. Then he came within an ace of beating Ferrari's Kimi Raikkonen to third overall in 2018, again winning twice as he assumed internal dominance over Ricciardo.

By 2019, with the team revolving around his efforts, people reckoned Max would be winning a lot more if he was in a Mercedes, but three wins was all he could manage – one more than he collected in 2020 when he trailed Hamilton and Valtteri Bottas.

TRACK NOTES

Nationality:	**DUTCH**
Born:	**30 SEPTEMBER 1997,**
	HASSELT, BELGIUM
Website:	**www.verstappen.nl**
Teams:	**TORO ROSSO 2015-16,**
	RED BULL RACING 2016-22

CAREER RECORD

First Grand Prix: **2015 AUSTRALIAN GP**

Grand Prix starts: **141**

Grand Prix wins: **20**
2016 Spanish GP, 2017 Malaysian GP, Mexican GP, 2018 Austrian GP, Mexican GP, 2019 Austrian GP, German GP, Brazilian GP, 2020 70th Anniversary GP, Abu Dhabi GP, 2021 Emilia Romagna GP, Monaco GP, French GP, Styrian GP, Austrian GP, Belgian GP, Dutch GP, United States GP, Mexican GP, Abu Dhabi GP

Poles: **11**

Fastest laps: **16**

Points: **1557.5**

Honours: **2021 F1 WORLD CHAMPION, 2013 WORLD & EUROPEAN KZ KART CHAMPION, 2012 WSK MASTER SERIES KF2 CHAMPION, 2011 WSK EURO SERIES CHAMPION, 2009 BELGIAN KF5 CHAMPION, 2008 DUTCH CADET KART CHAMPION, 2007 & 2008 DUTCH MINIMAX CHAMPION, 2006 BELGIAN ROTAX MINIMAX CHAMPION**

TURNING FROM GOOD TO GREAT

This was the first season in which Max had machinery as good as, and occasionally superior to, Lewis Hamilton's Mercedes. Not wanting to let this opportunity go begging, he grabbed it with both hands. It looked at the opening round, at Sakhir, that the shoe was on the other foot as he took on and passed Hamilton for the lead, but he had had all four wheels beyond the edge of the circuit and had to hand the place back. Still, it was clear that he was on an equal footing. A win next time out, at Imola, made Max feel better and he then spent much of the rest of the season swapping wins with Hamilton, enjoying a three-race winning streak in the summer at Paul Ricard and then the consecutive grands prix at the Red Bull Ring. Had it not been for a cruel blow-out when leading in Baku, that would have been four wins in a row. Then came his clash with Hamilton at Silverstone. This is when the championship developed an edge.

SERGIO PEREZ

Now accustomed to his new life at Red Bull Racing, where he plays a supporting role to Max Verstappen, expect Sergio to be even more effective in gathering points, providing that Red Bull's new car is as effective as last year's RB16B.

Sergio was good last year, winning again, but expect even more from him in 2022.

The recipe for Sergio's younger years was standard, competing in karting from the age of six, something that is permitted in Mexico, while drivers have to wait until eight in Europe. He was also ahead of his rivals when he stepped up to car racing aged just 14. That he did so away from home in the USA was unusual, but Sergio showed enough promise in the Skip Barber Dodge series to encourage

his family to send him even further away the following year: to Germany.

This upheaval had a reward when he finished second behind Nico Hulkenberg in the opening round of the 2005 ADAC Formula BMW series. However, consistent results came only in his second year when he ranked sixth, marking him out as good but not exceptional.

The next step for Sergio was to compete in British F3, running in the secondary – National – class which he won, for what was the only title of his racing career.

Aiming higher by going for overall British F3 honours in 2008, Sergio won four rounds, but this was good only for fourth place overall as Jaime Alguersuari took the spoils.

GP2 followed, starting with the Asian series, and Sergio used the experience gained in those 12 races to enter the FIA GP2 series, ending the year 12th in another championship dominated by Hulkenberg. There were few signs that Sergio was an F1 driver in the making, but he had a lot of sponsorship from Mexican companies and used it to advance to be

runner-up to Pastor Maldonado in 2010, displaying a new-found ability to be light on his tyres.

Sergio's F1 career began in 2011 with Sauber and he did well enough in ranking 10th for the Swiss team in 2012, but notably by finishing second at Sepang and Monza, to earn a ride with McLaren, but not enough to keep it.

Then began a seven-year stay at a team that was Force India when he joined it and Racing Point when he left, interestingly outscoring nemesis Hulkenberg when they were team-mates in 2015.

TRACK NOTES

Nationality:	**MEXICAN**
Born:	**26 JANUARY 1990,**
	GUADALAJARA, MEXICO
Website:	**www.sergioperezf1.com**
Teams:	**SAUBER 2011-12,**
	McLAREN 2013, FORCE INDIA 2014-18,
	RACING POINT 2019-20,
	RED BULL RACING 2021-22

CAREER RECORD

First Grand Prix:	**2011 BAHRAIN GP**
Grand Prix starts:	**213**
Grand Prix wins:	**2**
	2020 Sakhir GP, 2021 Azerbaijan GP
Poles:	**0**
Fastest laps:	**6**
Points:	**896**
Honours:	**2010 GP2 RUNNER-UP,**
	2007 BRITISH FORMULA THREE NATIONAL
	CLASS CHAMPION

LEARNING TO BE A NUMBER TWO

Late in 2020, it was clear that Sergio wasn't being kept on by the team that was set to become Aston Martin, with Sebastian Vettel having been signed to replace him. So, after 10 years, his F1 career was about to end without a win. Then, he came good in the penultimate race and that convinced Red Bull Racing to sign him. It was clear from the outset that he was going to have to play "the Bottas role" in support of Max Verstappen, not something that is easy to do after years as the top dog in a team. To start with, he had no choice in the matter, as his team-mate was simply faster. Then Sergio won the sixth round in Baku, after a blow-out for Verstappen and a mistake by Hamilton and his confidence grew. However, he never did become a match for the Dutchman's pace and so simply concentrated on scoring as many points as he could, with special delight when he became the first Mexican to stand on the podium at the Mexican GP.

There is no point guessing which team they are supporting. This is the *tifosi* cheering on all things Ferrari to add to the atmosphere at Monza.

FERRARI

Ferrari was on better form last year than in 2020 when it ranked sixth, something inexcusable for a team with such history and such a budget, but the *tifosi* wait with bated breath to see whether the team has mastered the new F1 rules for 2022.

Charles Leclerc and Carlos Sainz Jr are a strong pairing, but Ferrari must seize the introduction of new rules to race at the front again.

Ferrari had an appreciable headstart on its current F1 rivals, as it even brought experience from pre-war Grand Prix racing when the Scuderia entered the inaugural World Championship in 1950. In fact, that gave it a 16-year advantage at the very least over the oldest of the other current teams, McLaren. Yet, for all that, it hasn't always been the dominant team, even with invariably having one of the healthiest budgets. The main problem has been internal politics, something that has fortunately become less of a factor for F1's most popular team.

Ferrari's first world champion was Alberto Ascari who dominated 1952 and 1953. The titles became harder to come by when Mercedes joined and it took until 1956 for Ferrari to produce a second world champion, Juan Manuel Fangio. Then Mike Hawthorn edged out Vanwall's Stirling Moss to win the 1958 crown.

What Ferrari failed to heed was the rise of what Enzo Ferrari dubbed the

"*garagistes*" as he looked down at British teams like Cooper and Lotus. He was wrong, and their ingenuity, starting with putting the engine behind the driver, transformed F1. Fortunately, a rule change for 1961, reducing engine size to 1,500cc fell into Ferrari's hands and Phil Hill became its fourth world champion.

KEY PERSONNEL & 2021 ROUND-UP

JOCK CLEAR
Jock trained as a race engineer and gained knowledge by working for Lola then entering F1 with Benetton before moving on to Leyton House, then Lotus. He worked with first David Coulthard then Jacques Villeneuve at Williams before the latter took him with him to BAR. When this became Brawn GP, Jock helped Rubens Barrichello to wins and stayed on when it became Mercedes. In 2015, he joined Ferrari.

SMALL STEPS, BUT NO SHOT AT VICTORIES
There were immediately signs of improvement over its 2020 form in the early races of last year and Carlos Sainz Jr. gave the team cheer when he finished second in Monaco. This position was backed up by Charles Leclerc finishing second in the British GP and several other podium finishes. However, Sainz Jr. must have watched his old team, McLaren, with envy as their cars outstripped them, before Ferrari came on song and secured third place overall.

2021 DRIVERS & RESULTS

Driver	Nationality	Races	Wins	Pts	Pos
Charles Leclerc	Monegasque	21	0	159	7th
Carlos Sainz Jr	Spanish	22	0	164.5	5th

FOR THE RECORD

Country of origin:	**Italy**
Team base:	**Maranello, Italy**
Telephone:	**(39) 536 949111**
Website:	**www.ferrari.com**
Active in Formula One:	**From 1950**
Grands Prix contested:	**1030**
Wins:	**237**
Pole positions:	**230**
Fastest laps:	**253**

THE TEAM

Chief executive officer:	**John Elkann**
Team principal & technical director:	
	Mattia Binotto
Head of performance development:	
	Enrico Cardile
Head of power unit:	**Enrico Gualtieri**
Head of aerodynamics:	**Loic Bigois**
Sporting director:	**Laurent Mekies**
Driving academy director:	**Jock Clear**
Operations director:	**Gino Rosato**
Chief race engineer:	**Matteo Togninalli**
Reserve driver:	**Antonio Giovinazzi**
Chassis:	**Ferrari SF22**
Engine:	**Ferrari V6**
Tyres:	**Pirelli**

Three years later, John Surtees became its fifth, but the team's management handled him badly and he left.

It took the arrival of focused Niki Lauda to drag the team forwards again and, had it not been for the burns he suffered in the 1976 German GP, he might have won three titles in a row. Then those *"garagistes"* introduced ground effects and Ferrari got left behind again, until 1979 when Jody Scheckter came out on top.

A long wait followed as Brabham, McLaren, Williams and Benetton displayed an ability to interpret the rules best and their drivers won every title until Michael Schumacher finally got a car in his fifth year with Ferrari that was good enough to win the title in 2000. Four more titles followed, with his 2002 season being particularly dominant as he won 11 of the 17 grands prix, with Rubens Barrichello adding four more. The guidance of former rally chief Jean Todt and technical director Ross Brawn was also key as this triumvirate made this most Italian of teams less Italian, like Lauda had done in the 1970s when he combined with Luca di Montezemolo to reduce the political element as it became clear that F1 was won by focus and intellect rather than simply by nationality.

It seemed when he was winning grand prix after grand prix that Michael Schumacher's run would never end but, as ever, change came in the end, with Renault's Fernando Alonso outscoring him two to one in 2005 as Michael ranked third behind McLaren's Kimi Raikkonen too, taking just one win as a rule change banning tyre changes during pitstops left him unable to cope as the team's Bridgestone tyres were no match for their rivals' Michelins.

By the end of 2006, having chased Alonso hard, Schumacher retired and this opened the way for a new age at Ferrari as Felipe Massa was joined by Kimi Raikkonen who came on strong at season's end to steal the title from McLaren's Alonso and rookie Lewis Hamilton. And that was the team's last title, although Felipe Massa came within a few seconds of beating Hamilton to the crown in 2008. Alonso lost out to Sebastian Vettel at the final round in 2010 and just fell short in 2012.

Since then, the team has had no answers to the might of Mercedes. Looking ahead, the *tifosi* would settle for Ferrari becoming a winner again and would swoon with delight if it could land another title, as 2007 seems a very long time ago.

"Third place in last year's constructors' championship was down to the efforts of everyone in the team, at the track and back in Maranello, who worked really hard with determination, humility and in a united fashion."

Mattia Binotto

Scheckter and Villeneuve on the charge in the Italian GP in 1979, a great year for Ferrari.

CHARLES LECLERC

If Ferrari has interpreted the new technical rules better than its rivals to build its first truly competitive car for years, then Charles might be able to have his first true crack at becoming the first ever Monegasque driver to with the F1 title.

Charles knows that Carlos will push him harder in 2022 and will surely raise his game.

Charles was always likely to try a career in racing as his father Herve raced F3. So, into karting Charles went and he was good enough to land the French cadet title aged 11, the Junior Monaco title in 2010 and the FIA Karting Academy Trophy in 2011 before finishing as runner-up in world and European series in 2012.

Clearly, Charles was more than ready for car racing and finishing second in a regional Formula Renault series in his first year in single-seaters was impressive. In 2015, Charles elected to move directly to F3 and he took four wins against more experienced rivals to rank fourth, then travelled to the end-of-year invitational race around the streets of Macau and came second.

Charles's third year of car racing was spent in GP3 rather than GP2 which would have been the more natural progression, as there wasn't the backing for him to do the latter. Still, Charles did all he could and landed the title ahead of Alex Albon.

He also had an F1 test for Ferrari and did well enough to race in the last step before F1, F2, in 2017. It was a fabulous season, as seven wins were more than enough for Charles to make it two titles in two years. F1 beckoned, and Ferrari placed him with Sauber for 2018. The results were remarkable, as Charles starred for this less than competitive team, especially in qualifying, but also in coming sixth in Baku.

Joining Ferrari in 2019 was a big step up and Charles grabbed it with both hands and would probably have won on his second outing, at Sakhir, but for an engine glitch. He was a winner before the year was out, though, twice, and so ended the year ahead of much vaunted team-mate Sebastian Vettel, ranked fourth overall.

The 2020 season wasn't as easy as not only did Mercedes dominate, but Red Bull Racing easily outstripped Ferrari too, with Charles achieving a best finish of second in the opening race in Austria and ending up eighth overall as Ferrari fell to sixth.

TRACK NOTES

Nationality:	**MONEGASQUE**
Born:	**16 OCTOBER 1997,**
	MONTE CARLO, MONACO
Website:	**www.charles-leclerc.com**
Teams:	**SAUBER 2018,**
	FERRARI 2019-22

CAREER RECORD

First Grand Prix: **2018 AUSTRALIAN GP**

Grand Prix starts:	**80**
Grand Prix wins:	**2**
	2019 Belgian GP, Italian GP
Poles:	**9**
Fastest laps:	**4**
Points:	**560**

Honours: **2017 FIA F2 CHAMPION, 2016 GP3 CHAMPION, 2015 MACAU F3 RUNNER-UP, 2014 FORMULA RENAULT ALPS RUNNER-UP, 2013 WORLD KZ KART RUNNER-UP, 2012 UNDER 18 WORLD KART CHAMPIONSHIP RUNNER-UP & EURO KF KART RUNNER-UP, 2011 ACADEMY TROPHY KART CHAMPION, 2010 JUNIOR MONACO KART CUP CHAMPION, 2009 FRENCH CADET KART CHAMPION**

POLES, BUT NO RACE VICTORIES

There was a definite upswing in form for Ferrari last year after its poor 2020 season in which it ranked only sixth overall. Better still, early season form was then built upon and the increasingly competitive SF21 was then a real challenge for McLaren as the two teams scrapped to see which would end the year third overall. Charles was often a threat in qualifying, grabbing two poles in succession, first in Monaco and then in Baku. However, neither resulted in a win as over a race distance the Ferrari drivers simply couldn't match the four from Mercedes and Red Bull Racing. As the season unfolded, it seemed that a fourth place was the best result that this Monegasque racer could hope for, but then came the British GP at Silverstone and Charles left with second place behind Lewis Hamilton when he was helped by Hamilton's clash with Max Verstappen but hindered by his own engine stuttering.

Second place in Monaco was the highlight of Carlos' first year with Ferrari as he all but matched team-mate Charles Leclerc for points scored. This year, the Spanish driver will be seeing whether the new car suits him or Charles better.

Carlos is quietly spoken but has a steely determination to land a first grand prix win.

It would have come as no surprise had Carlos followed his namesake and father Carlos Sainz into rallying as Carlos Sr was a two-time World Rally Champion. Yet, Carlos Sr had also tried single-seaters back in the 1980s and it was to these that Carlos Jr turned in 2010 when he moved up after a high-achieving time in karts during which he won the Monaco Kart Cup and was runner-up in the European KF3 series.

Having been immediately on the pace in Formula BMW, ranking fourth, Carlos was second in the European Formula Renault series in 2011. So, F3 was the natural next step and Carlos won a round of the European championship as he ranked fifth and there became a question mark over his continuance on the Red Bull scholarship scheme. This became even more of a question mark when Carlos raced in GP3 the following year and was able to rank only 10th as Daniil Kvyat dominated. Yet, he did well enough in a few F1 tests to keep Red Bull interested and then stepped up to Formula Renault 3.5 with DAMS in 2014 and stormed to the title ahead of Pierre Gasly. This was enough, and F1 followed.

Carlos spent two years with Scuderia Toro Rosso, claiming three sixths in 2017, and was part way through a third, when he moved to Renault after the team dropped Jolyon Palmer. Carlos showed speed if a slight lack of consistency in 2018 but then joined McLaren for 2019.

His first year for the British team yielded sixth overall, albeit a long way behind the five highest scorers. Then Carlos was classified sixth again in 2020. The highlight was a career-best second place in the Italian GP when, had the race been a lap longer, he would probably have overhauled Gasly's AlphaTauri to go take the win. He then ended his time at McLaren strongly with a run of strong point-scoring drives to stay ahead of team-mate Lando Norris, knowing that he would be a Ferrari driver in 2021.

TRACK NOTES

Nationality:	**SPANISH**
Born:	**1 SEPTEMBER 1994, MADRID, SPAIN**
Website:	**www.carlossainzjr.com**
Teams:	**TORO ROSSO 2015-17, RENAULT 2017-18, McLAREN 2019-20, FERRARI 2021-22**

CAREER RECORD

First Grand Prix:	**2015 AUSTRALIAN GP**
Grand Prix starts:	**141**
Grand Prix wins:	**0** (best result: 2nd, 2020 Italian GP, 2021 Monaco GP)
Poles:	**0**
Fastest laps:	**1**
Points:	**536.5**
Honours:	**2014 FORMULA RENAULT 3.5 CHAMPION, 2011 EUROPEAN FORMULA RENAULT RUNNER-UP & NORTHERN EUROPEAN FORMULA RENAULT CHAMPION, 2009 MONACO KART CUP WINNER & EUROPEAN KF3 RUNNER-UP, 2008 ASIA/PACIFIC JUNIOR KART CHAMPION, 2006 MADRID CADET KART CHAMPION**

CARLOS'S SECOND SECOND PLACE

It may yet prove that Carlos has an F1 win in him, but he proved last year at least that he was good enough to take another second place. This season-high result came at Monaco, in the fifth round of the season, and it was something of a gift as Valtteri Bottas's race was wrecked at a pitstop. Still, when your team's cars are probably only third or fourth most competitive, behind those from Mercedes, Red Bull Racing and perhaps McLaren, you take what comes your way. Carlos also finished third at both the Hungaroring and at Sochi, keeping his cool as those around him lost theirs. What was notably impressive was the way that he settled into a team that was already being shaped around his team-mate Charles Leclerc and yet, without any political wrangling, Carlos seemed to settle in and get the team behind him as well. Carlos's excellent third place in the final race at Yas Marina will have given him confidence to carry into 2022.

If the 2020 season was one of solid progress for McLaren, then 2021 was a huge leap forward, as proved when not only did the team take its first win in nine years, but also when it claimed a one-two at Monza. This season will prove if these results were a fluke.

Lando Norris was strong at the start of 2021, leading McLaren's attack with third place. Expect Daniel Ricciardo to start faster this year.

Having watched his Cooper team-mate Jack Brabham become a successful racing car constructor alongside his continued racing exploits, Bruce McLaren decided to do the same. Although McLaren's initial F1 forays in 1966 were far from successful as Brabham won the F1 title in one of his own cars, McLaren would soon pull ahead as he hit on building sportscars for the lucrative American sportscar racing scene, landing the Can Am title each year from 1967 to 1972 and filling the team coffers as he was soon supplying cars to the majority of the grid. This is what helped McLaren to win in F1 from 1968 when the team ranked second behind only Lotus.

Then, in 1970, while testing the latest Can Am McLaren at Goodwood, Bruce was killed and the close-knit team lost its lynchpin. The following years were hard for the team as Tyrrell and Lotus assumed control of F1, with Denny Hulme winning occasionally as the driving mainstay.

Teddy Mayer ran a tight ship after assuming control and McLaren guided Emerson Fittipaldi to the 1974 drivers' crown, a feat replicated by James Hunt in 1976 after a dramatic battle with Ferrari's Niki Lauda.

Despite failing to keep up in the technology race that produced ground

KEY PERSONNEL & 2021 ROUND-UP

ANDREA STELLA
After graduating in aerospace engineering, Andrea joined Ferrari as a performance engineer for its test team and advanced to fulfil the same role for no less a talent than Michael Schumacher from 2002 to 2006 as he raced to three drivers' titles and then helped Kimi Raikkonen pip McLaren's drivers to the 2007 crown. He joined McLaren in 2015 as head of race operations and rose to become performance director then executive director of its racing division.

A RETURN TO THE WINNERS' CIRCLE
When Lando Norris finished fourth at round one, it was clear that McLaren was going to be competitive. It expected to be behind Mercedes and Red Bull, but being ahead of the rest was positive. Norris became the more frequent scorer, with the incoming Daniel Ricciardo struggling to get the feel of the MCL35B. By mid-season, Norris had three third places, Ricciardo nothing higher than a fifth. But then came Monza, and the Australian led home a one-two.

2021 DRIVERS & RESULTS

Driver	Nationality	Races	Wins	Pts	Pos
Lando Norris	British	22	0	160	6th
Daniel Ricciardo	Australian	22	1	115	8th

FOR THE RECORD

Country of origin:	**England**
Team base:	**Woking England**
Telephone:	**(44) 01483 261900**
Website:	**www.mclaren.com**
Active in Formula One:	**From 1966**
Grands Prix contested:	**903**
Wins:	**182**
Pole positions:	**156**
Fastest laps:	**159**

THE TEAM

Executive director:	**Zak Brown**
Team principal:	**Andreas Seidl**
Executive director, technical:	**James Key**
Executive director, racing:	**Andrea Stella**
Executive director, operations:	**Piers Thynne**
Chief engineering officer:	**Matt Morris**
Chief engineer, aerodynamics:	**Peter Prodromou**
Director of design & development:	**Neil Oatley**
Head of design:	**Mark Inham**
Team manager:	**Paul James**
Test driver:	**tba**
Chassis:	**McLaren MCL36**
Engine:	**Mercedes V6**
Tyres:	**Pirelli**

effects, McLaren found its form again after Ron Dennis took over the team and brought in John Barnard who produced F1's first carbon-fibre monocoque in 1980 and so moved McLaren to the front of the queue, with Lauda and then Alain Prost winning the title in 1984, 1985 and 1986 respectively as the team claimed its second and third constructors' titles, both powered by TAG engines.

Then Williams moved ahead, but McLaren took over its Honda engine-supply deal and entered its most purple of purple patches, with Ayrton Senna and Prost winning all but one of the 16 races in 1988 as Senna came out on top. Prost returned the favour in 1989 when the opposition could do nothing against the two best drivers in the two best cars. In 1990, after Prost had left for Ferrari, Senna made it three McLaren titles in a row.

The team's next golden age came from 1998 when designer Adrian Newey came up trumps with the pick of the chassis that combined well with Mercedes engines to better everything that Michael Schumacher could throw at Mika Häkkinen

and David Coulthard as the Finn landed the title, a feat he would repeat in 1999.

After Ferrari had assumed dominance when Schumacher was in his pomp, and despite fabulous form from Kimi Raikkonen as he raced to be second overall in both 2003 and 2005, McLaren had to wait almost another decade to win regularly again, with Fernando Alonso and rookie Lewis Hamilton taking points off each other in 2007 and so allowing Ferrari's Kimi Raikkonen to pip them both. Hamilton made no mistake the following year.

Losing Mercedes engines was a big setback for the team and its second spell with Honda power, starting in 2015, was a disappointment. Actually, it was a near disaster and it began to look as though this once dominant team had become a fading force as it ended up ninth of the 10 teams in the 2015 and 2017 rankings.

However, Renault engines arrived in 2018 and racer-turned-sponsorship guru Zak Brown gradually found the personnel that he sought to take McLaren forward, notably bringing in Andreas Seidl from the Porsche sportscar team to run the

team and this has guided it back to the front, with Carlos Sainz Jr. helping it to advance to sixth overall in 2019 then fourth in 2020 when Lando Norris began to mature and score not just points but podium finishes too on a more regular basis. At Monza in 2020, Sainz Jr. came within half of a second of winning.

> **"As a team, we'd been waiting for that [Monza] win for quite some time. We know we still have a lot of work to do on our journey, but it was a great motivation."**
>
> Andreas Seidl

Senna shares the podium with Patrese and team-mate Berger after winning in Brazil in 1991.

DANIEL RICCIARDO

It looked last year as though Daniel was being shown up by less experienced team-mate Lando Norris, but he learnt more about the car, advanced and took McLaren's first win in nine years. Expect even more from him in 2022.

Daniel took a while to get going in 2021, then grabbed McLaren's first win in 170 races.

One of the most popular characters on Netflix's *Drive To Survive* series because of his beaming smile, Daniel appears to really appreciate being an F1 driver. And well he might, as his journey to get there required the sacrifice of displacement.

Daniel's is a journey that required a lot of journeys, and long ones at that, for his childhood home in Western Australia was far from even the rest of Australia.

So he spent his first full year of single-seater racing after karts competing all around Asia, losing out to future Le Mans 24 Hours winner Earl Bamber in Formula BMW.

Next stop was Europe in 2007 at the age of 17, racing in the Italian Formula Renault series thanks to being signed for the Red Bull driver search scholarship. That was followed by a step up to the European series and finishing as runner-up to Valtteri Bottas in 2008. Then came Daniel's second car racing title as he took the British F3 championship for Carlin in 2009.

Having tried a couple of races in Formula Renault 3.5, Daniel moved up to that more powerful category in 2010 and ranked second with four wins to end up just two points behind the champion.

Daniel returned to Formula Renault 3.5 in 2011 but his season changed midway through when the short-lived HRT F1 team dropped Narain Karthikeyan and he was offered his drive, paid for by Red Bull and used to give Daniel experience.

Red Bull then placed Daniel with its junior F1 team, Scuderia Toro Rosso, in 2012 and he stayed for two years until

landing promotion to Red Bull Racing for 2014. And how his image changed, from hard trying charger to race winner, with three wins coming his way as he ranked third behind the Mercedes drivers Lewis Hamilton and Nico Rosberg. Third again in 2016, Daniel found himself outperformed by Max Verstappen and so joined Renault in 2019. It was a signing that meant he would be team leader, but his two years there were disappointing, and so he chose well to join McLaren.

TRACK NOTES

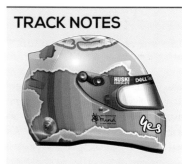

Nationality:	**AUSTRALIAN**
Born:	**1 JULY 1989, PERTH, AUSTRALIA**
Website:	**www.danielricciardo.com**
Teams:	**HRT 2011, TORO ROSSO 2012-13, RED BULL RACING 2014-18, RENAULT 2019-20, McLAREN 2021-22**

CAREER RECORD

First Grand Prix:	**2011 BRITISH GP**
Grand Prix starts:	**210**
Grand Prix wins:	**8**
	2014 Canadian GP, Hungarian GP, Belgian GP, 2016 Malaysian GP, 2017 Azerbaijan GP, 2018 Chinese GP, Monaco GP, 2021 Italian GP
Poles:	**4**
Fastest laps:	**16**
Points:	**1274**
Honours:	**2010 FORMULA RENULT 3.5 RUNNER-UP, 2009 BRITISH FORMULA THREE CHAMPION, 2008 EUROPEAN FORMULA RENAULT RUNNER-UP & WESTERN EUROPEAN FORMULA RENAULT CHAMPION**

IT WAS ALL SMILES AT MONZA

Daniel's early-season results weren't great compared to his team-mate Lando Norris's opening run, with the Australian finishing a minimum of three places behind in each of the first three grands prix. Then there was a sense that Daniel was getting to understand the MCL35M better when he finished ahead, in sixth place, in the Spanish GP. But this was a false dawn and it was straight back onto the back foot next time out and stayed that way for the next six races as Norris kept on finishing in front. Then, finally, at the 12th round at Spa-Francorchamps, when Daniel claimed fourth. Yet, Daniel was working hard to get to grips with the car and, two races later, at Monza, he proved that he had, by winning the Italian GP on a day in which the collision between Lewis Hamilton and Max Verstappen didn't change the outcome. The normal Ricciardo smile became supercharged, a weight off his shoulders.

LANDO NORRIS

Any sequence that goes 11th, ninth, fifth shows good progress, and this is the track of Lando's first three years in F1. In 2022, the target has to be to break into the top three overall, something that will only be possible if McLaren is stronger.

Lando raced hard and chased hard last year, but is still waiting for his first F1 win.

After being a stand-out kart racer, starting with a European title and then augmenting that with world titles at junior and senior levels, Lando made his first steps in car racing in the Ginetta Junior series at the of 14. He then took a maximalist approach to his first couple of years of single-seater racing, as he had the money behind him to race as much as he pleased. Experience was gained by racing in the British, German and Italian F4 series in 2015, and a first title secured when he won the MSA Formula title.

It was the same in 2016 when Lando spent the northern hemisphere winter in New Zealand winning the Toyota Racing Series title. Then he came back to Europe and added the European Formula Renault and northern European regional title too. When he rounded out the year by winning the McLaren Autosport BRDC Young Driver award, his name was up in lights.

For 2017, Lando stepped up to the European F3 series and became one of a select gang to win it at their first attempt and also enjoyed his first taste of an F1 car, courtesy of the McLaren Autosport BRDC award.

The target for 2018 was to see whether he could win the last FIA series before F1 and Lando's consistent F2 campaign resulted in an impressive second place, ending the year just a few points ahead of Alex Albon but appreciably behind the year's dominant driver George Russell in a three-way British title fight that had Lando win one race, George seven and Alex four.

Then came F1, joining McLaren for 2019 and impressing everybody when he raced to sixth place on his second outing. This was at Sakhir, but he failed to improve on that in the following 19 races, albeit adding another in Austria.

In 2020, Lando benefitted not just from his year of F1 experience but from a major upswing in form for McLaren, finishing third in the opening race at the Red Bull Ring and kept on scoring but was overhauled by team-mate Carlos Sainz Jr.

TRACK NOTES

Nationality:	**BRITISH**
Born:	**13 NOVEMBER 1999, GLASTONBURY, ENGLAND**
Website:	**www.landonorris.com**
Teams:	**McLAREN 2019-22**

CAREER RECORD

First Grand Prix:	**2019 Australian GP**
Grand Prix starts:	**60**
Grand Prix wins:	**0 (best result: 2nd, 2021 Italian GP)**
Poles:	**1**
Fastest laps:	**3**
Points:	**306**
Honours:	**2018 F2 RUNNER-UP, 2017 EUROPEAN F3 CHAMPION, 2016 EUROPEAN FORMULA RENAULT CHAMPION & FORMULA RENAULT NEC CHAMPION & TOYOTA RACING SERIES CHAMPION, 2015 MSA FORMULA CHAMPION, 2014 WORLD KF KART CHAMPION, 2013 WORLD KF JUNIOR KART CHAMPION & EUROPEAN KF KART CHAMPION & KF JUNIOR SUPER CUP WINNER**

STARTING WITH A BIG BANG

Lando hit the ground running at the start of last year's World Championship, helped in no small part by McLaren's change from Renault to Mercedes engines. His run of fourth place at Sakhir, third at Imola and then fifth at the Algarve International Circuit in the first three races of the season showed that both he and McLaren meant business. That he left new team-mate Daniel Ricciardo in his wake was a further boost to his morale. Adding third-place finishes at Monaco and the Red Bull Ring kept the 21-year-old British racer near the sharp end of the championship standings. Lando scored in each of the first 10 grands prix to rank third before a non-finish in Hungary. Then came the Italian GP, when Lando scored a career-best second place, though he crossed the line behind his team-mate. Then the Ferrari challenge began to become more potent and Sergio Perez came on strong in the second Red Bull to move him down the order to sixth overall.

ALPINE

The yellow and black livery was replaced with red, white and blue for 2021 as the Alpine branding dressed what had previously been Renault, but this brought little progress on the track and Fernando Alonso and Esteban Ocon will be hoping for better in 2022.

Fernando Alonso took a while to settle in after returning to F1 in 2021 but is bound to be stronger now he has bedded in with the Alpine team.

Having raced as the Renault F1 team for two spells, yet having no connection to the original Renault F1 team, at least this team based in Oxfordshire appears to have settled on racing as Alpine for now.

In truth, although this team has moved around little, simply moving its base up the road from Witney to Enstone back in 1992, its name has been in what seems like constant flux.

Life started when the Toleman team founded by car transport magnate Ted Toleman stepped up from an F2 championship one-two for Brian Henton and Derek Warwick to F1 in 1981. After an inauspicious start, things improved through the next two seasons as Rory Byrne's Hart-engined designs became more competitive. Toleman made giant strides in 1984, led by F1 rookie Ayrton Senna, highlighted by a second place in Monaco, but Senna joined Lotus in 1985.

There was a major change for 1986 when the team underwent its first name

change, being called Benetton after the Italian knitwear company that was sponsoring it. Running with very powerful BMW turbocharged engines, Byrne's cars were competitive and Gerhard Berger gave the team its first win in Mexico.

From fifth overall in 1987, Benetton ranked third in 1988 as Thierry Boutsen

KEY PERSONNEL & 2021 ROUND-UP

DAVIDE BRIVIO
This 57-year-old Italian brought something new to F1 when he joined Alpine last year after managing director Cyril Abiteboul's surprise departure, as his background was in motorbike racing. Davide rode in motocross, worked as a journalist before going to World Superbikes' PR department. He joined Yamaha in 1992, switched to MotoGP in 1992 and won four world titles with Valentino Rossi and one with Jorge Lorenzo. Suzuki lured him over in 2013.

A SHOCK WIN DOESN'T HIDE A LACK OF SPEED
Esteban Ocon was a deserving winner of last year's extraordinary Hungarian GP, as he mastered tricky conditions superbly, but the 2021 season wasn't a glorious success to give the Alpine sportscar brand its dream start in F1. The team wanted to build on the midfield consistency of Renault and start to trouble the big guns, but even getting top-six, let alone podium, results proved largely beyond Ocon and Alonso.

2021 DRIVERS & RESULTS

Driver	Nationality	Races	Wins	Pts	Pos
Fernando Alonso	Spanish	22	0	81	10th
Esteban Ocon	French	22	1	74	11th

ran hard behind the dominant McLarens and a few more wins were added in 1989 and 1990 through Alessandro Nannini then Nelson Piquet.

The team's greatest spell came when Michael Schumacher joined and developed from rookie in 1991 to race winner precisely a year after his F1 debut in Belgium and became world champion in 1994 after a scrap with Williams' Damon Hill. Schumacher won the title again in 1995 after a change from Ford to Renault power also gave the team its first constructors' title.

In 2002, with Ferrari dominant, the team was badged as Renault simply because it was part of the deal to secure Renault engines rather than because of any connection to the team based at Viry-Chatillon in France that introduced turbo engines to F1 when it arrived in 1977 and ran on until 1985. A remarkable element about the various name changes is that the team personnel has been kept largely constant, with Pat Symonds staying from its pre-F1 Toleman days to lead its technical side after Byrne and Ross Brawn

moved on to Ferrari in the late 1990s.

Fortunately, good times were around the corner as Fernando Alonso was adding experience to his natural speed and advanced to take his first F1 win with the team, in Hungary in 2003. In 2005 and 2006 Alonso won back-to-back F1 titles, the latter title push, including seven wins, was augmented by consistent scoring from Giancarlo Fisichella. It landed the team its second constructors' championship.

What followed when Alonso left and then returned was less glorious as name change number three followed in 2012 when the team became Lotus Renault GP, named after Lotus Cars rather than having any connection Team Lotus of old. The deal to race as Lotus ran through until 2016 when it reverted to being called Renault again. A highlight of the Lotus period was when former World Champion Kimi Raikkonen, just one year after coming back from a two-year spell as a rally driver, triumphed in Australia in 2013.

Racing as Renault for a second spell from 2016, the team enjoyed good form

FOR THE RECORD

Country of origin:	**England**
Team base:	**Enstone, England**
Telephone:	**(44) 01608 678000**
Website:	**www.alpinecars.com**
Active in Formula One:	**As Toleman 1981-85, Benetton 1986-2001, Renault 2002-11 & 2016-2020, Lotus 2012-15, Alpine 2021 on**
Grands Prix contested:	**694**
Wins:	**49**
Pole positions:	**34**
Fastest laps:	**56**

THE TEAM

President:	**Jerome Stoll**
Racing director:	**Davide Brivio**
Executive director:	**Marcin Budkowski**
Chassis technical director:	**Pat Fry**
Chief aerodynamicist:	**Dirk de Beer**
Sporting director:	**Alan Permane**
Operations director:	**Rob White**
Chief engineer:	**Ciaron Pilbeam**
Team manager:	**Paul Seaby**
Test drivers:	**Oscar Piastri**
Chassis:	**Renault A522**
Engine:	**Renault V6**
Tyres:	**Pirelli**

from Nico Hulkenberg, Carlos Sainz Jr. and Daniel Ricciardo, albeit with the best of those years, 2018, being good enough only for fourth overall behind Mercedes, Ferrari and Red Bull Racing as Lewis Hamilton dominated ahead of Sebastian Vettel with Renault's Hulkenberg ranked seventh overall.

"The drama that Max Verstappen and Lewis Hamilton created in 2021 only made us hungrier to be up at the top of the grid fighting for wins and championships in the near future. That is our ultimate goal."

Laurent Rossi

Michael Schumacher races towards his second F1 title with Benetton at Hockenheim in 1995.

» FERNANDO ALONSO

Slotting back into F1 after three years away isn't as easy as people might think, even for a former World Champion, as shown by Michael Schumacher when he joined Mercedes. However, Fernando knuckled down and got faster through the year.

Fernando will have to relish the challenge of getting Alpine to the front to succeed.

Fernando gathered Spanish karting titles for fun as a teenager before winning the world title in 1996. The car racing world had a good idea of what was coming their way in 1999 and he delivered, winning the Formula Open by Nissan title in his rookie season.

Stepping up to E3000 in 2000, he didn't just win the final round at Spa-Francorchamps, but dominated it, elevating him to fourth in the final rankings. Not surprisingly, talent scouts paid attention and Benetton got his name on a contract.

Fernando got his F1 break in 2001, placed at Minardi to learn his craft. He then spent 2002 away from racing but gaining a lot of testing time before joining the Renault team (formerly Benetton) for 2003. Fernando was a winner just after the middle of the season, triumphing in Hungary.

Michael Schumacher was dominating for Ferrari, but Fernando was fourth in 2004, then won seven rounds to be champion in 2005 ahead of Kimi Raikkonen, then seven more to make it two titles in a row. A move to McLaren almost gave him a third, but his squabble with rookie team-mate Lewis Hamilton cost them both and allowed Ferrari's Raikkonen to pip them.

So it was back to Renault for 2008 but, after two poor years, Fernando went to Ferrari and came within a whisker of being crowned in 2010, only to be overtaken at the final round by Red Bull's Sebastian Vettel. That season produced five wins and it was downhill from here, with four years at declining McLaren notably disappointing.

Fernando sought new adventures and took two wins in the Le Mans 24 Hours, one in the Daytona 24 Hours plus a World Endurance title. He then returned to F1 at the age of 39 and his team of old, now called Alpine, welcomed him back.

TRACK NOTES

Nationality:	**SPANISH**
Born:	**29 JULY 1981, OVIEDO, SPAIN**
Website:	**www.fernandoalonso.com**
Teams:	**MINARDI 2001, RENAULT 2003-06, McLAREN 2007, RENAULT 2008-09, FERRARI 2010-14, McLAREN 2015-18, ALPINE 2021-22**

CAREER RECORD

First Grand Prix: **2001 AUSTRALIAN GP**

Grand Prix starts: **336**

Grand Prix wins: **32**
2003 Hungarian GP, 2005 Malaysian GP, Bahrain GP, San Marino GP, European GP, French GP, German GP, Chinese GP, 2006 Bahrain GP, Australian GP, Spanish GP, Monaco GP, British GP, Canadian GP, Japanese GP, 2007 Malaysian GP, Monaco GP, European GP, Italian GP, 2008 Singapore GP, Japanese GP, 2010 Australian GP, German GP, Italian GP, Singapore GP, Korean GP, 2011 Bitish GP, 2012 Malaysian GP, European GP, 2013 Chinese GP, Spanish GP

Poles:	**22**
Fastest laps:	**23**
Points:	**1980**

Honours: **2019 DAYTONA 24 HOURS WINNER, 2018/2019 WORLD ENDURANCE CHAMPION, 2018 & 2019 LE MANS 24 HOURS WINNER, 2005 & 2006 F1 WORLD CHAMPION, 2012 & 2013 F1 RUNNER_UP, 1999 FORMULA NISSAN CHAMPION, 1997 ITALIAN & SPANISH KART CHAMPION, 1996 WORLD & SPANISH KART CHAMPION, 1994 & 1995 SPANISH JUNIOR KART CHAMPION**

WAITING FOR A BETTER CAR

Any double World Champion has to be watched carefully when they return to F1 after time away. There is no guarantee that they will immediately be on the pace, despite their obvious skills, as cars and tyres can change a lot in just a few years. And so it was when he rejoined the team with which he achieved his title success. Admittedly, this was way back in 2005 and 2006, back when Alpine raced as Renault. However, after being shown the way by team-mate Esteban Ocon in the early-season races, Fernando began to get back into the swing of things and was able to do more than claim his season's best finish of fourth place in Hungary, as he also drove defensively enough to hold back Lewis Hamilton's Mercedes and so protect the lead that Ocon would convert into his first F1 victory. The highlight of the remainder of the season was his run to third place on F1's first visit to the Losail circuit in Qatar.

ESTEBAN OCON

Any season that contains a driver's maiden victory is good for their morale, and Esteban will have been bolstered by his success in the Hungarian GP and hope that Alpine can also find steps forward as F1 welcomes new technical rules.

Esteban took a popular victory last year, but life will continue to be tough in 2022.

Esteban showed form in kart racing that suggested that he was special. However, when he started he first had to prove that he was one of the best of the young French stars at the head of the pack. Pierre Gasly had his nose just in front, but he was chased hard by Esteban and Anthoine Hubert.

They all graduated to car racing as soon as they were able, with Esteban starting in Formula Renault in 2012 in the year he turned 16. At the second time of asking, he advanced from a podium appearance in the European championship to winning races and ranking third as Gasly took the crown. Importantly, his skill had been noticed as he was put on the books of the Lotus F1 Junior Team and in 2014 he had his first F1 test.

The focus of 2014, though, was the FIA F3 Euro series and he won that by taking nine wins for Prema Powerteam, enough to leave racing rookie Max Verstappen third.

Although he wanted to step up to F2, he didn't have the budget, so he moved slightly sideways to try GP3. Fortunately, Esteban won that title as well, this time for ART Grand Prix. Two days of testing for the Force India F1 team kept him in the frame, but no budget was there to advance, so Esteban headed to touring cars instead, to a pair drive in the DTM, placed there by Mercedes. Amazingly, his allegiance to Mercedes gave him his break before the year was out, as the Manor F1 team dropped Ryo Haryanto and Esteban took his place.

A move to Force India in 2017 was a step up and Esteban impressed by ranking eighth, just a few points behind experienced team-mate Sergio Perez, with a best finish of fifth, achieved twice.

Esteban didn't score as well in 2018 and dropped to 12th, then losing his ride to Lance Stroll. However, Esteban tested for Renault and then raced for the team the following year and finished well by taking second in the Sakhir GP.

TRACK NOTES

Nationality:	**FRENCH**
Born:	**17 SEPTEMBER 1996,**
	EVREUX, FRANCE
Website:	**www.esteban-ocon.com**
Teams:	**MANOR 2016, FORCE INDIA**
	2017-18, RENAULT 2020, ALPINE
	2021-22

CAREER RECORD

First Grand Prix:	**2016 BELGIAN GP**
Grand Prix starts:	**89**
Grand Prix wins:	**1**
	2021 Hungarian GP
Poles:	**0**
Fastest laps:	**0**
Points:	**272**
Honours:	**2015 GP3 CHAMPION, 2014 FIA**
	EUROPEAN FORMULA THREE CHAMPION

ESTEBAN'S BREAKTHROUGH WIN

The 2021 Hungarian GP will be remembered for a long time and not necessarily because it was Esteban's first F1 win. What most fans will recall is that it was a chaotic race with a shunt at the first corner that necessitated a restart and then that Lewis Hamilton had to immediately pit to go on to the correct – dry weather – tyres. The Mercedes driver then mounted a fantastic charge but, with help from team-mate Fernando Alonso, Esteban was able to hang on to win. So, at the very least he took the 25 points for a win but, in his eternal battle with former karting rival Pierre Gasly, he now had parity again following his compatriot's win at Monza in 2020. Showing how out of the ordinary this result was, Esteban didn't get within a sniff of another podium finish, with his second best result of 2021 coming in the second last grand prix in Saudi Arabia GP when he came home fourth.

» SCUDERIA ALPHATAURI

This team that once ploughed around at the back of the field far away from scoring points in its Minardi days is maturing nicely and its now comfortably part of F1's midfield, looking even more consistent than it was when it ran as Scuderia Toro Rosso.

Japanese racer Yuki Tsunoda gives AlphaTauri a cosmopolitan feel, but it is French ace Pierre Gasly who leads the Italian team's attack.

Many people increasingly had a lot of time for the Minardi F1 team. This wasn't because it won a lot of grands prix. In fact, it never won any or even scored more than the very occasional point. However, people admired the team and its mainly black and yellow cars simply for keeping going, for plugging onwards despite achieving little of note.

The team – which changed identity twice before becoming AlphaTauri – was founded by Fiat dealer Giancarlo Minardi in 1980 after he had run teams in the junior formulae in Italy and then around Europe in F2. Building his own cars was the next step and Giancarlo was soon rewarded when rising star Michele Alboreto won in one in 1981. Although frontrunners over the next few seasons, notably with Alessandro Nannini, no more wins followed. The demise of F2 after 1985 encouraged Minardi to try F1, but it was only in the third year that it found any decent form.

The first real step forward for Minardi came in 1988 when it replaced its heavy and unreliable Motori Moderni engines with Ford units. It took until the arrival of Aldo Costa though, for the team to get a wieldy chassis. All their travails were rewarded when the team took fifth and sixth places in the 1989 British GP

KEY PERSONNEL & 2021 ROUND-UP

HELMUT MARKO

Helmut cut his teeth in Formula Super Vee, then tried F3 and sportscars, finishing third in the 1970 Le Mans 24 Hours, before winning it in a Porsche in 1971. He also made his F1 debut, renting a BRM. After finishing eighth at Monaco in 1972, his career ended when a stone flew into one of his eyes in the French GP. Marko went on to run teams in F3 then F3000 before befriending Red Bull founder Dietrich Mateschitz for whom he oversees its driver development programme.

GASLY STARS AGAIN, BUT TO WHAT REWARD?

There were no wins in 2021, after Pierre Gasly's amazing win at Monza in 2020, but none were expected. That said, no one would have predicted that Gasly would stand on the podium at Baku, but he did. For all his heroics, there was to be a return to parent team Red Bull Racing. Rookie team-mate Yuki Tsunoda looked hugely promising by finishing ninth at the opening race, but he then fell away, until coming good to lead Gasly home in a fourth/fifth finish in Abu Dhabi.

2021 DRIVERS & RESULTS

Driver	Nationality	Races	Wins	Pts	Pos
Pierre Gasly	French	22	0	110	9th
Yuki Tsunoda	Japanese	21	0	32	14th

FOR THE RECORD

Country of origin:	**Italy**
Team base:	**Faenza, Italy**
Telephone:	**(39) 546 696111**
Website:	**www.scuderialphatauri.com**
Active in Formula One:	**As Minardi 1985-2005, Toro Rosso 2006-19, AlphaTauri 2020 on**
Grands Prix contested:	**648**
Wins:	**2**
Pole positions:	**1**
Fastest laps:	**2**

THE TEAM

Team owner:	**Dietrich Mateschitz**
Team principal:	**Franz Tost**
Technical director:	**Jody Egginton**
Chief designer:	**Paolo Marabini**
Head of aerodynamics:	**tba**
Head of vehicle performance:	**Guillaume Dezoteux**
Team manager:	**Graham Watson**
Team co-ordinator:	**Michele Andreazza**
Chief engineer:	**tba**
Chief race engineer:	**Jonathan Eddols**
Test driver:	**Liam Lawson**
Chassis:	**AlphaTauri AT03**
Engine:	**Honda V6**
Tyres:	**Pirelli**

at Silverstone, Pierluigi Martini finishing ahead of Luis Perez Sala. Later in the year, Martini led the Portuguese GP at Estoril for a single lap when, during late-race tyre-changing pitstops, he fell back to fifth. Then, making the most of Pirelli tyres that worked brilliantly in qualifying, Martini started the United States GP at Phoenix on the front row before falling back to a seventh place finish.

A move to run with Ferrari engines in 1991 paid off when the team ranked seventh overall, chiefly down to Martini going well at Estoril again, this time finishing fourth. The deal didn't last though and the next year saw the cars powered by Lamborghini engines before changing to Ford HBs for 1993 boosted the team to eighth overall as Christian Fittipaldi went well.

In the years that followed, Minardi stuck to its aim of giving rising Italian drivers their F1 breaks, including Giancarlo Fisichella and Jarno Trulli, while also providing an opening later on for Spain's great hope, Fernando Alonso.

However, it was increasingly difficult to keep up financially and so any point-scoring result that eluded them hurt considerably. Indeed, none more so than when Luca Badoer was heading to fourth place in the European GP at the Nurburgring in 1999, only for his gearbox to fail.

The inevitable happened in 2001 when Paul Stoddart took over the team and Mark Webber cheered his fellow Australian enormously at the start of 2002 when he finished fifth in Melbourne.

By the start of 2006, however, the team had a new identity as money from the Red Bull group turned it into Red Bull Racing's junior team, now with the name of Scuderia Toro Rosso ("Team Red Bull" in Italian). The aim was to try out its best scholarship drivers and see if they could cut it in F1. If they could, then a year or two with Toro Rosso would give them a shot at stepping up to drive for Red Bull Racing.

They never expected them to win while at Toro Rosso, although this is what Sebastian Vettel did at a wet Italian GP in 2008, embarrassingly before the senior team registered the first of its victories. Vettel's reward was promotion. Others have followed since, but some have then been demoted again, including Daniil Kvyat and Pierre Gasly. The latter then came second in the 2019 Brazilian GP, then went one better when he won the Italian GP in 2020.

Gerhard Berger celebrates with Sebastian Vettel at Monza in 2008 after the team's first win.

"We finished the season on our highest points total in the history of the team and only 13 behind Alpine. The team made a big step forward in all areas and I'm looking forward to 2022 with hopefully a competitive new car to fight for strong positions."

Franz Tost

PIERRE GASLY

There were no repeat wins for Pierre in 2021, but he displayed his undoubted talent with another podium performance for AlphaTauri and backed that up with a fourth place, making him the best driver awaiting a break with a top team.

Pierre was consistently strong in 2021 and this may be his last year before moving on.

Many times, a driver has displayed all the right credentials to have a shot at making it to the top. Yet, usually because of a lack of finance, that hasn't happened. Fortunately, Pierre is one who managed to keep rising through the ranks.

Pierre has always done enough to facilitate the next step. So, the skills that landed him second place in European KF3 kart series in 2010 were used to become

European Formula Renault champion three years later. However, this was at his second attempt, having been 10th in 2012 and his career might have fizzled out had he not finished on top of the pile.

Pierre's next target was Formula Renault 3.5, importantly with sponsorship from Red Bull as he joined its make-or-break driver-search programme. These cars offered much more power and he took to them well enough to harry Carlos Sainz Jr for the title, ending up second.

This accelerated Pierre's career and he stepped up to GP2, and he took the title at the second attempt in 2016, pipping Antonio Giovinazzi. Unfortunately, there were no openings in F1 and so Red Bull elected to pay for him to spend a year racing in Super Formula in Japan. This was out of the spotlight to an extent, but gave him longer races in diverse weather conditions, all on circuits he had to learn. And learn he did, as Pierre not only won twice but beat every driver other than the hugely experienced Hiroaki Ishiura to end the year as runner-up.

Late in 2017, his F1 break came when Scuderia Toro Rosso dropped Daniil

Kvyat. Pierre was then kept on for 2018 and because he claimed a fourth place, he was promoted to Red Bull Racing for 2019.

Pierre was then overshadowed by Max Verstappen and dropped back to Toro Rosso before the year was out.

The team was renamed as Scuderia AlphaTauri for 2020 and Pierre produced the drive of the year to win the Italian GP, which made it all the more surprising that he didn't get reinstated at Red Bull Racing for 2021 so he had no choice but to keep on pressing on where he was.

TRACK NOTES

Nationality: **FRENCH**
Born: **7 FEBRUARY 1996, ROUEN, FRANCE**
Website: **www.pierregasly.com**
Teams: **TORO ROSSO 2017-18 & 2019, RED BULL RACING 2019, ALPHATAURI 2020-22**

CAREER RECORD

First Grand Prix: **2017 MALAYSIAN GP**
Grand Prix starts: **86**
Grand Prix wins: **1 (2020 Italian GP)**
Poles: **0**
Fastest laps: **3**
Points: **309**
Honours: **2017 JAPANESE SUPER FORMULA RUNNER-UP, 2016 GP2 CHAMPION, 2014 FORMULA RENAULT 3.5 RUNNER-UP, 2013 EUROPEAN FORMULA RENAULT CHAMPION, 2010 EUROPEAN KF3 KART RUNNER-UP**

ANOTHER YEAR OF EXCELLENCE

Pierre likely felt vexed that Sergio Perez was selected instead of him to fill the seat vacated at Red Bull Racing by Alex Albon's departure at the end of 2020, given his own long-term connection with Red Bull. Yet, he got on with the job and followed up an impressive sixth place at Monaco with a stunning third around the streets of Baku, ironically a race won by Perez. From then on, Pierre drove better than Sergio, gathering a string of top-six finishes for what is, don't forget, Red Bull's second-string team. His fourth place in the Dutch GP was another highlight, a result that he matched in the Mexican GP. That Pierre scored points in four of the final five grands prix emphasised how the team had made progress with its Honda-engined AT02 and he simply did the rest. Finishing fifth in the final race of the season ought to have been a fillip, but it will play on Pierre's mind all winter than this was one place behind his junior team-mate Tsunoda.

YUKI TSUNODA

Japanese F1 fans had been wanting a driver of their own to cheer on for six years and last year Yuki showed that he might become their hero, but only if he learns the lessons from his first year at the sport's top level.

Yuki has a lot to learn but can certainly produce the speed to impress on occasion.

Stepping into Formula 4 just after his 16th birthday, Yuki showed that he could be competitive in the Japanese series. So, he returned for a full campaign in 2017 and lived up to that promise as he became a race winner then added two more later in the year and went on to rank third in this entry-level category. Electing to come back to try to win the title in 2018, he secured 10 poles, seven

wins and the title he was seeking.

With an eye on trying his luck in Europe, Yuki had three days testing a GP3 car. Encouraged by this, and with backing from Red Bull as one of its junior drivers, he committed instead to the FIA F3 series in 2019 and added a parallel season in Euroformula Open, a second division F3 series. This gave him extra seat time and Yuki took a win in that at the third round at Hockenheim. Bolstered by this, Yuki then moved ever closer to the front of the field, finally taking his first FIA F3 victory for Jenzer Motorsport at the penultimate round at Monza, elevating him to ninth in a series dominated by Robert Schwartzman.

In 2020, anxious to gain as much experience as possible, Yuki began his racing season contesting the Toyota Racing Series in New Zealand and was a creditable fourth in that before heading to Europe.

Yuki's appeal was obvious to Scuderia AlphaTauri's engine supplier Honda and what was also a consideration was that young Japanese fans in particular would

like his "maximum attack" approach.

Yuki's main focus in 2020, though, was stepping up to F2, joining the Carlin team. As early as the opening meeting at the Red Bull Ring, Yuki demonstrated that he was up for the challenge by grabbing a second place. Wins followed, albeit with his first one coming after Nikita Mazepin was given a penalty at Spa-Francorchamps. He then won again at Silverstone and at Sakhir, and this was enough for Yuki to end the year ranked third overall behind Ferrari junior drivers Mick Schumacher and Callum Ilott. Thus Yuki earned his F1 seat, to become the first Japanese F1 driver since Kamui Kobayashi raced for Caterham in 2014.

TRACK NOTES

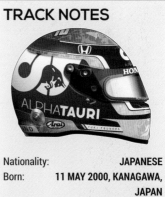

Nationality:	**JAPANESE**
Born:	**11 MAY 2000, KANAGAWA, JAPAN**
Website:	**www.yukitsunoda.com**
Teams:	**ALPHATAURI 2021-22**

CAREER RECORD

First Grand Prix:	**2021 AUSTRALIAN GP**
Grand Prix starts:	**21**
Grand Prix wins:	**0**
Poles:	**0**
Fastest laps:	**0**
Points:	**32**
Honours:	**2018 JAPANESE F4 CHAMPION**

STARTING WITH A BANG

Scoring points on his debut by finishing ninth in Bahrain was a great start to small but feisty Yuki's F1 career, and triggered much excitement in his native Japan. However, what followed was not as impressive as Yuki made mistakes, some through being overly aggressive, and was seldom as competitive. Importantly, though, Yuki listened and learned and was back on form in the second half of the season. He was notably rewarded with sixth place in the crash-hit Hungarian GP. Yuki had an excellent yardstick in team-mate Pierre Gasly and clearly learned a great deal from the Frenchman as the campaign progressed. Proof that he was taking his weaknesses into consideration, Yuki calmed down and took a good ninth in the United States GP, before rounding out with a brilliant fourth in the final round in Abu Dhabi.

It's not just the teams that bring transporters to races. These are Pirelli's with the F1 TV pop-up production facility in the background.

» ASTON MARTIN F1 TEAM

Aston Martin F1 Team has bold plans for the future, with an enlarged facility in Silverstone under construction, but it will be hoping that the new rules in 2022 will give it a chance to move back up the order after a troubled first season racing with its latest identity.

Second place in the Azerbaijan GP was the first glint of promise for Sebastian Vettel in 2021, and now he is looking to aim for more top scores.

Ferrari has been Ferrari since before the start of the World Championship in 1950. Yet, in less than half that time, the team based across from the main gates at Silverstone, the team that became Aston Martin F1 Team in 2021, has raced in F1 previously as Jordan, Midland, Spyker, Force India and Racing Point.

Irish racer Eddie Jordan went as far as he could behind the wheel but then elected to use his renowned bartering skills to better effect, by running cars for others. Eddie Jordan Racing had a modicum of success in British F3, but then really made a name for itself in what was F1's immediate feeder formula, F3000, in the late 1980s, guiding Jean Alesi, Johnny Herbert and Martin Donnelly to many successes.

Jordan was nothing if not ambitious and so elected to try to graduate to F1 in 1991. Fellow Irishman Gary Anderson designed the car, custom Ford HB engines were sourced and they made a near instant impact, amazingly ranking fifth in their maiden season.

This initial success was hard to replicate as Jordan sought to find a works engine deal to help cut costs, with the team's first notable result being a two-three finish in the 1995 Canadian GP in a year with Peugeot engines.

KEY PERSONNEL & 2021 ROUND-UP

MARTIN WHITMARSH

Martin worked on fighter plane production at British Aerospace. These skills were sought by McLaren when it signed him as head of operations in 1989. By 1997, he had become managing director and ran the F1 team under Ron Dennis. Titles for Mika Hakkinen in 1998 and 1999 put McLaren on top and Whitmarsh stayed at the helm until 2014. Moving to a new area, Martin joined Britain's America's Cup yachting project, working with Ben Ainslie before Aston Martin signed him.

A CHANGE OF NAME DIDN'T LEAD TO GAINS

From fighting over third place with McLaren in 2020, the renamed Aston Martin team regressed in 2021 as Sebastian Vettel seemed out of sorts in the first part of the year before racing to second in Baku and again in Hungary before being disqualified. Lance Stroll was more consistent, but finished in lesser positions. However, with Ferrari, Renault and AlphaTauri having upped their game, the season proved a long and unsatisfactory one for the team in dark metallic green.

2021 DRIVERS & RESULTS

Driver	Nationality	Races	Wins	Pts	Pos
Sebastian Vettel	German	22	0	43	12th
Lance Stroll	Canadian	22	0	34	13th

Three years later, now with Mugen Honda power, Eddie Jordan had his day of days when he found himself in the luxurious position in having to ask Ralf Schumacher to back off in the closing laps of the Belgian GP so that the team could be sure of taking not just its first win, but a one-two that helped it rank a then record fourth at the year's end.

What marked the team out was its rock-and-roll nature, its image as being the upstart ruffling the feathers of the establishment and this was carried through to 1999 when Jordan advanced to third as Heinz-Harald Frentzen won in France and in Italy too.

The next Jordan win didn't come until 2003 when Giancarlo Fisichella triumphed in Brazil. By this point, F1 was becoming ever more expensive and Jordan sold the team to steel magnate Alex Shnaider at the end of 2004. The rebranding as Midland didn't last long, as a second name change followed for 2007 when it was named Spyker after an old Dutch sportscar brand. That lasted all of one year before Indian millionaire and sometime racer Vijay Mallya bought them out and renamed the team Force India.

Always battling to find even a mid-sized budget, the team punched above its weight, with Fisichella, Sergio Perez, Paul di Resta and Nico Hulkenberg going well.

Unfortunately, the Indian authorities wanted to question Mallya about financial matters and the wolf was only kept from the door by Lawrence Stroll paying off the debts and taking over the team from 2019. At last the team had some financial stability. The staff were certain their wages would be met and suppliers could be sure their invoices would be paid.

This reignited their ambition, as seventh overall in 2019 was followed by fourth in 2020, behind only Mercedes, Red Bull and McLaren. In fact, if it had not been for a 15-point deduction for some of its parts looking as if they had been copied from the 2019 Mercedes, it would have been good for third. The season did end well, though, as long-time servant Perez took his first F1 win in the penultimate round after being told that he wouldn't be being kept on for 2021.

Perhaps the boldest statement of intent that the team means business is the signing of former McLaren chief Martin Whitmarsh to guide its programme.

FOR THE RECORD

Country of origin:	England
Team base:	Silverstone, England
Telephone:	(44) 01327 850800
Website:	www.astonmartinf1.com
Active in Formula One:	As Jordan 1991-2004, Midland 2005-06, Spyker 2007, Force India 2008-18, Racing Point 2019-20, Aston Martin 2021 on
Grands Prix contested:	557
Wins:	5
Pole positions:	4
Fastest laps:	7

THE TEAM

Chief executive officer:	Martin Whitmarsh
Chief technical officer:	Andrew Green
Technical director:	Dan Fallows
Sporting director:	Andy Stevenson
Factory engineering director:	Luca Furbatto
Production director:	Bob Halliwell
Chief designers:	Akio Haga & Ian Hall
Aerodynamics director:	Simon Phillips
Performance engineering director:	Tom McCullough
Operations manager:	Mark Gray
Test driver:	tba
Chassis:	Aston Martin AMR22
Engine:	Mercedes V6
Tyres:	Pirelli

41

Giancarlo Fisichella, heading for second at Spa in 2009, was one of the Force India stars.

"We learned a lot through the 2021 World Championship season and that will put us in good stead for 2022. It was great to be a part of Aston Martin's first year back in F1 and I am sure that there is a bright future ahead."

Lance Stroll

»SEBASTIAN VETTEL

There were times last year when Sebastian looked out of sorts at Aston Martin, but there were also times when all his old skills shone through. If the team's new car is a good one, expect this German veteran to shine again.

Sebastian said racing in the midfield didn't interest him so he's aiming high in 2022.

In the decade following Michael Schumacher's remarkable ascent, German fans wondered which of their young drivers might be able to follow in his wheel tracks and become a World Champion. Ralf Schumacher would become a grand prix winner, but Sebastian was the driver who looked next most likely to land an F1 title.

A driver with a German and a European karting title to his name, he clearly had a good pedigree, then proved that when he advanced to single-seaters, blitzing the opposition in Formula BMW with 18 wins from 20 in 2004. Top rookie in his first year of European F3, he ended 2006 second to Paul di Resta, but won once in Formula Renault 3.5. So he opted for that for 2007.

However, Sebastian was an F1 driver before the year was out, getting his chance when Robert Kubica was injured. This was a one-off but a few races later he took over the second Toro Rosso seat from Scott Speed. In 2008, Sebastian gave Red Bull's second F1 team its greatest day when he dominated the Italian GP. Unsurprisingly, he was promoted to Red Bull Racing. After finishing second to Brawn GP's Jenson Button in 2009, he took the 2010 title, becoming F1's youngest champion at just 23, then followed that up with the next three for good measure, taking 12 wins in 2011 and 13 two years later.

Sebastian joined Ferrari in 2015, but couldn't keep up with Lewis Hamilton and Mercedes. Second in 2017 and 2018, he then fell out of favour when Charles Leclerc became the team's choice, so elected to move on after 2020.

TWO SECONDS, BUT LITTLE ELSE

Racing Point had ranked fourth overall in 2020 and would have ended up third if it hadn't had a points deduction. So, when Sebastian joined the team he must have had high hopes that life after Ferrari – sixth in 2020 – might not be so bad after all. Wrong. Although the team had a new identity as it was renamed as Aston Martin, its AMR21 was simply not as competitive as the RP20 had been, as shown by Sebastian's first races producing a pair of 15ths followed by a pair of 13ths. These were not results befitting a four-time World Champion, as team-mate Lance Stroll finished ahead of him in three of these. However, the car improved and a fifth place in Monaco elicited the first smile of the year. Sebastian raced to second place in Baku, and there was another second place in the Hungarian GP, but this then turned into disqualification as there hadn't been enough fuel left for a post-race sample to be taken.

TRACK NOTES

Nationality:	**GERMAN**
Born:	**3 JULY 1987,**
	HEPPENHEIM, GERMANY
Website:	**www.sebastianvettel.de**
Teams:	**BMW SAUBER 2007,**
	TORO ROSSO 2007-08, RED BULL
	RACING 2009-14, FERRARI 2015-20,
	ASTON MARTIN 2021-22

CAREER RECORD

First Grand Prix:	**2007 UNITED STATES GP**
Grand Prix starts:	**280**
Grand Prix wins:	**53**

2008 Italian GP, 2009 Chinese GP, British GP, Japanese GP, Abu Dhabi GP, 2010 Malaysian GP, European GP, Japanese GP, Brazilian GP, Abu Dhabi GP, 2011 Australian GP, Malaysian GP, Turkish GP, Spanish GP, Monaco GP, European GP, Belgian GP, Italian GP, Singapore GP, Korean GP, Indian GP, 2012 Bahrain GP, Singapore GP, Japanese GP, Korean GP, Indian GP, 2013 Malaysian GP, Bahrain GP, Canadian GP, German GP, Belgian GP, Italian GP, Singapore GP, Korean GP, Japanese GP, Indian GP, Abu Dhabi GP, United States GP, Brazilian GP, 2015 Malaysian GP, Hungarian GP, Singapore GP, 2017 Australian GP, Bahrain GP, Monaco GP, Hungarian GP, Brazilian GP, 2018 Australian GP, Bahrain GP, Canadian GP, British GP, Belgian GP, 2019 Singapore GP

Poles:	**57**
Fastest laps:	**38**
Points:	**3061**

Honours: **2010, 2011, 2012 & 2014 F1 WORLD CHAMPION, 2009, 2017 & 2018 FORMULA ONE RUNNER-UP, 2006 EUROPEAN FORMULA THREE RUNNER-UP, 2004 GERMAN FORMULA BMW ADAC CHAMPION, 2003 GERMAN FORMULA BMW ADAC RUNNER-UP, 2001 EUROPEAN & GERMAN JUNIOR KART CHAMPION**

LANCE STROLL

Lance has shown flashes of speed through his career but, as this will be his sixth season in F1, he must be hoping that he can have a car to challenge at the very least the other teams at the front of the midfield.

Lance will have learnt a lot from Vettel in 2021 and must now put that into practice.

Anyone looking at this Canadian racer's career will see that he has pace aplenty and bravado too. However, it's impossible to ignore the fact that he has, far more than most, always been in a position to learn from his mistakes and keep on attacking, as he has a billionaire as a father. In fact, these days, a motor racing mad billionaire who happens to be ploughing a great deal of money into

turning Aston Martin around.

While his father Lawrence was racing Ferraris, Lance got stuck in to karting and did well enough to rank sixth in the World KF series. That was in 2013 when he was 14 and this was enough for him to join the Ferrari Driver Academy and he kicked off the 2014 in the Ferrari-backed Florida Winter Series. The main target in the 15-year-old's season, however, was the Italian F4 championship and Lance won that at a canter.

Heading to New Zealand during the southern hemisphere summer, Lance won the Toyota Racing Series, then stepped up to European F3 and finished fifth, behind both Antonio Giovinazzi and Charles Leclerc in a season that was peppered with accidents.

So, the target in 2016 was to stay on with Prema Powerteam, eliminate those mistakes and win the title. Lance did both, grabbing 14 wins to take the title in style.

Lance also ended his Ferrari tie as his father invested in the financially beleaguered Williams team and so Lance skipped F2 and went straight into F1 at the age of 18 in 2017. And his first

season was a considerable success as not only did he all but match the points tally of veteran team-mate Felipe Massa, but he raced to third place in the Azerbaijan GP.

Unfortunately, Williams was a team going backwards and so Lance followed Lawrence's investment to Racing Point for 2019 and then spent a couple of seasons racing alongside Sergio Perez. These were going learning years and although outperformed by the Mexican both years, a pair of third places at Monza and Sakhir were good reward.

TRACK NOTES

Nationality:	**CANADIAN**
Born:	**29 OCTOBER 1998,**
	MONTREAL, CANADA
Website:	**www.lancestroll.com**
Teams:	**WILLIAMS**
	2017-18, RACING POINT 2019-20,
	ASTON MARTIN 2021-22

CAREER RECORD

First Grand Prix:	**2017 AUSTRALIAN GP**
Grand Prix starts:	**100**
Grand Prix wins:	**0 (best result: 3rd, 2017**
Azerbaijan GP, 2020 Italian GP, Sakhir GP)	
Poles:	**1**
Fastest laps:	**0**
Points:	**176**
Honours:	**2016 FIA EUROPEAN**
FORMULA THREE CHAMPION, 2015 TOYOTA	
RACING SERIES CHAMPION, 2014 ITALIAN	
FORMULA FOUR CHAMPION	

WAITING FOR 2022 TO COME

Last year was a setback for Lance. It was his fifth year in F1 and one of his most troubled. There were no podium finishes to match the two third places he achieved in 2020. In fact, the Canadian's best finish was a seventh place in the Italian GP at Monza. However, this was more to do with Aston Martin being less competitive compared to its midfield rivals than Racing Point had been in the previous season. Of course, it's nigh on impossible for a driver to maintain career momentum in a team that is losing ground, so the chief point of interest was how Lance would perform against a new team-mate who happened to be a multiple World Champion. This was, of course, Sebastian Vettel, and at first he fared well, but then Sebastian got around car problems to show his class. So, as the year drew to a close, all Lance could do was to pray that the designers were creating a car for 2022 that will be relatively more competitive when the new technical rules are introduced.

» WILLIAMS

George Russell's second place at Spa last year turned out to be an anomaly, but this is a team that is starting to turn the corner under new ownership and it's great for F1 when vital parts of its history, such as the Williams name, are reinvigorated.

Nicholas Latifi was seldom a match for George Russell but this year will be hoping that he can come out ahead of new team-mate Alex Albon.

Formula One teams come and they go and one of the best things since founder Frank Williams' family relinquished control towards the end of the 2020 season is that there was no change. There might be new ownership, new management, a new livery and new ideas, but its illustrious history hasn't been buried.

People might have laughed at Frank Williams' early days in F1 in the 1970s when his attempts to run his own F1 team always lacked that vital main ingredient: money.

Yet Frank pressed on and after going into partnership with engineer Patrick Head, the corner began to be turned in the late 1970s when the team had a sensible amount of backing for the first time. Alan Jones was a great driver and he gelled with the Head-designed FW07B so well that he landed the 1980 drivers' title and, supported by Carlos Reutemann, the team won the constructors' title too.

As in most sports, success begat

success and Williams won the title again in 1981, although Reutemann blew his title chance in the last round at Las Vegas. Williams then signed Keke Rosberg and

he promptly won the drivers' title in an extraordinarily close 1982 season.

Moving to Honda engines in the mid-1980s helped Williams to find a

KEY PERSONNEL & 2021 ROUND-UP

JOST CAPITO
Williams' team principal raced motorbikes and won the truck sector of the Paris-Dakar Rally before joining BMW's engine development division. After spells at VW and Porsche, Jost got taste of F1 with Sauber in 1996 before helping to guide Ford to two World Rally titles, then VW to three more WRC titles. His return to F1 in 2016 with McLaren lasted just three months and he then ran VW's R performance division before joining Williams.

SECOND IN BELGIUM IS A MASSIVE FILLIP
The take-over from the Williams family late in the 2020 season wasn't expected to lead to a sudden improvement, but the signs were there that points might be achievable. This proved correct when Nicholas Latifi and George Russell grabbed seventh and eighth in the crash-strewn Hungarian GP. That was nothing to what happened next time out when Russell qualified second in the wet at Spa and took points for second place when the race was halted because of awful conditions.

2021 DRIVERS & RESULTS

Driver	Nationality	Races	Wins	Pts	Pos
George Russell	British	22	0	16	15th
Nicholas Latifi	Canadian	22	0	7	17th

competitive edge and only a blowout in the 1986 finale in Adelaide prevented Nigel Mansell from becoming the team's third world champion. This was a further blow to the team after Frank had a road accident on his return from a pre-season test at Paul Ricard and became confined to a wheelchair. Some cheer was provided when Nelson Piquet got the job done in 1987 before the subsequent loss of Honda power to McLaren knocked Williams back. Adrian Newey joined in 1991 and began to make great chassis that combined with excellent Renault V10 engines to move the team back to the front in the early 1990s. And so started the team's greatest days, with a run of five constructors' titles in six years, first with a runaway title for Mansell in 1992 when he won eight of the first ten grands prix to build up an unassailable lead.

Williams has, like Enzo Ferrari before him, been ruthless in his driver choice, shown by the way that he immediately replaced Mansell with Alain Prost who took the 1993 crown. He too was dropped,

to make way for Ayrton Senna in 1994, but the Brazilian great was killed on his third outing. Damon Hill stepped up and came close to winning that year's title before getting one over Michael Schumacher in 1996 then Jacques Villeneuve became Williams' most recent champion in 1997.

Nothing stays the same forever and Newey moved on to McLaren and success only returned when Williams went into partnership with BMW, leading to wins but not titles for Juan Pablo Montoya and Ralf Schumacher in 2001 and 2002.

Since then, though, this team that had moved to third in the all-time list of F1 winners stopped winning, save for an extraordinary day in 2012 when Pastor Maldonado came good at the Spanish GP. Not winning races didn't just mean a lack of points, but a lack of prize money and a loss of prestige, followed by the drying up of a supply of competitive engines.

Despite the team's dwindling form, there was still tremendous respect for Frank in the pitlane, but it was operating

FOR THE RECORD

Country of origin:	**England**
Team base:	**Grove, England**
Telephone:	**(44) 01235 777700**
Website:	**www.williamsf1.com**
Active in Formula One:	**From 1972**
Grands Prix contested:	**822**
Wins:	**114**
Pole positions:	**128**
Fastest laps:	**133**

THE TEAM

Chairman:	**Matthew Savage**
Team principal:	**Jost Capito**
Chief technical officer:	
	Francois-Xavier Demaison
Chief designer:	**David Warner**
Deputy chief designer:	**Jonathan Carter**
Design consultant:	**Willy Rampf**
Chief engineer:	**Doug McKiernan**
Head of aerodynamics:	**Dave Wheater**
Head of vehicle performance:	
	Dave Robson
Team manager:	**David Redding**
Test driver:	**Logan Sargeant**
Chassis:	**Williams FW44**
Engine:	**Mercedes V6**
Tyres:	**Pirelli**

at the 'wrong' end of the grid from 2018 onwards and so something had to change or risk the team either folding or being suffocated in a take-over bid. Fortunately, a consortium of people with a racing soul took it over in 2020 and everyone would love to see this once great team rise to the top again as reward for those years of toil.

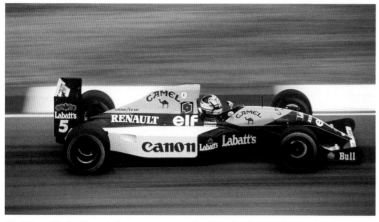

Nigel Mansell led Williams in its best ever season in 1992, when he won nine grands prix.

> **"The long history was a big part of me joining Williams, and the fact that Williams had been so successful but was now having hard times. I absolutely believe that Williams can win again."**
>
> Jost Capito

ALEX ALBON

After a year spent on the sidelines, Alex is back in F1, this time with Williams. The former Red Bull Racing racer has shown he is rapid and will be determined to make sure that he makes his mark this time around.

Alex is back in F1 after a year on the sidelines and should have the pedigree to do well.

Racing is in Alex's blood, as his father competed in Ferraris and in the British Touring Car Championship. So, it was into karts for Alex and the Super 1 Honda title was his in 2009 before he became a European champion the following year and then runner-up in the world KF1 series in 2011 when he was 15.

Alex was snapped up for Red Bull's scholarship scheme for Formula Renault, then dropped when the results didn't come. Convinced he had the skills, Alex stayed on for a third year and ranked third in the European series. Next came F3 in 2015, but ranking seventh didn't do much for his name. On, then, to GP3 in 2016 and Alex found redemption as he ended the year second to Charles Leclerc.

Remaining with ART Grand Prix, Alex stepped up to F2 in 2017 and stood on the podium twice, but was only 10th overall. Giving F2 another shot, Alex hit form in 2018 and was part of a three-way title battle with George Russell and Lando Norris in which Russell dominated and Alex ended up third behind Norris despite outscoring him by four wins to one.

Alex's first season of F1 in 2019 was an interesting one. Signed to race for Scuderia Toro Rosso, he matched more experienced team-mate Daniil Kvyat, advancing to an impressive sixth place in the German GP. Then, after just 12 grands prix, Alex was propelled from Toro Rosso upwards to Red Bull Racing, with Pierre Gasly being demoted in this mid-season swap. This could have been the sort of setback that could end a career, but Alex went away and worked hard.

Alex was expected to go after podium finishes to help the team to beat Ferrari to second in the championship. None came, but his best result of fourth place at Suzuka was backed up with a gaggle of fifth place finishes and so he got to keep his ride alongside Max Verstappen.

In 2020, while Verstappen was taking the battle to Mercedes, Alex couldn't respond and, despite taking two third place finishes, he ranked seventh to the Dutchman's third overall, getting no offer of a further contract.

TRACK NOTES

Nationality:	**BRITISH/THAI**
Born:	**23 MARCH 1996,**
	LONDON, ENGLAND
Website:	**www.alexalbon.com**
Teams:	**TORO ROSSO 2019,**
RED BULL 2019-2020, WILLIAMS 2022	

CAREER RECORD

First Grand Prix:	**2019 AUSTRALIAN GP**
Grand Prix starts:	**38**
Grand Prix wins:	**0 (best result:**
3rd 2020 Tuscan GP, Bahrain GP)	
Poles:	**0**
Fastest laps:	**0**
Points:	**197**
Honours:	**2016 GP3 RUNNER-UP,**
2011 WORLD KF1 KART RUNNER-UP, 2010 EUROPEAN KF3 KART CHAMPION, 2009 SUPER 1 HONDA KART CHAMPION	

STILL RACING, JUST NOT IN F1

One minute you're an F1 driver, and then you're not. This was the situation that faced Alex at the end of the 2020 season when he was dropped by Red Bull Racing. Not back to its second team, renamed as AlphaTauri, instead, Alex found himself competing in the DTM (Deutsche Tourenwagen Meisterschaft). For some reason, in 2021, it was no longer for touring cars but had become a series for GT cars. Alex was entered in a Ferrari 488 GT3 alongside Kiwi Liam Lawson and run by Ferrari specialists AF Corse, both paid for by Red Bull. Lawson did better, winning three rounds to be runner-up, while Alex won a race at the Nurburgring and ended the year sixth after missing the final round so that he could do his other job. This was mentoring Yuki Tsunoda in his maiden F1 year with AlphaTauri. And it was good as it kept Alex in the F1 paddock, staying current, while his ink was drying on a contract with Williams for 2022.

NICHOLAS LATIFI

Back for a third year with Williams, this affable Canadian will be praying that recent investment in the team has enabled it to build a car to the new regulations that is more competitive than those that have gone before it.

Nicholas is facing his third year in F1 and will be praying that the team finds new form.

There are no championship titles on Nicholas's curriculum vitae but, if you look closely, you will notice that there was almost no time spent in karts, putting him at a major disadvantage to his rivals when he started car racing at the tender age of 16.

Ambitiously, Nicholas went straight to F3, contesting the Italian series. Then he spent the winter gaining further experience by competing in New Zealand's Toyota Racing Series, followed by a combined programme of European and British F3.

Kicking off 2014, Nicholas raced in the Florida Winter Series and then spent a second season in European F3 in which he ranked 10th. Fortunately, Nicholas comes from a family of wealth and this led to him testing the more powerful Formula Renault 3.5 cars and then racing one right at the end of the year. His outing at Jerez was a revelation as Nicholas finished second in the final round.

So, there were high hopes as he set off into a Formula Renault 3.5 campaign in 2015, but he failed to match that result, never even visiting the podium.

Time was then spent in GP2, then the level immediately beneath F1. In fact, four years were spent at this level, albeit with it being renamed as F2 from 2017. Although Nicholas visited the podium just once in 2016, finishing second in the first race of the opening round, he made clear progress in his second season with DAMS in 2017, winning the sprint race at Silverstone to rank fifth overall as Charles Leclerc won the title with ease. Yet, although he took another win in 2018, at Spa-Francorchamps, Nicholas was good enough only for ninth overall. He was good, but not F1 standard.

Then came 2019, Nicholas's best season to date. He started strongly, taking three early-season wins, but Nyck de Vries was better, leaving Nicholas to be runner-up. Fortunately, he had been doing a number of days testing F1 cars and this experience was useful, as was his considerable wealth, so a seat was secured for his F1 debut season with Williams in 2020.

Nicholas got down to learning as he went, his best finish 11th at Imola.

TRACK NOTES

Nationality:	**CANADIAN**
Born:	**29 JUNE 1995,**
	TORONTO, CANADA
Website:	**www.nicholaslatifi.com**
Team:	**WILLIAMS 2020-22**

CAREER RECORD

First Grand Prix:	**2020 Australian GP**
Grand Prix starts:	**39**
Grand Prix wins:	**0 (best result:**
	7th 2021 Hungarian GP)
Poles:	**0**
Fastest laps:	**0**
Points:	**7**
Honours:	**2019 FORMULA 2 RUNNER-UP**

SOLID, BUT NOT SPECTACULAR

For any driver who managed to score a point for Williams in the past few years, respect must be offered, for the cars have been far from competitive. Indeed, points are likely to be collected only when drivers from teams further up the order stumble, so all the Williams team could ask was for their drivers to press on and seize the moment if it arose. This was the case when Nicholas grabbed seventh place at the crash-affected Hungarian GP, with George Russell following him home in eighth for a double team celebration. Ninth place next time out at Spa-Francorchamps was another delight, one that was earned by managing to qualify well in horrendously wet conditions. However, the fact that team-mate Russell claimed an exceptional second place in that rain-hit washout reflected their respective skill levels. This is no matter of disrespect, as Russell is a rare talent. Indeed, Nicholas has pushed hard, with many a strong drive going unrecognized.

It took a while to get used to Williams' new livery last year, but there can be no mistaking the backdrop, Monaco's Grand Hotel Hairpin.

ALFA ROMEO RACING ORLEN

It is difficult to see from where the Alfa Romeo team may find the extra performance to advance up the field in F1 and, although Valtteri Bottas will bring vital experience with him from Mercedes, points will surely be hard to come by once again in 2022.

Neither Antonio Giovinazzi (above) nor Kimi Raikkonen were kept on by Alfa Romeo, with Valtteri Bottas being brought in to lead its attack.

As rival teams like Benetton and Jordan changed their names, this Swiss team remained for decades named after its founder Peter Sauber. Yet, true to the way of the day, it too has been racing under a different identity for the past three seasons, that of Alfa Romeo.

Sauber had competed in hillclimbs, as circuit racing had been banned in his native Switzerland since the Le Mans 24 Hours disaster of 1955. However, he soon moved to racing sportscars on circuits around Europe and then began to construct his own. Better still, he soon started selling these as well and by the late 1980s his cars were entered in the World Sports-Prototype Championship sponsored by Mercedes, winning the title in 1989. This was followed by a big push as it financed a programme for junior drivers to race against more experienced ones, to help bring them along, and it boosted the careers of Michael Schumacher, Heinz-Harald Frentzen and Karl Wendlinger.

Sauber had an ambition to try F1 and he thought that Mercedes might supply him with engines to do this, but it declined, so he went it alone in 1993 and his cars shone

immediately, with JJ Lehto getting straight into the points. Mercedes put its name on the team's engines for 1994, but then took those V10s away for the following year,

KEY PERSONNEL & 2021 ROUND-UP

JAN MONCHAUX
This Franco-German aerodynamicist joined Toyota in 2002 for his first F1 posting. His next move took Jan to Ferrari in 2010, but he quit F1 in 2013 to start working with Audi Sport when its sports-prototypes were doing so well in the Le Mans 24 Hours. Then, in 2018, he came back to F1 when he joined Sauber just before it changed its name to Alfa Romeo. He was then promoted from head of aerodynamics to technical director in the second half of 2019 after Simone Resta left.

ALWAYS CHASING, BUT SELDOM SCORING
The team celebrated its 500th F1 start at the Turkish GP last year, but its return at Istanbul was typical of its recent time in F1: two finishes, eleventh for Antonio Giovinazzi and twelfth for Kimi Raikkonen, but no points. The drivers' best result all year was an eighth place for the Finn in the Russian GP at Sochi, when the team chose the right time to change to rain tyres, but then Raikkonen added another eighth place in Mexico and Giovinazzi a ninth in Saudi Arabia.

2021 DRIVERS & RESULTS

Driver	Nationality	Races	Wins	Pts	Pos
Kimi Raikkonen	Finnish	20	0	10	16th
Antonio Giovinazzi	Italian	22	0	3	18th
Robert Kubica	Polish	2	0	0	20th

when the deal went to McLaren instead.

However, Sauber sailed on and in 1997 started to use Ferrari engines. Naturally, these were a spec behind the Ferrari's teams engines, but they enabled Sauber to continue in F1, although largely leaving it ranked sixth, seventh or eighth. Then it vaulted to fourth overall in 2001 with great showings from Nick Heidfeld and rookie Kimi Raikkonen.

This spiked the interest of BMW when it considered entering F1 with a team of its own, and the team raced as BMW Sauber from 2006, with this financial shove propelling the team to second overall behind Ferrari in 2007. Then, in 2008, not only did the team score its one and only win, but it grabbed second as well in the Canadian GP as Robert Kubica led Heidfeld home. Life has never been as sweet again, especially after BMW moved on after 2010.

Being based in Switzerland has held the team back in the hunt for key designers and engineers, with employment costs being higher than elsewhere in Europe and the many candidates preferring not to uproot their families from houses and schools near the predominantly British-based teams.

Failing to keep up with the leading teams as budgets soared is another problem, and this was what led to Peter Sauber being moved aside, as investment in 2016 from Longbow Finance headed by Finn Rausing landed a seat for Marcus Ericsson and part of the deal was that Frederic Vasseur was brought in as team principal. Good times followed in 2018, thanks to rookie Charles Leclerc who raced to a sixth place, but then he left to join Ferrari. To bring in more money, the team was renamed as Alfa Romeo from 2019.

The team's form in the past few seasons, when points have been rare, will leave new F1 fans considering that it has always been thus for this team, but that sole win for Robert Kubica in Canada in 2008 seems almost a lifetime ago.

Rumours swirled last year that the team was up for sale after six years of ownership by Rausing. Then other rumours circulated that Michael Andretti might be the person to head the takeover.

FOR THE RECORD

Country of origin:	**Switzerland**
Team base:	**Hinwil, Switzerland**
Telephone:	**(41) 44 937 9000**
Website:	**www.sauber-group.com**
Active in Formula One:	**As Sauber 1993-2018 (as BMW Sauber 2006-2010), Alfa Romeo 2019 on**
Grands Prix contested:	**524**
Wins:	**1**
Pole positions:	**1**
Fastest laps:	**5**

THE TEAM

Owner:	**Finn Rausing**
Chairman:	**Pascal Picci**
Team principal:	**Frederic Vasseur**
Technical director:	**Jan Monchaux**
Chief designer:	**Eric Gandelin**
Head of aerodynamics:	**tba**
Head of engineering:	**Giampaolo Dall'ara**
Head of track engineering:	**Xevi Pujolar**
Head of aerodynamic development:	**Mariano Alperin-Bruvera**
Head of aerodynamic research:	**Seamus Mullarkey**
Head of vehicle performance:	**Elliot Dason-Barber**
Team manager:	**Beat Zehnder**
Third driver:	**Robert Kubica**
Chassis:	**Alfa Romeo C42**
Engine:	**Ferrari V6**
Tyres:	**Pirelli**

This deal was derailed late last year and Rausing may have been wise in this as the value of F1 teams has recently taken a major upturn.

Raikkonen raced for the team when it was Sauber, shown heading for points on his debut in 2001.

> "Last year, we let some big chances get by and didn't get everything we deserved. There is a lot of work to do in the winter but we are prepared for it and can't wait to see the results of all our efforts when we line up on the grid in 2022."
>
> Frederic Vasseur

VALTTERI BOTTAS

It's going to feel very different for Valtteri in 2022 as not only has he changed team from Mercedes to Alfa Romeo, but he will be operating as team leader after having had to perform a supporting role for years.

Valtteri should enjoy being in a less pressured environment than it was at Mercedes.

After his mid teens were spent karting, Valtteri graduated to single-seaters at 17 and was quick in Formula Renault, finishing third in the lesser Northern European Countries series in 2007 before landing the title and, more importantly, the full European title too, resisting a late-season push from Daniel Ricciardo.

Then Valtteri spent two years in F3, finishing third in the European championship each time and also winning the Marlboro Masters F3 invitation race in both 2009 and 2010.

With money not in abundance, Valtteri gambled in 2011 by racing at a similar level in GP3. It really was a case of having to win the title or his career momentum was gone. Fortunately, driving for ART, he did. What made this so pivotal was that part of the prize for being champion was an F1 test with Williams. And this is what started Valtteri on the path to becoming a multiple grand prix winner, as the team was impressed by his approach.

A year testing for Williams convinced the team to give Valtteri a race seat for 2013 and he came home eighth in the penultimate round at the Circuit of the Americas. Valtteri's second season was a quantum leap as he ranked fourth, peaking with two second place finishes at Silverstone and Hockenheim. Despite slipping to fifth in 2015 and eighth in 2016, Valtteri got a major break for 2017 when Nico Rosberg quit suddenly after winning the title and left a seat vacant at Mercedes, which he was selected to fill.

His first win followed, in Sochi, followed by two more as Valtteri settled into supporting Lewis Hamilton. He improved further to be runner-up in 2019 and 2020 before George Russell was lined up to replace him.

While moving from Mercedes to midfielders Alfa Romeo is a backward step, it does at least keep Valtteri in F1. It also reunites him with team principal Frederic Vasseur who ran ART Grand Prix for whom Valtteri drove in his F3 and GP3 days.

TRACK NOTES

Nationality:	**FINNISH**
Born:	**28 AUGUST 1989,**
	NASTOLA, FINLAND
Website:	**www.valtteribottas.com**
Teams:	**WILLIAMS 2013-16,**
	MERCEDES 2017-21, ALFA ROMEO 2022

CAREER RECORD

First Grand Prix:	**2013 AUSTRALIAN GP**
Grand Prix starts:	**178**
Grand Prix wins:	**10**
2017 Russian GP, Austrian GP, Abu Dhabi GP, 2019 Australian GP, Azerbaijan GP, Japanese GP, US GP, 2020 Austrian GP, Russian GP, 2021 Turkish GP	
Poles:	**20**
Fastest laps:	**19**
Points:	**1738**
Honours:	**2019 & 2020 F1 RUNNER-UP, 2011 GP3 CHAMPION, 2009 & 2010 FORMULA 3 MASTERS WINNER, 2008 EUROPEAN & NORTHERN EUROPEAN FORMULA RENAULT CHAMPION**

A WAVERING YEAR IN SUPPORT

Last year's 22 grands prix resulted in just one win for Valtteri, this coming in the Turkish GP just outside Istanbul. And, however one looks at this, it's a poor return while driving for one of F1's two most competitive teams. There were the occasional pole positions to put a smile on Valtteri's face, but his role at Mercedes was that relentlessly wearing one of being instructed to score points for the team rather than for himself. Lewis Hamilton remained the focus of Mercedes' attack. That said, Valtteri was occasionally simply not at the races, a charge that could never have been aimed at his team-mate. Valtteri's worst day was triggering the first corner accident in the Hungarian GP. Still, with a second place at the Red Bull Ring and a cluster of third place finishes, Valtteri was good for third in the championship but perhaps he had lost heart by the final round as his race performance in Abu Dhabi was lacklustre.

GUANYU ZHOU

Zhou will break new ground in 2022 with Alfa Romeo Racing by becoming the first Chinese driver to race in F1, going a step further than Ma Qing Hua who had a few outings as an F1 test driver a decade ago.

Zhou's rookie year in F1 is sure to attract considerable attention in China.

China has been waiting a very long time to get one of its young drivers into F1. Certainly, when it hosted a round of the World Championship for the first time as long ago as 2004, it wouldn't have expected to wait until 2022 for one of its own drivers to make the grade. Pleasingly, now that one has, Zhou has the pedigree to be more than a makeweight at the sport's highest level.

He started to make a mark as soon as he stepped up to try single-seaters at the age of 15 in 2015, the year after competing at World and European level in karting.

To begin with, Zhou focused on the Italian F4 series and finished second with three wins. With clear interest in the Chinese market, Ferrari made Zhou part of its driver academy programme. Then he headed down to New Zealand in the northern hemisphere winter, to rank sixth in the Toyota Racing Series as Lando Norris took the title.

Then it was time for the European F3 championship in 2016, twice reaching the podium as Lance Stroll dominated. Back for another crack at the series in 2017, Zhou ranked eighth, visiting the podium five times but taking no wins. So, determined to land the series, he came back again in 2018 for a second season with Prema Powerteam, and Zhou was twice a winner, but was classified eighth again as Mick Schumacher took the title.

Fortunately, there was backing available for Zhou to move on to the FIA F2 Championship in 2019 as he had been signed by the Renault Sport Academy, so he was able to join the UNI-Virtuosi outfit. On the podium by the fifth race of the 24-race championship, Zhou went on to score four more third place finishes. In his second crack at F2 in 2020, Zhou took a win at Sochi and started to look like having F1 potential.

If all goes well and Zhou excites Chinese sports fans, he could develop the largest fan base of any driver in F1.

TRACK NOTES

Nationality:	**CHINESE**
Born:	**30 MAY 1991, SHANGHAI, CHINA**
Website:	**tba**
Teams:	**ALFA ROMEO 2022**

CAREER RECORD

First Grand Prix:	**2022 BAHRAIN GP**
Grand Prix starts:	**0**
Grand Prix wins:	**0**
Poles:	**0**
Fastest laps:	**0**
Points:	**0**
Honours:	**ASIAN FORMULA 3 CHAMPION, 2015 ITALIAN FORMULA 4 RUNNER-UP**

GOING FOR GOLD AT THIRD TRY

Having finished seventh in the FIA F2 series in 2019 then sixth in 2020, only the title would really suffice last year and so winning one of the three races at the opening round at Sakhir was a good start. Staying on for a third year with the UNI-Virtuosi team, he made the most of the experience he had gained and his familiarity with the team, to then add further wins at Monaco, earning considerable coverage at home in China for that, and later in the season at Silverstone. In a season in which no driver stood out by winning multiple rounds, Zhou's consistent scoring kept him in the hunt for the title. However, failing to start the first race at a wet Sochi after spinning out on the way to the grid, dented his hopes and he headed to the final two triple-header rounds 36 points behind the even more consistent Australian Oscar Piastri. Zhou was able to win a race at the Yas Marina finale but ended the year third.

⟫ HAAS F1

The big question is where does Haas F1 go from here after finishing 2021 stone last? Simone Resta might boost its hopes for the new season, but its drivers have only one year of F1 experience to fall back on which is not a recipe for success.

Mick Schumacher settled in well, but both he and Nikita Mazepin would have gone better if there had been an experienced pro to learn from.

Gene Haas is an incredibly successful businessman who loves motor racing. Having joined those two factors together with considerable success in NASCAR, first on his own from 2002 and then in partnership with multiple champion Tony Stewart from 2009, with his cars regular winners in the premier stock car division over the past decade – with drivers' titles for Stewart in 2011 and for Kevin Harvick in 2014 – his machining business gained an enormous amount of exposure because of this.

The next step was to try to expand this publicity onto a global stage, thus F1. That was always going to cost a whole lot more, especially when he decided to set up a team from scratch rather than save money by buying an existing team, and it was all the more surprising as Haas had no single-seater background. Then Haas F1 added to that complication by being determinedly based in the USA rather than in Europe like all other teams. This was considered

to be a point of near madness as although it was just next door to the Haas-Stewart NASCAR team at Kannapolis in North Carolina and could share some of its

facilities, it was far from F1's European centre of excellence, so recruiting the best technical brains and practitioners was going to be hard. Wisely, a satellite base

KEY PERSONNEL & 2021 ROUND-UP

SIMONE RESTA

Formerly head of chassis engineering at Ferrari, Simone joined Haas for 2021. Inspired to work in motor racing after spending his childhood near Imola, he advanced into F1 after leaving Bologna University to join Minardi in 1998. He started with the Scuderia back in 2001 and was promoted to become its chief designer in 2014. He moved to Sauber for a short spell in 2018 to help boost its chassis department before returning to Ferrari.

A REAL STRUGGLE FOR TWO F1 ROOKIES

This was never going to be an easy year for a team that had had the better only of Williams through 2019 and 2020. That it had been seen fit to replace both Romain Grosjean and Kevin Magnussen cost it continuity and also known speed. In their place came rookies Mick Schumacher and Nikita Mazepin, with the latter looking out of place as he made a string of errors. However, the Russian settled down, but was seldom a match for his team-mate.

2021 DRIVERS & RESULTS

Driver	Nationality	Races	Wins	Pts	Pos
Mick Schumacher	German	22	0	0	19th
Nikita Mazepin	Russian	21	0	0	21st

FOR THE RECORD

Country of origin:	USA
Team bases:	Kannapolis, USA, & Banbury, England
Telephone:	(001) 704 652 4227
Website:	www.haasf1team.com
Active in Formula One:	From 2016
Grands Prix contested:	122
Wins:	0
Pole positions:	0
Fastest laps:	3

THE TEAM

Team owner:	Gene Haas
Team principal:	Guenther Steiner
Chief operating officer:	Joe Custer
Technical director:	Simone Resta
Vice-president of technology:	Matt Borland
Team manager:	Dave O'Neill
Chief aerodynamicist:	Ben Agathangelou
Group leader aerodynaicist:	Christian Cattaneo
Head of logistics:	Peter Crolla
Chief engineer:	Ayao Komatsu
Test driver:	tba
Chassis:	Haas VF-22
Engine:	Honda V6
Tyres:	Pirelli

in Britain was added and then the Haas F1 team headed into 2016 to see what they could achieve.

Few F1 debuts have had a more magical outcome, but Romain Grosjean started 19th of the 22 starters in Melbourne and was still lapping at the finish, coming home in an unexpected sixth place. When he followed that by starting ninth and finishing fifth in Bahrain, people sat up and paid attention. Although he never finished as well again and team-mate Esteban Gutiérrez failed to score at all, Haas F1 ranked eighth, easily ahead of Renault, Sauber and Manor.

Kevin Magnussen replaced Gutierrez in 2017 and used the experience that he had gained at McLaren and Renault to push Grosjean, as Haas ranked eighth again. In their second year together, though, Grosjean and Magnussen took the Ferrari-powered team to fifth overall as Grosjean gave the team a new high with fourth place in the Austria GP while Magnussen outscored him with a pair of fifths, one of which was on Grosjean's tail at the Red Bull Ring. Remarkably, the team scored more points than multiple champions McLaren that had no less a driver than Fernando Alonso leading its attack.

Watching the team's new confidence be pricked in 2019 was frustrating for all concerned as the cars and their custom Ferrari engines underperformed, falling away increasingly through the course of a race, and the drivers crashed into each other more than once. This provided theatrical viewing on the Netflix *Drive to Survive* series, making the famously curt and exasperated team principal Guenther Steiner into something of a cult hero, but it did nothing to help the team advance.

Then, for no clear reason other than needing an influx of money, the team sacked its experienced and capable drivers and brought in Mick Schumacher and Nikita Mazepin from F2 for 2021 and this really got them nowhere.

For a man like Haas, who is used to succeeding in all that he does, one wonders why he is sticking it out and if life might be easier for him to sell the team to Mazepin's billionaire father rather than pouring more of his own money into a team that looks destined to be cemented to the foot of the order without considerable investment.

Another alternative, having banked the experience gained through six seasons of F1, is to go more American in approach and turn into a breeding ground for American designers, engineers and, of course, drivers.

"Our last race in 2021 was the best that we did. Mick did a fantastic job and cars that beat us all year ended up behind us, so it was very good to go into the winter season knowing that we're ready for a better season in 2022."

Guenther Steiner

Kevin Magnussen did well in the 2018 Bahrain GP, racing to a fifth place finish at Sakhir.

MICK SCHUMACHER

With his rookie F1 season behind him, Mick will be looking to demonstrate that he has absorbed the lessons learnt in 2021 and attempt to show that, in the future, he might be worthy of a ride with a team further up the order.

Mick will be wanting to score points in 2022, but this might require others to drop out.

It's safe to say that racing is in Mick's blood, with karting a particular favourite, as his grandfather Rolf ran a kart circuit and of course father Michael progressed from there to seven F1 titles. So, karting was a natural course of action for Mick and he proved good at it. Good enough to shine at European KF level, ranking third in 2013 when he was 14. The following year, he was second in both the World and European series.

Then came the move to car racing, alas with the head injury that Michael suffered in a skiing accident denying Mick his staunchest supporter and someone with so much knowledge to pass on as well as pride in his achievements.

Starting in the German F4 series in 2015, Mick finished second in that and the Italian series too in 2016. Then, after spending the winter racing in the MRF Challenge in India, he moved up to F3, coming 12th with one podium visit. Back for a second attempt in 2018, Mick went way better and won the title in a season that started slowly before rattling off eight wins. It was a bit of a gamble, but if Mick could bring even a few of his father's genes, then things might turn out alright.

Remaining with the Prema team, Mick graduated to F2 in 2019, winning the sprint race at the Hungaroring and going on to be classified 12th at the end of the year. He rounded out the year with a couple of F1 tests with Ferrari and Alfa Romeo, courtesy of being a member of the Ferrari Driver Academy.

Then, just as he had in F3, Mick improved by fully 11 championship positions in his second year in F2, becoming champion in a season in which he won but twice, yet this was enough to edge out fellow Ferrari academy drivers Callum Ilott and Yuki Tsunoda.

There was an obvious attraction to getting the Schumacher name back into F1, which is why Haas F1 signed Mick for 2021, and it has to be one of the reasons that the team was prepared to replace Romain Grosjean and Kevin Magnussen with a pair of rookies.

TRACK NOTES

Nationality:	**GERMAN**
Born:	**22 MARCH 1999, VUFFLENS-LE-CHATEAU, SWITZERLAND**
Website:	**www.mickschumacher.ms**
Teams:	**HAAS F1 2021-22**

CAREER RECORD

First Grand Prix:	**2021 BAHRAIN GP**
Grand Prix starts:	**22**
Grand Prix wins:	**0 (best result: 12th 2021 Hungarian GP)**
Poles:	**0**
Fastest laps:	**0**
Points:	**0**
Honours:	**2020 FIA F2 CHAMPION, 2018 FIA F3 EUROPEAN CHAMPION, 2016 ADAC & ITALIAN F4 RUNNER-UP, 2014 WORLD & EUROPEAN KF JUNIOR KART RUNNER-UP**

LEARNING WITHOUT FIREWORKS

Life with Haas was never going to be about winning grands prix, standing on a podium or, barring a major incident, even about scoring points. For Mick and fellow rookie team-mate Nikita Mazepin, 2021 was about gaining experience. Both drivers spun more than once at the season-opening meeting at Sakhir, but Mick was the one who settled down to life in F1 more quickly was invariably the faster of the pair, although Nikita got closer as the season advanced. Mick peaked with a 12th place finish at the crash-hit Hungarian GP, but the American team's lack of competitive machinery meant that all he could aim for was making sure that he finished ahead of Mazepin rather than taking the battle to the drivers from Alfa Romeo and Williams. Both drivers would surely have benefitted from having either Kevin Magnussen or Romain Grosjean kept on board to mentor them.

NIKITA MAZEPIN

The money is there to keep Nikita in F1, but the Russian must demonstrate that he has learnt from his many mistakes last year to keep the critics off his back. Don't expect points, as he drives for Haas, but do look for improvement.

Nikita must learn from the mistakes he made last year if he wants to advance in 2022.

There have been scions of wealthy families in F1 before, think Lance Reventlow (Woolworths stores) who formed his own team – Scarab – in 1960 and Rikki von Opel (Opel cars) who asked Ensign to step into F1 with him in 1973. However, the scale of money required to have a team of your own is vastly more now. Yet, remarkably, two of the 20 drivers on the grid have fathers who wield the

wealth to buy a team for them. Obviously, Lance Stroll is one, as his father is the major shareholder in Aston Martin's F1 team, and Nikita is the other thanks to his father's Uralchem conglomerate that had tried to buy the same outfit when it raced as Force India. In both cases, this wealth has paved their passage through the junior formulae and then opened a door to F1 that, certainly in Nikita's case, would never have been opened otherwise.

Nikita's career started promisingly in karting and he developed by the time he was 15 to end 2014 as runner-up to Lando Norris in the world KF series. Then he stepped up to race cars, albeit not with spectacular success in the MRF Challenge, the Toyota Racing Series or regional Formula Renault. However, with a budget being no matter of concern, Nikita simply moved up to F3 for 2016, again without getting close to a win. Yet he had his first taste of F1 in a test with Force India.

The 2017 season was far better as Nikita made onto the European F3 podium three times as he ranked 10th in a season dominated by Norris. Incidentally, 2022 team-mate Mick Schumacher was 12th in

his rookie F3 season.

There was more improvement in 2018 when Nikita moved across to marginally more powerful GP3 and took his first high-level car racing wins, four in all, to end the year second overall.

Then came a two-year project in F2, with 18th overall in 2019 with just a couple of eighths being followed by fifth for the family-owned Hitech GP team in 2020, with wins at Silverstone and Mugello. This upswing in form, plus the family fortune, ensure that the door swung open for Nikita to enter F1.

TRACK NOTES

Nationality:	**RUSSIAN**
Born:	**2 MARCH 1999, MOSCOW, RUSSIA**
Website:	**www.nikitamazepin.com**
Teams:	**HAAS F1 2021-22**

CAREER RECORD

First Grand Prix:	**2021 BAHRAIN GP**
Grand Prix starts:	**21**
Grand Prix wins:	**0 (best result: 14th 2021 Azerbaijan GP)**
Poles:	**0**
Fastest laps:	**0**
Points:	**0**
Honours:	**2018 GP3 RUNNER-UP, 2014 WORLD KF KART RUNNER-UP**

EARLY SPINS ARE PUT BEHIND HIM

Nikita could hardly have started his rookie season in F1 in worse style as he followed spin with spin in practice and incident with incident. Spinning at Turn 2 on the first lap of your maiden grand prix was unfortunate. Fortunately, Nikita began to eliminate the errors, gradually, sometimes by simply being less aggressive. Of course, driving a Haas VF21 meant being at the very back of the field, with only team-mate Mick Schumacher to fight and gauge himself against. In this comparison, the more highly-ranked German came out ahead. Indeed, it took until the ninth race, the British GP at Silverstone, before the Russian was higher up the order – one of only two occasions on which that happened, the other time being at the Brazilian GP. Nikita's best result was 14th place in the Azerbaijan GP, when records show that he finished ahead of Lewis Hamilton, albeit after the latter fell to the tail of the field while challenging for the lead.

TALKING POINT: **IT'S A NEW START FOR FORMULA ONE IN 2022**

It has long been a quest to change F1 cars to make the racing more of a spectacle. So, for 2022, there is a new set of technical rules aimed at doing just that by shaping them so that cars will be able to run closer to each other and so have more of a chance of overtaking.

It was clear that last year's F1 cars made life difficult for any driver to catch and pass them. One look at these figures and you will understand why. A car travelling three car lengths behind will lose just over one-third of their downforce, with an obvious reduction in their ability to handle when they most need it. If they are running just one car length behind, that deficit increases to 47%. For this year, the new rules will lead to those downforce deficits tumbling to 4% and 18% respectively.

The primary changes that have been mandated by F1's Motorsport team, in conjunction with the sport's governing body, are to reduce the amount of turbulent wake to the following parts of the all-new F1 cars: the front wing, the winglets above the front wheels, the wheels and tyres, plus the rear wing.

The front wing has been made simpler and redesigned in a way that will make it less ineffective when following closely behind a rival's car. As with the other key elements that have been changed, a key tenet is the reduction of "messy" air coming out of the back of the car and the new front wing has been designed so that it will channel air around the car rather than straight to the rear wing or under the car itself.

Winglets are to be allowed above the front wheels and these will be used to tidy up the air flow and move it outwards, thus away from the rear wing, helping to reduce turbulent air heading back into the path of a chasing car. Another change in the wheel department is the return of wheel covers that are there to prevent air being channelled through the wheels.

Tyres front and back will be wider, at 18 inches, with the change being implemented to give the tyres more grip. This, in turn, stops them sliding and reduces the amount by which they overheat, enabling the drivers to control them better and thus be able to attack more easily. You can't often see, without the benefit of a slow-motion replay, just how tyres deflect under load, but being low-profile will reduce that by cutting the size of the sidewalls and thus reducing how much they can move around and create turbulent air.

The rear wing has been reshaped so that it doesn't kick as much air upwards and outwards, forming instead a narrower wake and thus allowing a cleaner flow of less disturbed air to any car following close behind.

There will be changes F1 fans won't be able to see that will also shift the way that the cars handle. The stepped undersides to the cars are being replaced by venturi ducts beneath the car that are shaped to increase downforce without creating a great deal more turbulence for following cars. The cars which raced in 2021 and earlier used other aerodynamic devices to generate extra downforce, but these winglets and barge boards really lost their bite when a car was tucked into the draft of another.

These rule changes had been proposed for the 2021 season, but the onset of the pandemic meant that their introduction was pushed back to this year.

A big question will be the efficacy of these car changes, whether there will immediately be more of the overtaking that F1 fans crave. However, the drivers weren't sure that they liked the new-gen cars on first inspection. Indeed, after trying a mock up on a simulator last autumn, McLaren's Lando Norris described the experience as being "very different and not as nice". You can be sure that the designers and engineers have been working flat-out ever since to improve the way that they feel and handle.

There are no major changes on the engine front. Indeed, their specification will be frozen for four years, and this will be great news for the teams that have the best engine this year, less so for others. What has changed is that these 1.6-litre turbocharged hybrids will have more standard components to help keep costs in check but, more importantly, they will run with a greater proportion of biocomponents in their fuel, up from 5.75% to 10%, making it E10, the same proportion as in the fuel used in today's road cars.

Opposite: A demonstration prototype of the 2022 Formula 1 car was shown to the drivers when it was launched at last year's British GP, allowing the drivers to check out its refined shape.

TALKING POINT: **MIAMI GIVES THE USA ANOTHER F1 CHANCE**

Getting America to embrace F1 has been a struggle for six decades. Yet, anyone who saw the huge crowds at last autumn's US GP at COTA will appreciate that F1 might finally be getting some traction. So, the timing of a second American race in Miami is perfect, while there is serious talk of the USA wanting a third.

Any story about the future of the United States GP needs to run through the long list of circuits that have hosted a grand prix to outline how it has flitted around but seldom settled. Discounting the period in which the Indy 500 made up a leg of the World Championship, Sebring was first off in 1959, then Riverside was another one-hit wonder in 1960. Watkins Glen in upstate New York was a stayer, lasting from 1961 until 1980 when it became outmoded. From 1976 until 1983, there was a second American race each year, on the streets of Long Beach in California. This started a trend of holding a race on temporary venues. In 1981 and 1982, Las Vegas hosted a grand prix in the parking lot of the Caesars Palace casino. In fact, the USA hosted a third race in 1982 when its motor city, Detroit, joined the party, with yet another street circuit, and held the event for the next six years. Dallas in Texas became the third one-hit wonder when it held a grand prix in 1984 and the oil-rich city didn't deserve another go as its surface broke up awfully. Five years later, Phoenix in Arizona held the US GP on a street circuit from 1989 to 1991.

Then the Indianapolis Motor Speedway stepped forward and created a road circuit that used part of its famous banked oval. That lasted from 2000 until 2007. And then in 2012 came COTA, the Circuit of the Americas, in Texas, a circuit designed with the express aim of attracting F1. It was a hit in that it showed F1 cars at their best around its wonderful mixture of corner types, but it does mean that American

F1 fans from either the west coast or the eastern seaboard have to travel a very long way to see an F1 car in full flight. There are some brilliant road circuits, namely Road America, Mid-Ohio and Road Atlanta, all of them scenic too, but their safety levels aren't commensurate with the speed of today's F1 cars. That said, the teams still love going to old school circuits like Spa-Francorchamps and Suzuka, but none of this trio is close enough to a major city to make it worth them paying the not insubstantial fee to host a grand prix.

While these circuits had their shot at F1, there has been talk for nigh on four decades of Miami wanting one, with its largely Hispanic population more attracted to F1 than motor racing fans in the rest of the USA. F1 supremo Bernie Ecclestone long pushed for a race in New York and got a long way down the line with one set for just across the river in New Jersey, but that didn't happen.

So, after all this movement, and thwarted plans, it is fabulous news that Miami has finally got what it wanted and it follows along the lines of taking F1 to the people. This is how F1 owners Liberty Media envisages expanding its American audience. The success of Netflix's *Drive to Survive* series has already shown in ticket sales. Obviously, having an American driver in F1 would be a real help, too, yet the only American team, Haas F1, has yet to go down that route. Colton Herta is the name on people's lips, but it looks as though the Indycar race winner might have to wait until 2023.

Talk of Michael Andretti – McLaren racer in 1993 and son of 1978 World Champion Mario – buying the Sauber team circulated at the end of last year, and that would help too. Having two races is certain to help keep F1 in the public eye, albeit with the organisers both at COTA and Miami preferring for them to be held at different ends of the championship. This American surge may also bring in more American sponsors, something that will clearly be good for all involved.

So, while Miami has finally landed its race, stories continue that Las Vegas is extremely keen to have a second crack at F1 after its weak attempt four decades ago. The driving force of this is, of course, that it wants to draw people into town to leave their money at the casinos and, perhaps, now that F1 is far bigger business than it was when it went there in the early 1980s, it might be done properly this time around.

Opposite top left: Checking out how it can be done, Miami GP managing partner Tom Garfinkel attended the Dutch GP at Zandvoort.

Opposite top right: The state police look on as Lewis Hamilton's McLaren flashes past them at Indianapolis in 2007.

Opposite middle: Ayrton Senna was in a class of his own in his McLaren in the 1991 United States GP on the streets of Phoenix.

Opposite bottom: The multi-purpose Hard Rock Stadium will provide a distinctive backdrop for the temporary track used for the Miami GP.

TALKING POINT: **ARE GREAT DAYS RETURNING FOR FRENCH DRIVERS?**

There was a time in the 1980s when French drivers were not only in the majority in F1 but also set the pace. It took until 1985 for a French driver to land the title, when Alain Prost did so. There have been years since in which the French have had no driver in F1 at all, but now their numbers are growing.

For the country that hosted the first ever motor race – the Paris to Rouen road race in 1894 – and then the first grand prix – the 1906 French GP on a road circuit near Le Mans – the French have always been involved at the top level of the sport, but amazingly it took until the 36th season of the World Championship for a French driver to become champion.

That was Alain Prost, one of the sport's all-time greats who then added the 1986, 1989 and 1993 crowns to his accolades, but incredibly there have been no other French world champions. However, in Pierre Gasly and Esteban Ocon, they have two grand prix winners who could, given the right breaks, become France's second world champion. They also have a young charger looking to make his break in F1 who could outshine them both: Theo Pourchaire.

French drivers in the 1950s tended to be held back by driving Lago-Talbots that were no match from the best Italian cars from Alfa Romeo, Ferrari and Maserati. Jean Behra was quick, but excitable and talked himself out of a good drive, while Maurice Trintignant was twice a winner at Monaco.

Through the 1960s, as the British teams took control of F1, French drivers were only also-rans and the title went to English-speaking drivers in every year, as American Phil Hill set the ball rolling followed by Brits Graham Hill, Jim Clark and John Surtees before antipodeans Jack Brabham and Denny Hulme hit the top and Jackie Stewart rounded out the decade.

The next bright French light was Johnny Servoz-Gavin in the late 1960s, but he left

as fast as he arrived. Jean-Pierre Beltoise took a one-off win at Monaco in 1972. However, it was at this point that the first likely French World Champion emerged. It was François Cevert and he was all set to lead Tyrrell's attack in 1974 after Jackie Stewart's retirement, when he was killed at the end of 1973.

Stung by this lack of success, France's motorsport administrators then decided to make a concerted push to develop its best talent, finding sponsors for a series of scholarship schemes that selected the drivers at the bottom of the racing tree, Formula Renault, and kept backing the best of the crop through the single-seater formulae, so F3, F2, *et voila*, F1. The outcome was sensational, as the Pilote Elf scheme in particular gave a leg-up to Didier Pironi, Prost, Patrick Tambay and Olivier Panis, with the French petrochemicals giant also helping Rene Arnoux and Jean-Pierre Jabouille when their careers were already underway, much as BP France did for Jacques Laffite.

Thanks to this, even though the two French teams, Renault and Ligier, had challenged but not hit the top as Lotus, Brabham, McLaren and then Williams assumed control, French drivers were a real factor.

The oil companies gradually withdrew their support, and Marlboro filled the gap by sponsoring drivers in F3000, but then a law was passed to ban tobacco sponsorship in sport in France, and that hit the scholarship schemes with the result that the supply of French drivers largely dried up. Panis was a

notable exception and scored a famous win in the wet at Monaco in 1996.

French fans were cheered at the start of the 21st century when a group of its young kart-racers were shining on the world stage and then moving rapidly up the single-seater ladder, often trying to climb the greasy pole of Red Bull's scholarship programme. These were Esteban Ocon, Pierre Gasly and Anthoine Hubert, along with Charles Leclerc from neighbouring Monaco. Sadly, Hubert was killed in an F2 race at Spa-Francorchamps in 2019. Since that dark day, though, Gasly bounced back from being dropped by Red Bull Racing to become an F1 winner at the 2020 Italian GP for AlphaTauri, a feat matched by Ocon for Alpine at last year's Hungarian GP.

Coming up behind them, but without an F1 ride for 2022, is Pourchaire, a precociously talented 18-year-old who took his first F2 win at Monaco in his first full season at this level and then added another at Monza to be in the title hunt until Australian Oscar Piastri pulled clear in the second half of the season.

Opposite top: The French trio of Prost, Arnoux and Pironi celebrate on the podium after locking out the 1982 French GP at Paul Ricard.

Opposite middle: Pierre Gasly put French drivers back on the map by winning the 2020 Italian GP at Monza for Scuderia AlphaTauri.

Opposite bottom left: Fernando Alonso celebrates with Esteban Ocon after the Frenchman won for Alpine at last year's Hungarian GP.

Opposite bottom right: Theo Pourchaire is the French coming man and drove to victory in one of the F2 races at Monaco last year.

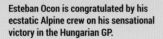
Esteban Ocon is congratulated by his ecstatic Alpine crew on his sensational victory in the Hungarian GP.

⟫ KNOW THE TRACKS 2022

Formula 1 fans have become accustomed over the past two years to the World Championship dates being rejigged to fit around the pandemic, but should be pleased that the 23-grands prix schedule is missing just one of its regulars, with only the Chinese GP not in place for the season ahead, balanced by a return for Imola and new venue in Miami.

Travel restrictions aside, one of the most difficult things for World Championship organisers Liberty Media is how to find a natural flow for its record number of grands prix to limit the degree of team personnel burn-out as they plot their route between the 23 venues.

It makes logical sense that a week after the season-opener in Bahrain, Jeddah will hold round two. This buys a little more time for Australia to improve its low vaccination rate. The teams will be delighted to return to Melbourne as it's such a great city that always provides a superbly well supported event.

Replacing the Chinese GP, which has been put on ice until 2023, is Imola, which will host its third grand prix in three years after its 14-year break from F1, again run under the courtesy title of the Emilia Romagna GP.

This year's only new venue comes at the start of May, with Miami finally landing a race of its own after numerous previous events over the decades. After a fortnight's gap, in mid-May, the European season begins in Spain followed, a week later, by the annual blast around the streets of Monaco. There are more back-to-back races in the middle of June, first in Azerbaijan, then in Canada.

There are two pairs of back-to-back races in July, leading up to the summer break. First are the grands prix at Silverstone and then the Red Bull Ring. At the end of month, the French GP is followed by the race in Hungary. Both pairs fit well together.

Teams then return for a couple of intense three-race blocks, first at Spa-Francorchamps, Zandvoort and Monza, which are not too far apart. The second trio requires more of a logistical scramble, involving air freight rather than road transport, as the teams bounce from the final Russian GP at Sochi to Singapore and then on to the much-desired return to Suzuka in Japan.

Then it's off to the Americas, with the United States GP at Circuit of the Americas followed a by a relatively short hop to Mexico City. The circus heads south for the Brazilian GP after a week's break. However, in order to avoid a clash with the football World Cup in Qatar in late November, the last race of the year will be held the very next weekend, in Abu Dhabi, which will be an exhausting combination as it rounds out the 23 races being squeezed into just 35 weeks.

The introduction last year of shorter sprint races on the Saturday of three rounds, with qualifying being pushed forward to the Friday, was an interesting experiment. Many teams protested that they added considerably to their costs and so ate into their capped budgets. However, Liberty Media wants to have six sprints in 2023, as it attempts to boost F1's popularity and airtime over the coming seasons.

These 23 race weekends might, of course, have to be amended in the months ahead, with Australia's first grand prix since its aborted one in 2020 already having a tentative feel about it, while the Japanese are known to be wary about another spike of infection, as the country suffered one last year when it hosted the Olympic Games.

Naturally, China will want a race of its own again in 2023 and Qatar will be ready for its second grand prix after the one-year break caused by its hosting of the FIFA World Cup. So, for future seasons the question will be which of the other races will be culled to make space for their inclusion? With the calendar already overstuffed and teams doing their best to accommodate more races than ever, you can't imagine all of the teams agreeing to take their race tally to 25 in 2023.

» SAKHIR

The teams have come to get to know the Sakhir circuit well in recent years and even got to use two different circuit layouts in 2020 so that it could host a pair of grands prix.

The Middle East has long been a place that the World Championship has wanted to go. This isn't just because the Arab nations have oil money to finance their hosting deal, but because its time zone works for most of the F1 watching nations that continue to be Eurocentric. So, instead of having a midday start for European viewers, the race will start later and be run under floodlights. This means the start time will be mid-afternoon in Europe.

The circuit is divided into two parts. The first part represents an oasis, with well-watered grass verges. This marks the area along the main straight and around the paddock. The other part, echoing the local landscape, is desert, albeit with the rocky areas around the track sprayed with glue to limit the amount of dust that would otherwise blow onto the circuit.

The first two corners are typical of circuit-designer Hermann Tilke, with a tight first corner followed almost immediately by a second turn that folds the track in the opposite direction. From here, the drivers accelerate hard through a kink and then on along a straight that climbs to the Turn 4 hairpin.

From this high point, the track drops through a fifth-gear esse and on to tight Turn 8, which is a popular passing place. Drivers also try to pass into Turn 10 where the track loops around the rear of the paddock.

The track turns uphill again at one of the key corners, Turn 11, rising to Turn 13 where it doubles back and the drivers come down the slope to the double-apex sweep onto the start-finish straight and top 200mph as they blast past the pits.

INSIDE TRACK

BAHRAIN GRAND PRIX

Date:	**20 March**
Circuit name:	**Bahrain International Circuit**
Circuit length:	**3.363 miles/5.412km**
Number of laps:	**57**
Email:	**info@bic.com.bh**
Website:	**www.bahraingp.com.bh**

PREVIOUS WINNERS

2013	**Sebastian Vettel**	RED BULL
2014	**Lewis Hamilton**	MERCEDES
2015	**Lewis Hamilton**	MERCEDES
2016	**Nico Rosberg**	MERCEDES
2017	**Sebastian Vettel**	FERRARI
2018	**Sebastian Vettel**	FERRARI
2019	**Lewis Hamilton**	MERCEDES
2020	**Lewis Hamilton**	MERCEDES
2020	**Sergio Perez**	RACING POINT
2021	**Lewis Hamilton**	MERCEDES

Location: The Bahrain International Circuit, to give it its official name, is located at Sakhir, around 20 miles south of the capital city Manama, built on a gently sloping patch of rocky desert.

Its first grand prix: Michael Schumacher dominated the inaugural Bahrain GP for Ferrari in 2004, beating team-mate Rubens Barrichello easily as the drivers learnt not to run wide and bring sharp stones back onto the circuit.

A race to remember: Tyre life is important at every grand prix venue, but it's an extra gamble at Sakhir and yet by opting not to make a second tyre stop in 2018, Ferrari helped Sebastian Vettel to beat Valtteri Bottas's Mercedes. Vettel was really struggling for grip near the end, but hung on to win.

Rising Bahraini star: Bahraini drivers remain thin on the ground, especially in the junior single-seater series, with Bahrainis preferring to contest the Middle East Porsche Carrera Cup, with Jaber Al-Khalifa and Ali Al Khalifa finishing in the top 12 of that last year.

Its toughest corner: Turn 11 is the trickiest of the lot, with the uphill left-hander continuing to tighten as the drivers try to get the power down, then turning to the right just afterwards.

BAHRAIN INTERNATIONAL CIRCUIT

Speed
0   100   200   300

325.6km/h maximum

⏱1 Timing sector   ▬ DRS   DRS detection   ⚙ Gear   ▲ Overtaking opportunity

2021 POLE TIME: **VERSTAPPEN (RED BULL), 1M28.997S, 136.030MPH/218.919KPH**
2021 WINNER'S AVERAGE SPEED: **122.630MPH/197.355KPH**
2021 FASTEST LAP: **BOTTAS (MERCEDES), 1M32.090S, 131.461MPH/211.566KPH**
LAP RECORD: **M SCHUMACHER (FERRARI), 1M30.252S 134.262KPH/216.074KPH, 2004**

JEDDAH

Built with the aim of being the fastest ever street circuit, the Jeddah Street Circuit certainly didn't disappoint on its debut. Not only could cars average 150mph, but the lap had a good flow.

Singapore set the gold standard when it constructed the Marina Bay circuit for its maiden F1 visit in 2008. The illuminated central business district provides a spectacular backdrop to the racing action. This will have been a consideration for the circuit management as they planned to make a splash for Saudi Arabia by providing a similar lightshow for its night race, with several buildings and grandstands suspended over the circuit aping elements of Singapore's circuit and also the Yas Marina venue in Abu Dhabi, all of which gain a special atmosphere as the light fails and day turns to night.

The 6.175km lap at the Jeddah Street Circuit is F1's second longest after the 7.004km of Spa-Francorchamps, and it's packed with 27 corners. What stands out is the great flow that can be attained through its long sequences of corners between the few low-speed ones. Take the sequence from Turn 4 to Turn 12, a run of nine corners through which the speed never drops below 240kph. The run from Turn 18 to Turn 26 is faster still, with a long arc to the left out of Turn 24 taking the cars towards the final corner of the lap at up to 315kph which certainly doesn't make the drivers feel as though they are hemmed in on a traditional street circuit.

There are two points on the lap where the cars get close to 200mph, firstly through the esses at Turn 21 and then just before braking on the approach to the lap's final corner, Turn 27.

It is possible that at some stage in the future, the Saudi Arabian GP will move on from the Jeddah Street Circuit to a purpose-built venue.

INSIDE TRACK

SAUDI ARABIAN GRAND PRIX

Date:	**27 March**
Circuit name:	**Jeddah Street Circuit**
Circuit length:	**3.830 miles/6.175km**
Number of laps:	**50**
Email:	**tba**
Website:	**www.saudiarabiangp.com**

PREVIOUS WINNERS

2021	**Lewis Hamilton**

Location: The circuit has been built about eight miles north of the centre of Jeddah on a west-facing stretch of the coastline that has been built out into the Red Sea to provide a couple of lagoons.

Its first grand prix: The 2021 Saudi Arabian GP was an extraordinary event that resulted in a series of clashes between Lewis Hamilton and Max Verstappen as they tussled over the lead, with the Dutchman being hit with several penalties and having to accept finishing in second place, which meant that they would head to the final race in Abu Dhabi equal on 369.5 points apiece.

A race to remember: Frankly, the race to get the Jeddah Street Circuit completed in time for its World Championship debut last November was a testament to the organisers' desire to put on a good show on a circuit that they were sure would impress with its runs of high-speed corners.

Greatest Saudi Arabian driver: Abdulaziz Al Faisal, a member of the Saudi royal family and the country's minister of sport, remains the most successful Saudi racing driver, having won the annual Dubai 24 Hours GT race in both 2015 and 2018, both times driving a Black Falcon-entered Mercedes after winning the Middle East Porsche GT3 series in 2010 and 2012. He also contested the Le Mans 24 Hours each year between 2011 and 2015.

Rising Saudi Arabian star: Reema Juffali continues to be that rarest of things: a female Saudi racing driver. The 30-year-old has been racing single-seaters since 2018, and spent last year on the British club scene, in the GB3 category that was formerly BRDC F3.

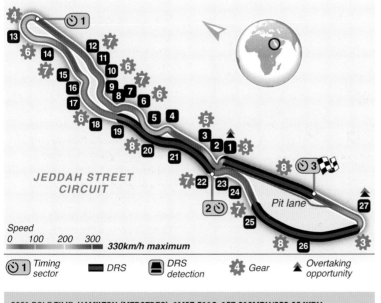

JEDDAH STREET CIRCUIT

Pit lane

Speed
0   100   200   300
330km/h maximum

🕐1 Timing sector   ▬ DRS   DRS detection   ⚙ Gear   ▲ Overtaking opportunity

2021 POLE TIME: HAMILTON (MERCEDES), 1M27.511S, 157.818MPH/253.984KPH
2021 WINNER'S AVERAGE SPEED: 91.085MPH/146.587KPH
2021 FASTEST LAP: HAMILTON (MERCEDES), 1M30.734S, 152.212MPH/244.962KPH
LAP RECORD: HAMILTON (MERCEDES), 1M30.734S, 152.212MPH/244.962KPH, 2021

» MELBOURNE

Australia's extreme entry requirements during the pandemic made entry to the country all but impossible and so this sporting nation had to do without F1 and F1 had to do without its traditional season-opener.

Melbourne's Albert Park is a pleasant municipal park, a green space with a lake at its centre with a golf course and other sporting facilities sprinkled around its fringes. It is here that F1 likes to visit every March to race on a circuit laid out around the lake. The open feel of the place will feel extra welcoming this year as F1 has had to skip its popular Australian opening race last year after a false start there in 2020 when COVID outbreaks during the event led the teams to pack up and go home again without getting to race.

The lap starts with a gentle right-left esse, but there is more often than not some contact into the first turn on the opening lap. If not there, then it may come down to the third turn, which is usually one of the best passing places.

Approached down a narrow, concrete-walled run, it hides its 100-degree turn to the right until the drivers are nearly at the apex. Martin Brundle had an aerobatic ride there in the inaugural Melbourne race because of the field bunching.

The track then opens out a bit as it passes the sport stadium, but only really feels open once it turns right at Turn 8 and leaves the trees behind. Now running between golf course and lake, it allows the drivers to let loose and hit 190mph before the left-right esse before the sailing club.

At Turn 13, the second-best passing place as the cars decelerate from 190mph, the lap tightens up again and feels more like the first part of the lap as it runs through a series of slower corners between the trees.

INSIDE TRACK

AUSTRALIAN GRAND PRIX

Date:	**10 April**
Circuit name:	**Albert Park**
Circuit length:	**3.295 miles/5.300km**
Number of laps:	**58**
Email:	**enquiries@grandprix.com.au**
Website:	**www.grandprix.com.au**

PREVIOUS WINNERS

2010	**Jenson Button** McLAREN
2011	**Sebastian Vettel** RED BULL
2012	**Jenson Button** McLAREN
2013	**Kimi Raikkonen** LOTUS
2014	**Nico Rosberg** MERCEDES
2015	**Lewis Hamilton** MERCEDES
2016	**Nico Rosberg** MERCEDES
2017	**Sebastian Vettel** FERRARI
2018	**Sebastian Vettel** FERRARI
2019	**Valtteri Bottas** MERCEDES

Location: This is a circuit that is as easy to reach from a city centre as any circuit apart from Monaco and Singapore, as it's just a one-mile tram ride away.

Its first grand prix: The 1996 Australian GP was the first after the race transferred from Adelaide and it nearly went to Jacques Villeneuve on his debut, but his Williams' engine lost oil pressure and team-mate Damon Hill raced by to win.

A race to remember: The rush to the first corner on the opening lap has often been fraught with danger, but never more so than in 2002 when Ralf Schumacher's Williams got airborne after hitting the back of Rubens Barrichello's Ferrari. Six other cars were eliminated in the incident.

Greatest Australian driver: Jack Brabham put Australian racers on the map by landing the 1959 and 1960 F1 titles with Cooper. He then formed his own team and won the 1966 F1 title. Mark Webber, with nine wins for Red Bull between 2009 and 2012 deserves a mention.

Rising Australian star: Oscar Piastri is the real deal. He's enjoyed a great run through the junior categories, as he won the European Formula Renault title in 2019, the FIA F3 crown in 2020 and then F2 honours last year.

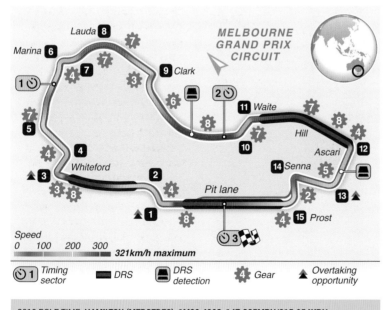

MELBOURNE GRAND PRIX CIRCUIT

Speed
0   100   200   300
321km/h maximum

(🕐)1 Timing sector   ▬ DRS   🅿 DRS detection   ⚙4 Gear   ▲ Overtaking opportunity

2019 POLE TIME: **HAMILTON (MERCEDES), 1M20.486S, 147.385MPH/215.954KPH**
2019 WINNER'S AVERAGE SPEED: **134.187MPH/223.075KPH**
2019 FASTEST LAP: **BOTTAS (MERCEDES), 1M25.580S, 138.612MPH/223.075KPH**
LAP RECORD: **M SCHUMACHER (FERRARI), 1M24.125S 141.016MPH/226.944KPH, 2004**

IMOLA

This old school Italian circuit won new fans in 2020 when it stood in to host a round of a scrambled World Championship, with its gradient change and picturesque setting.

Although Imola hosted the San Marino GP 24 times between 1981 and 2006, it's not actually in the landlocked principality of San Marino. Instead, it's to the north-west – in Italy – and the title was used as a courtesy one so that Italy could give the *tifosi* two home races each year.

The lap at Imola starts on the level, little more than 50m in from the edge of the river that forms one side of the circuit's plot and curves gently to the left through Targuardo. What was once the long Tamburello corner had a chicane inserted there after Ayrton Senna's death when his Williams speared off into the wall on the right-hand side of the track in 1994.

A further chicane was inserted towards the end of what had been a kinked straight to the hairpin at Tosa, which was a shame,

as the approach to the corner used to be the best spot for overtaking.

From Tosa, the track doubles back to the left, then immediately rises towards Piratella. This is taken in fifth gear and the hillside drops away sharply towards Acque Minerali where it fires the drivers through a left then reaches a turnaround point before snapping uphill again to climb towards the lap's tightest chicane – Variante Alta – at the crest of the hill.

Running down a corridor of trees, the track then offers a pair of downhill lefts before reaching the riverbank again. From here, it's just a flat-out blast through a right-hand kink onto the start-finish straight and then on past the pits and through Targuardo – the fastest point on the lap, where cars hit 180mph – as they start another lap.

INSIDE TRACK

EMILIA ROMAGNA GRAND PRIX

Date:	**24 April**
Circuit name:	**Autodromo Enzo & Dino Ferrari**
Circuit length:	**3.048 miles/4.906km**
Number of laps:	**63**
Email:	**info@autodromoimola.it**
Website:	**www.autodromoimola.it**

PREVIOUS WINNERS

1999*	**Michael Schumacher**	FERRARI
2000*	**Michael Schumacher**	FERRARI
2001*	**Ralf Schumacher**	WILLIAMS
2002*	**Michael Schumacher**	FERRARI
2003*	**Michael Schumacher**	FERRARI
2004*	**Michael Schumacher**	FERRARI
2005*	**Fernando Alonso**	RENAULT
2006*	**Michael Schumacher**	FERRARI
2020	**Lewis Hamilton**	MERCEDES
2021	**Max Verstappen**	RED BULL

* Run as the San Marino GP

Location: The circuit is built between the River Santerno and rolling hills on the southern flank of Imola, a town roughly twenty miles south-east of Bologna.

Its first grand prix: After hosting a non-championship F1 race in 1963, won by Jim Clark for Lotus, Imola had to wait until 1980 to host the Italian GP while Monza was out of favour following Ronnie Peterson's death in 1978. This race reverted to Monza, though, leaving Imola to wait only until 1981 to gain a second Italian race under the title of the San Marino GP. This was won by Nelson Piquet for Brabham.

A race to remember: Michael Schumacher had an incredible hit rate at Imola, but he didn't win here for Ferrari until his fourth attempt after three second-place finishes. Finally, in 1999, he got the adulation he was seeking after Mika Häkkinen crashed out of the lead and then Ferrari outthought McLaren, denying David Coulthard victory.

Greatest driver: The principality of San Marino has yet to produce an F1 driver, with Christian Montanari being a frontrunner in World Series by Renault in 2005 and 2006 before turning to sportscar racing and going well in GT1 in 2007.

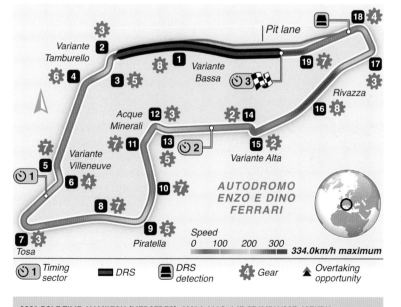

2021 POLE TIME: **HAMILTON (MERCEDES), 1M14.411S, 147.574MPH/237.497KPH**

2021 WINNER'S AVERAGE SPEED: **93.998MPH/151.276KPH**

2021 FASTEST LAP: **HAMILTON (MERCEDES), 1M16.702S, 143.166MPH/230.403KPH**

LAP RECORD: **HAMILTON (MERCEDES), 1M15.484S 145.476MPH/234.121KPH, 2020**

» MIAMI

This new race on the World Championship calendar for 2022 has been a long time in the making and had to negotiate local opposition before settling on this new venue.

Plans have come and plans have gone to host a grand prix in downtown Miami after first being discussed as a distant possibility as long ago as the 1990s, but local opposition thwarted them all. Then new plans were hatched to move the race away from assorted mooted venues near the heart of the city to a temporary circuit built on land around the home stadium of the Miami Dolphins NFL team on its outskirts. Finally, these plans got the go-ahead. So, the USA gets a second race alongside the regular United States GP at the Circuit of the Americas.

The 19-corner lap design is unusual in that it runs its course in an anti-clockwise direction, with a short blast from the grid to Turn 1, a medium-speed right feeding into an esse then an open right. A longer three-part esse follows before a long left leads onto a lightly arcing flat-out blast all the way to heavy braking for the sharp left at Turn 11. This will see the cars top 200mph (320kph) before dropping to a quarter of that speed for Turn 11 and so providing a clear passing opportunity, something that the circuit architects were keen to ensure.

The lap tightens up here as it enters a run of slow corners. From Turn 16, though, there's a complete change of nature as the lap's longest straight follows all the way to a left-hand hairpin at Turn 17 before a sweeping left-right combination in front of large temporary grandstands that brings the cars back to a short start-finish straight.

American circuits haven't always had a long hold on F1 visits, but the Miami International Autodrome has a 10-year contract from 2022.

INSIDE TRACK 🇺🇸

MIAMI GRAND PRIX

Date:	**8 May**
Circuit name:	**Miami International Autodrome**
Circuit length:	**3.362 miles/5.411km**
Number of laps:	**56**
Email:	**info@f1miamigp.com**
Website:	**www.f1miamigp.com**

PREVIOUS WINNERS
First race

Location: This new circuit is in the Miami Gardens suburb on the northern side of the city, on the grounds of the Hard Rock Stadium.

Its best corner: Turn 17 looks to be the pick of the 19 corners, as it is approached by the lap's longest straight and could be a good corner for attacking, but also for defending.

Florida's racing history: The state is best known for two of the USA's classic circuits, Daytona International Speedway and Sebring, both used for annual sportscar races, with Daytona also the venue for the most prestigious NASCAR stock car race. Florida has previously hosted Indycar races on temporary street circuits in Miami, firstly at Bicentennial Park and Tamiami Park then, after an unpopular spell at the Homestead oval, at Bayfront Park from 2002, and now the series uses the St Petersburg street circuit on the state's gulf coast.

Greatest Floridian driver: No one from Florida has starred in F1, but Ryan Hunter-Reay – from nearby Fort Lauderdale – has performed consistently in Indycar. Since stepping up from Formula Atlantic 19 years ago, he has won 16 Indycar rounds, four of which came in the year that he won the title with Andretti Autosport, and one of which was the 2014 Indy 500. In 2020, Hunter-Reay won the Sebring 12 Hours sportscar race.

Rising Floridian star: Kyle Kirkwood won last year's Indy Lights title, his fourth different single-seater title in five years, and with it a cheque for $1.3m to help him gain an Indycar ride for 2022.

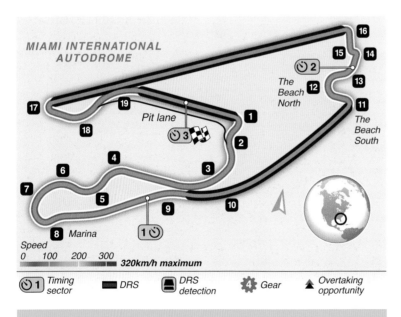

MIAMI INTERNATIONAL AUTODROME

The Beach North

The Beach South

Pit lane

Marina

Speed
0   100   200   300
320km/h maximum

🕐1 Timing sector ▪ DRS ▪ DRS detection ⚙4 Gear ▲ Overtaking opportunity

DESIGNED BY APEX, IS LAID OUT IN A MANNER THAT EARLY STREET CIRCUITS SELDOM WERE, WITH THE AIM OF ALLOWING THE CARS TO TRAVEL AT SPEED RATHER THAN SIMPLY AROUND A SEQUENCE OF 90-DEGREE BENDS, SOMETHING THAT IT WAS ABLE TO DO AS ITS COURSE IS IN A PARKING LOT.

BARCELONA

The home of the Spanish GP used to be popular when F1 teams had unlimited testing, as it provided all sorts of corner types. Now, it is seen as a less than special race venue.

The Spanish GP became part of the World Championship in 1951, running on a street circuit in the Pedralbes district of Barcelona. It dropped off the calendar after 1952 before returning in 1968 on the Jarama circuit outside Madrid to alternate with the Montjuich Park circuit in central Barcelona until the mid-1970s. In 1986, the Jerez circuit in the southwest took over.

However, since 1991, the race has been held at the Circuit de Barcelona-Catalunya. The circuit uses its gradient to make it interesting, but its lap is not one that offers many opportunities for overtaking, bar into the first corner.

The run from the startline is gently downhill to the first two corners that are very much connected as the track feeds right then left. A gentle climb follows as the track arcs through Turn 3 before it levels out for the run to Turn 4, where it goes right and gently uphill again before a notable drop out of tighter Turn 5.

Turn 7 is at the foot of the hill and the track snaps uphill from there, with Campsa being over a blind brow and exit speed from here is critical as it feeds onto the infield straight. The track descends to a Turn 10 that has been tweaked slightly in recent years, so passing is now possible – rather than expected – from where it turns uphill again.

The track flattens for the run out of Turn 12 then turns hard right at Turn 13 and drops through the fiddly chicane all the way to the final corner. With an appreciable straight to follow, on which cars top 200mph, a good tow is required for anyone trying to pass into Turn 1.

SPANISH GRAND PRIX

Date:	**22 May**
Circuit name:	**Circuit de Barcelona-Catalunya**
Circuit length:	**2.892 miles/4.654km**
Number of laps:	**66**
Email:	**info@circuitcat.com**
Website:	**www.circuitcat.com**

PREVIOUS WINNERS

2011	**Sebastian Vettel**	RED BULL
2012	**Pastor Maldonado**	WILLIAMS
2013	**Fernando Alonso**	FERRARI
2014	**Lewis Hamilton**	MERCEDES
2015	**Nico Rosberg**	MERCEDES
2016	**Max Verstappen**	RED BULL
2017	**Lewis Hamilton**	MERCEDES
2018	**Lewis Hamilton**	MERCEDES
2019	**Lewis Hamilton**	MERCEDES
2021	**Lewis Hamilton**	MERCEDES

Location: The Circuit de Barcelona-Catalunya lies in rolling hills 15 miles to the north of the city. When the circuit opened, this was open countryside, but industrial sprawl has changed the nature of the place.

Its first grand prix: Spain had long been in thrall to motorcycle racing, but its car racing fans were delighted when the grand prix moved from distant Jerez to a track closer to many more of them. Opened in 1991, it immediately hosted a grand prix, and this was won at a canter by Nigel Mansell for Williams.

A race to remember: For sheer surprise, few Spanish GPs can match 2012, when Williams scored its most recent grand prix success courtesy of fast but crash-happy Pastor Maldonado who did everything right in a year in which his next best finish was fifth. This came eight years after Williams' previous victory.

Greatest Spanish driver: Fernando Alonso is by far the greatest of Spain's racing stars, becoming the nation's first grand prix winner in 2003 and then, in 2005, its first World Champion.

Rising Spanish star: The pick of the pack is Rafael Villagomez, who raced in Euroformula Open – a second-rank F3 series – last year.

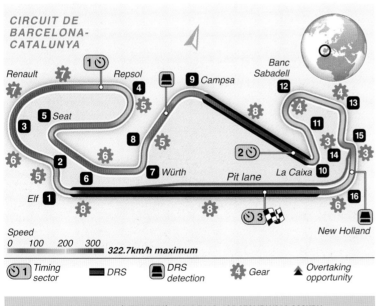

CIRCUIT DE BARCELONA-CATALUNYA

Renault · Repsol · Banc Sabadell · Campsa · Seat · Würth · Pit lane · La Caixa · Elf · New Holland

Speed
0 100 200 300 **322.7km/h maximum**

⏱1 Timing sector · DRS · DRS detection · Gear · ▲ Overtaking opportunity

2021 POLE TIME: **HAMILTON (MERCEDES), 1M16.741S, 136.272MPH/219.309KPH**
2021 WINNER'S AVERAGE SPEED: **123.472MPH/198.709KPH**
2021 FASTEST LAP: **VERSTAPPEN (RED BULL), 1M18.149S, 133.816MPH/215.357KPH**
LAP RECORD: **VERSTAPPEN (RED BULL), 1M18.149S 133.816MPH/215.357KPH, 2021**

The circuit has remained little changed, but the yachts in Monaco's harbour have grown since the principality held its first grand prix.

MONACO

This most famous of street circuits remains something truly distinct in the world of F1. It is a nearly impossible place to race or work but a brilliant backdrop for the sport nonetheless.

Monte Carlo is a beautiful location with a wonderful climate, a district of Monaco nestled between mountain and sea with pavements made of gold. Well, perhaps not, but the sheer wealth packed into such a tiny area is staggering. Some of the yachts berthed in the harbour are the size of several houses and, come the grand prix, they are moved out to make space for even larger superyachts occupied by plutocrats.

There's racing too, but the circuit is never less than cramped. There have been modifications in the past decade to the end of the lap and proper pits too, but the barriers are seldom more than a few metres from the racing line.

The start-finish straight is curved and there's even a slight esse before the first corner, Sainte Devote. Fortunately, there's an escape road there too, as it often gets a little too tight on the first lap.

Then it's off up a surprisingly steep climb towards Casino Square, with the wonderful left at its crest, Massenet; a tricky twister. Bursting clear from the barriers for a moment, the cars then turn right through Casino Square before diving down to Mirabeau and then snaking down further to the Grand Hotel hairpin and on down through Portier to the seafront.

The drivers have no time for the view as they then plunge into the tunnel under the hotel and keep arcing to the right until they emerge, hit 180mph and then brake for the harbour-front chicane. After this left/right/left flick, they blaze past the yachts through Tabac to the four-corner Piscine complex. La Rascasse, an uphill right-hand hairpin checks their pace, as does the final corner, before they blast back past the pits.

INSIDE TRACK

MONACO GRAND PRIX

Date:	**29 May**
Circuit name:	**Circuit de Monaco**
Circuit length:	**2.075 miles/3.339km**
Number of laps:	**78**
Email:	**info@acm.mc**
Website:	**www.acm.mc**

PREVIOUS WINNERS

2011	**Sebastian Vettel**	RED BULL
2012	**Mark Webber**	RED BULL
2013	**Nico Rosberg**	MERCEDES
2014	**Nico Rosberg**	MERCEDES
2015	**Nico Rosberg**	MERCEDES
2016	**Lewis Hamilton**	MERCEDES
2017	**Sebastian Vettel**	FERRARI
2018	**Daniel Ricciardo**	RED BULL
2019	**Lewis Hamilton**	MERCEDES
2021	**Max Verstappen**	RED BULL

Location: The circuit is in the heart of Monte Carlo, starting between the Grimaldi castle and the harbour before snaking through the town.

Its first grand prix: The first World Championship round was held here in 1950. Juan Manuel Fangio won for Alfa Romeo, finishing a lap clear of Alberto Ascari's Ferrari.

A race to remember: For sheer drama, no Monaco GP can have had a finish as crazy as in 1982. With three laps to go, Alain Prost led for Renault, but he slid off the wet track. Then Riccardo Patrese took over but slid off too. He rejoined the race, but Didier Pironi raced past to lead onto the last lap. His Ferrari stopped in the tunnel, the electrics in Andrea Cesaris's Alfa Romeo failed, so Patrese took the win for Brabham.

Greatest Monegasque driver: Louis Chiron finished third here in 1950, but his achievement has been eclipsed by Charles Leclerc who was snapped up by Ferrari for his second year of F1 in 2019 and became a winner.

Rising Monegasque star: Arthur Leclerc, younger brother of Charles, is the principality's next big hope for F1 stardom. The 20-year-old was a race winner in 2021's FIA Formula 3 Championship racing for Prema Racing.

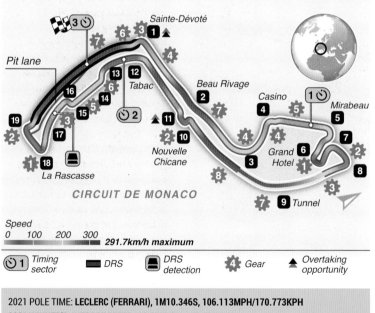

CIRCUIT DE MONACO

Speed
0   100   200   300
291.7km/h maximum

⏱1 Timing sector   ▬ DRS   DRS detection   ⚙4 Gear   ▲ Overtaking opportunity

2021 POLE TIME: **LECLERC (FERRARI), 1M10.346S, 106.113MPH/170.773KPH**
2021 WINNER'S AVERAGE SPEED: **98.073MPH/157.833KPH**
2021 FASTEST LAP: **HAMILTON (MERCEDES), 1M12.909S, 102.383MPH/164.769KPH**
LAP RECORD: **HAMILTON (MERCEDES), 1M12.909S, 102.383MPH/164.769KPH, 2021**

BAKU

The teams will all be concerned about tyre failures after both Lance Stroll and Max Verstappen crashed out when their tyres let go coming onto the main straight at 180mph last year.

Some circuits seldom produce exciting races while others never fail to provide spectacular moments and, ever since its introduction to the World Championship in 2016, this street circuit in the capital of Azerbaijan has fitted the latter description, whether for better or for worse. Last year's pair of top-gear blowouts was something that no one will wish to see repeated.

The format is effectively a two-part circuit around Baku, split between the modern area outside the city walls and the ancient area within.

The start straight runs parallel with the seafront, separated only by a park. The first four corners suggest a typical street circuit, as they are all 90-degree bends, three to the left and one to the right, and their format makes overtaking difficult, although Turn 1 is wider than the others so it can work.

After a chicane and a tight right, the track reaches the foot of the citadel and then changes nature as it flashes past shops, runs along the city wall in a claustrophobic climb before regaining light and space as it bursts into a park.

One of the reasons that Azerbaijan wanted a grand prix was to showcase its capital, and the track opens out past its banks, government buildings and embassies, rising gently until Turn 15 where it plunges downhill, drivers turning sharply to the left at Turn 16 before a flat-out sprint through the remaining corners and on all the way to Turn 1. Although there are still four corners to the end of the lap, these are no more than kinks and the drivers are hitting 200mph even before entering the start-finish straight, going on to top 201mph before braking for Turn 1.

INSIDE TRACK

AZERBAIJAN GRAND PRIX

Date:	**12 June**
Circuit name:	**Baku City Circuit**
Circuit length:	**3.753 miles/6.006km**
Number of laps:	**51**
Email:	**info@bakugp.az**
Website:	**www.bakugp.az**

PREVIOUS WINNERS

2016	**Nico Rosberg**	MERCEDES
2017	**Daniel Ricciardo**	RED BULL
2018	**Lewis Hamilton**	MERCEDES
2019	**Valtteri Bottas**	MERCEDES
2021	**Sergio Perez**	RED BULL

Location: Baku sits midway up the western coast of the Caspian Sea on the Absheron Peninsula and the circuit sits bang in the middle of the capital, where high temperatures can be fanned by high winds.

Its first grand prix: Mercedes was the dominant team for Baku's first grand prix in 2016 and Nico Rosberg won easily from pole position, while team-mate Lewis Hamilton qualified only tenth after clipping a wall and had no chance from there, finishing fifth.

A race to remember: Nothing has yet deposed Baku's second grand prix in 2017 for sheer drama. It is rare to witness one driver ramming another running at reduced pace behind the safety car. This happened here when Sebastian Vettel did that to Lewis Hamilton, having been frustrated when the Mercedes driver failed to accelerate out of Turn 15 and he clipped his tail, leaving Daniel Ricciardo to take victory.

Greatest Azerbaijani driver: There were no Azerbaijani drivers when the grand prix debuted in 2016. There are still none on the horizon, in no small part because of this being a temporary circuit in a country that offers nowhere else for its aspiring drivers to hone their skills.

Its toughest corner: Turn 16, a third gear lefthander, isn't particularly noteworthy in itself, but exit speed from here is critical as it feeds onto the longest flat-out blast that continues all the way to Turn 1.

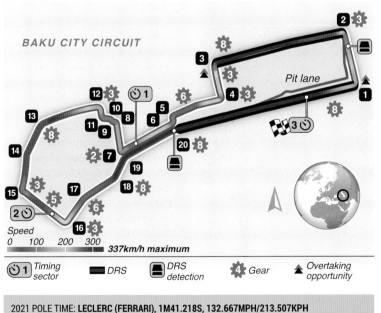

BAKU CITY CIRCUIT

Pit lane

Speed
0   100   200   300
337km/h maximum

⏱1 Timing sector	▬ DRS
🏁 DRS detection	⚙4 Gear
▲ Overtaking opportunity	

2021 POLE TIME: **LECLERC (FERRARI), 1M41.218S, 132.667MPH/213.507KPH**
2021 WINNER'S AVERAGE SPEED: **85.401MPH/137.440KPH**
2021 FASTEST LAP: **VERSTAPPEN (RED BULL), 1M44.481S, 128.524MPH/206.839KPH**
LAP RECORD: **LECLERC (FERRARI), 1M43.009S 130.360MPH/209.795KPH, 2019**

MONTREAL

The Canadian leg of the World Championship has long been one of the most popular, not chiefly for the circuit itself, but because the teams love the city and its party vibe.

INSIDE TRACK 🇨🇦

CANADIAN GRAND PRIX

Date:	19 June
Circuit name:	Circuit Gilles Villeneuve
Circuit length:	2.710 miles/4.361km
Number of laps:	70
Email:	info@circuitgillesvilleneuve.ca
Website:	www.circuitgillesvilleneuve.ca

The Circuit Gilles Villeneuve is named after Canada's beloved F1 driver whose son Jacques became Canada's only F1 World Champion. However, its tight nature is not the sort of circuit that would have ranked among this daredevil's favourites.

The problem faced when the circuit was created in the late 1970s was the lack of space, as it was squeezed onto the narrow end of an island in the St Lawrence River, hemmed in further by starting its course alongside the rowing lake used in the 1976 Olympic Games.

The run to the first turn kinks to the right then turns hard left, and this is where many a driver has run out of track or into a rival in opening lap action across the years.

The Senna Hairpin follows, and the track runs right to the edge of the island before snaking through an esse, a fast right and then a pair of two-corner combinations before opening out onto a run to the tighter of the lap's hairpins. There is definitely scope to overtake into here.

Perhaps more important is to get the power down quickly, as the lap's longest straight follows. Drivers can touch 200mph before having to brake for the two corners that end the lap. As Turns 13 and 14 are a chicane, they need to scrub off around 115mph and this always offers a chance to try a passing move. They don't always work though, and many a driver has ended up hitting the wall on their exit at the start of the pit straight. What makes this such a feature is the fact that the walls are right on the track's edge.

PREVIOUS WINNERS

2010	**Lewis Hamilton**	McLAREN
2011	**Jenson Button**	McLAREN
2012	**Lewis Hamilton**	McLAREN
2013	**Sebastian Vettel**	RED BULL
2014	**Daniel Ricciardo**	RED BULL
2015	**Lewis Hamilton**	MERCEDES
2016	**Lewis Hamilton**	MERCEDES
2017	**Lewis Hamilton**	MERCEDES
2018	**Sebastian Vettel**	FERRARI
2019	**Lewis Hamilton**	MERCEDES

Location: The Ile Notre-Dame was chosen for the circuit as it was the largest available space close to the city centre and it had a metro connection, making access easy and removing the need for much space for car parking.

Its first grand prix: It was cold and damp when Montreal hosted a grand prix for the first time in 1978 and Jean-Pierre Jarier, filling in at Lotus after Ronnie Peterson's death, was racing clear until his car broke and this handed victory to Canada's own, Gilles Villeneuve.

A race to remember: Jenson Button's triumph in 2011 was special as he overcame a drive-through penalty to hunt down Sebastian Vettel and pressure him into a final-lap error.

Greatest Canadian driver: Jacques Villeneuve became Canada's only World Champion to date in 2007, but his father Gilles is acknowledged as the country's best ever F1 talent. He ranked second to Ferrari team-mate Jody Scheckter but was then killed at Zolder in 1982 before he could claim a title of his own.

Rising Canadian star: Canada is short on rising stars at present, with no-one following family-backed Lance Stroll and Nicholas Latifi. Mac Clark looked good in US F4 last year.

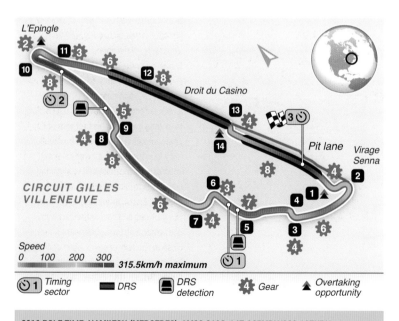

L'Epingle

Droit du Casino

Pit lane

Virage Senna

CIRCUIT GILLES VILLENEUVE

Speed
0   100   200   300
315.5km/h maximum

🕐1 Timing sector	DRS	DRS detection	⚙️ Gear	▲ Overtaking opportunity

2019 POLE TIME: **HAMILTON (MERCEDES), 1M28.319S, 147.965MPH/238.127KPH**
2019 WINNER'S AVERAGE SPEED: **136.606MPH/219.846KPH**
2019 FASTEST LAP: **VETTEL (FERRARI), 1M32.740S, 140.911MPH/226.775KPH**
LAP RECORD: **VETTEL (FERRARI), 1M32.740S 140.911MPH/226.775KPH, 2019**

SILVERSTONE

This classic circuit continues to pack in the fans and their passion for racing is as much of its appeal as its sheer longevity and clear connection with the many great ages of F1.

Silverstone started life as a simple airfield during the Second World War. After the war was over, it didn't really have a purpose, but racing fans decided that a combination of its defunct runways and perimeter roads would make a good circuit. And now, 74 years after it opened, there is still a semblance of that original layout despite a myriad developments and layout changes over the decades.

The first corner, Abbey, is a very fast, top-gear sweep, but the drivers need to brake heavily to get around the tight right at Village before snaking around The Loop. There can be a great deal of overtaking through these three corners when the field is bunched at the start.

A good exit onto the Wellington Straight can make an overtaking move possible into Brooklands. Likewise, a good run through Luffield can help a driver to try to pass at Copse, like Lewis Hamilton tried on Max Verstappen last year. Clearly, not all moves come off through this sixth-gear right.

Then comes one of the best stretches of track in use in F1, the run through Becketts, a set of esses that start in seventh gear before drivers have to drop a gear for each subsequent twist, with the change of direction so fast that it's hard to comprehend.

The Hangar Straight is a rare chance for drivers to rest, but they need to ensure that no rival tries to dive up the inside into Stowe. Then the track drops into a depression before drivers have a last chance to pass into Vale before having to hang on through the seemingly endless right-hander, Club, that completes the lap.

INSIDE TRACK

BRITISH GRAND PRIX

Date:	**3 July**
Circuit name:	**Silverstone**
Circuit length:	**3.659 miles/5.900km**
Number of laps:	**52**
Email:	sales@silverstone-circuit.co.uk
Website:	www.silverstone-circuit.co.uk

PREVIOUS WINNERS

2013	**Nico Rosberg**	MERCEDES
2014	**Lewis Hamilton**	MERCEDES
2015	**Lewis Hamilton**	MERCEDES
2016	**Lewis Hamilton**	MERCEDES
2017	**Lewis Hamilton**	MERCEDES
2018	**Sebastian Vettel**	FERRARI
2019	**Lewis Hamilton**	MERCEDES
2020	**Lewis Hamilton**	MERCEDES
2020*	**Max Verstappen**	RED BULL
2021	**Lewis Hamilton**	MERCEDES

*In the 70th Anniversary GP

Location: Silverstone is located 16 miles southwest of Northampton, straddling the Buckinghamshire and Northamptonshire border.

Its first grand prix: Its first British GP was in 1948 but two years later it hosted the opening round of the first F1 World Championship and this was a cakewalk for Alfa Romeo, with its red 158s far superior to all the opposition. Giuseppe Farina led home a one-two-three finish ahead of Luigi Fagioli and Reg Parnell, all of them two laps clear of the rest.

A race to remember: Having been so close to landing the title in his first year of F1, Lewis Hamilton bounced back in 2008. His win in the British GP was his most impressive as he mastered challenging conditions to win by nigh on a minute.

Greatest British driver: Jim Clark won two F1 titles and Jackie Stewart went one better with three, but neither can close to the tally of seven titles collected four decades on by Lewis Hamilton.

Rising British star: Either Lando Norris or George Russell could be the next British world champion, but the driver next in line to shine in F1 could have been fast but hot-headed Dan Ticktum, but he parted company with his Williams role while shining in F2.

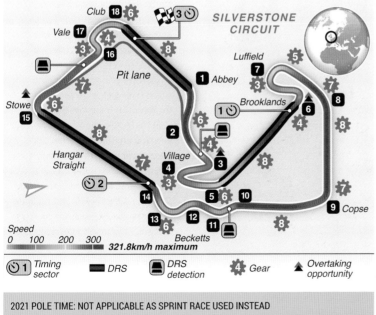

SILVERSTONE CIRCUIT

Club · Vale · Luffield · Abbey · Brooklands · Stowe · Hangar Straight · Village · Pit lane · Copse · Becketts

Speed 0 100 200 300 **321.8km/h maximum**

Timing sector	DRS
DRS detection	Gear
Overtaking opportunity	

2021 POLE TIME: NOT APPLICABLE AS SPRINT RACE USED INSTEAD
2021 WINNER'S AVERAGE SPEED: **96.426MPH/155.183KPH**
2021 FASTEST LAP: **PEREZ (RED BULL), 1M28.617S, 148.704MPH/239.317KPH**
LAP RECORD: **VERSTAPPEN (RED BULL), 1M27.097S 151.300MPH/243.494KPH, 2020**

RED BULL RING

This circuit in the Styrian Mountains has been busy of late; hosting two grand prixes per year for the past two seasons and the circuit seems to be tailor-made for incidents.

Gradient change is one of the ultimate ingredients for a great racing circuit, and this Austrian venue is blessed with plenty of that as it runs up and down the gentle lower slopes. It's a truncated version of the original track on this site, the Österreichring, which opened for business in 1969, but it contains the heady essence of the original.

The run to the first corner is the steepest section of all, with drivers seeing a lot of sky as they power up the hill before arriving at the lip, right at the apex. Fortunately, there is plenty of run-off straight ahead, as many drivers have to scramble wide as the track flattens out as it turns right.

From there, the drivers accelerate up a steepening incline, arcing left before having to hit the brakes for the right-hand hairpin at the top. Many a driver is overambitious here and contact is almost inevitable. Then the track climbs a little more before dipping down to Schlossgold. This is another tight right, but it has enough space on the exit for drivers to leave side-by-side, although this didn't work in 2020 when Alex Albon was tipped into a spin by Lewis Hamilton.

The track drops back down the slope through Turns 6 and 7 before it bottoms and then rises again through Turn 8. It dips again sharply into the penultimate corner and almost cradles the cars through a compression at the apex of the final corner. Accelerating hard along the start-finish straight, they will top 200mph as the track veers up to start another lap.

Heavy storms can blow in quickly in the mountains, so teams need to have a wet-weather strategy.

INSIDE TRACK

AUSTRIAN GRAND PRIX

Date:	10 July
Circuit name:	Red Bull Ring
Circuit length:	2.688 miles/4.326km
Number of laps:	71
Email:	information@projekt-spielberg.at
Website:	www.projekt-spielberg.at

PREVIOUS WINNERS

2014	**Nico Rosberg**	MERCEDES
2015	**Nico Rosberg**	MERCEDES
2016	**Lewis Hamilton**	MERCEDES
2017	**Valtteri Bottas**	MERCEDES
2018	**Max Verstappen**	RED BULL
2019	**Max Verstappen**	RED BULL
2020	**Valtteri Bottas**	MERCEDES
2020*	**Lewis Hamilton**	MERCEDES
2021*	**Max Verstappen**	RED BULL
2021	**Max Verstappen**	RED BULL

*In the Styrian GP

Location: The Red Bull Ring is remote from Austria's few major cities, with Graz the closest, and that's 45 miles away to the southeast.

Its first grand prix: The Österreichring held a sportscar race in 1969. Then in 1970, it timed its F1 debut just right as Austrian star Jochen Rindt was challenging for the world title. It wasn't to be his day, though, and victory went to his title rival, Ferrari's Jacky Ickx.

A race to remember: One of the wackiest Austrian GPs was in 1975 and it yielded victory to the first of three first-time winners in an extraordinary three-year streak. On this occasion, it was Vittorio Brambilla who was leading when the race was stopped early because of heavy rain. He then celebrated too wildly and crashed his March.

Greatest Austrian driver: Gerhard Berger won ten grand prixes and Niki Lauda three world titles, but, to many, Rindt remains the country's greatest, as he was dominant in F2 and F1 but was denied the chance to add to his six wins when he was killed in the 1970 Italian GP. He is the sport's only posthumous world champion.

Rising Austrian star: Since Lucas Auer quit Super Formula, Austrian fans have not one rising star in single-seaters.

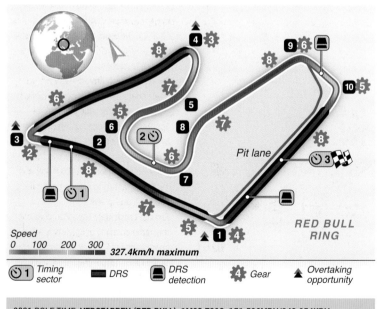

Speed			
0	100	200	300

327.4km/h maximum

(◷) 1 Timing sector   ▬ DRS   DRS detection   4 Gear   ▲ Overtaking opportunity

Pit lane

RED BULL RING

2021 POLE TIME: **VERSTAPPEN (RED BULL), 1M03.720S, 151.586MPH/243.954KPH**

2021 WINNER'S AVERAGE SPEED: **138.797MPH/223.373KPH***

2021 FASTEST LAP: **VERSTAPPEN (RED BULL), 1M06.200S, 145.907MPH/234.815KPH**

LAP RECORD: **SAINZ JR (MCLAREN), 1M05.619S 147.199MPH/236.894KPH, 2020***

PAUL RICARD

This French circuit's second spell of hosting the F1 World Championship has yet to produce any classic grands prix, but the teams at least like it for its ultra-modern facilities.

Circuit Paul Ricard really was a brave new world when it opened in 1970, as it was probably the first circuit built with driver safety in mind, championing having run-off areas rather than having barriers or even trees close to the racing line.

Financed by pastis manufacturer Paul Ricard it was super modern and spacious as well as being very fast in places, most notably at the end of the back straight.

It has been chopped and changed over the years, but its shape, when it welcomed F1 back in 2018 after a 28-year hiatus, was little altered. There was one big difference, though, in that the barriers had been moved even further back and the entire circuit was ringed with coloured bands of increasingly abrasive asphalt the further a driver strays off track.

The first turn is approached down a gentle slope and the track drops away even more by the time the cars have reached its exit. Its format attracts passing moves on lap 1, with some scraps still being contested when they have reached the Turn 3/4/5 chicane.

From Turn 6, Sainte-Beaume, the drivers then point their cars up the slope again, with a rapid entry onto the Mistral Straight vital to get maximum speed on the approach to the left-right-left chicane that bisects what was once just one long blast.

The next turn, Signes, is a fabulously fast right, taken in eighth gear at around 170mph. It's possible to pass here, but more likely to succeed at Turn 11, Beausset.

The lap then becomes tighter all the way to the final corner, a notably sharp right onto the start-finish straight. Overtaking isn't expected here, but it can be into Turn 1.

INSIDE TRACK

FRENCH GRAND PRIX

Date:	**24 July**
Circuit name:	**Circuit Paul Ricard**
Circuit length:	**3.630 miles/5.842km**
Number of laps:	**53**
Email:	**circuit@circuitpaulricard.com**
Website:	**www.circuitpaulricard.com**

PREVIOUS WINNERS

1983	**Alain Prost**	RENAULT
1985	**Nelson Piquet**	BRABHAM
1986	**Nigel Mansell**	WILLIAMS
1987	**Nigel Maansell**	WILLIAMS
1988	**Alain Prost**	McLAREN
1989	**Alain Prost**	McLAREN
1990	**Alain Prost**	FERRARI
2018	**Lewis Hamilton**	MERCEDES
2019	**Lewis Hamilton**	MERCEDES
2021	**Max Verstappen**	RED BULL

Location: The circuit is built on a plateau 20 miles northwest of Toulon, surrounded by pine trees and a mountainous backdrop.

Its first grand prix: Jackie Stewart led home a Tyrrell one-two in 1971, followed by his understudy Francois Cevert.

A race to remember: Ivan Capelli was three laps short of taking a shock win in 1990, but he could no longer keep Alain Prost's Ferrari behind his Leyton House and fell to second.

Greatest French driver: There are no challengers to Alain Prost with his four F1 world titles. He allied a cerebral approach to his speed and was a winner by the middle of his second year in F1. "The Professor" went on to win three titles with McLaren, in 1985, 1986 and 1989, before taking a comeback title with Williams in 1993.

Rising French star: Theo Pourchaire is the name on many people's lips after impressing in F2 last year, winning one of the races supporting the Monaco GP when still 17. Anyone who can win in their first season of F2 is marked out as special, and the fact that this followed him finishing as runner-up in the FIA F3 series in 2020 in his first year out of karting emphasizes his ability.

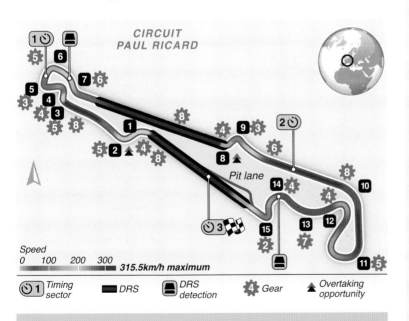

CIRCUIT PAUL RICARD

Pit lane

Speed
0   100   200   300
315.5km/h maximum

- ⏱ **1** Timing sector
- ▬ DRS
- 🖥 DRS detection
- ⚙ **4** Gear
- ▲ Overtaking opportunity

2021 POLE TIME: **VERSTAPPEN (RED BULL), 1M29.990S, 145.217MPH/233.705KPH**
2021 WINNER'S AVERAGE SPEED: **132.060MPH/212.530KPH**
2021 FASTEST LAP: **VERSTAPPEN (RED BULL), 1M36.404S, 135.556MPH/218.156KPH**
LAP RECORD: **VETTEL (FERRARI), 1M32.740S 140.911MPH/226.775KPH, 2019**

» HUNGARORING

It's tight, twisty, undulating, and as shown at the first corner last year, a circuit that can provide moments of chaos. Add tyre-melting temperatures, and it's a tricky place to go racing.

The setting is what makes the Hungaroring, for its use of the hills and valleys provides interest as the track starts high on one side of the valley, drops to the foot then rises to the far side and returns, with many a vantage point allowing views of at least a third of the lap.

The start-finish straight dips noticeably on the run down to the first corner, then drops at an even greater rate through the second apex. Continuing down into the valley, it reaches Turn 2 which is a second passing opportunity, but only on the opening lap when drivers don't have much opportunity to change line as there are so many other cars around them.

Doubling back to the left and pouring downhill, the drivers then get the power on, taking Turn 3 in sixth gear. They go on to hit 190mph as the track reaches the bottom of the valley then veers up. What follows, Turn 4, is probably the toughest corner of the lap, as it's largely blind until committed to, in fifth.

After turning uphill and right through Turn 5, the drivers reach a level stretch of track all the way to Turn 11, with the Turn 6/7 chicane interrupting the flow.

Out of Turn 11, the drivers enter the return leg, dropping down to the valley floor again before dropping to third gear for Turn 12 then snaking up the sharp slope behind the paddock. The final corner, if got right, allows a driver to catch a tow past the pits, up to 195mph before looking to make a passing manoeuvre into Turn 1.

To many of the teams, the Hungarian GP feels special as it usually marks the last race before the much-needed summer break.

INSIDE TRACK

HUNGARIAN GRAND PRIX

Date:	**31 July**
Circuit name:	**Hungaroring**
Circuit length:	**2.722 miles/4.381km**
Number of laps:	**70**
Email:	**office@hungaroring.hu**
Website:	**www.hungaroring.hu**

PREVIOUS WINNERS

2012	**Lewis Hamilton** McLAREN
2013	**Lewis Hamilton** MERCEDES
2014	**Daniel Ricciardo** RED BULL
2015	**Sebastian Vettel** FERRARI
2016	**Lewis Hamilton** MERCEDES
2017	**Sebastian Vettel** FERRARI
2018	**Lewis Hamilton** MERCEDES
2019	**Lewis Hamilton** MERCEDES
2020	**Lewis Hamilton** MERCEDES
2021	**Esteban Ocon** ALPINE

Location: Head northeast out of capital city Budapest and continue for a dozen miles until the start of rolling hills and the circuit is located close to the village of Mogyorod.

Its first grand prix: It came as a shock when communist-run Hungary was awarded a grand prix for 1986, but the circuit was built, the fans came, more than 200,000 in all, and it's been on the calendar ever since. Nelson Piquet won that first one for Williams ahead of compatriot Ayrton Senna's Lotus.

A race to remember: Races at the Hungaroring provide close action but overtaking is rare. To make it happen, rain is near essential, and this is what happened in 2006 when Jenson Button mastered the conditions to rise from 14th on the grid to give Honda its first win in the modern age of F1.

Greatest Hungarian driver: Despite having had a grand prix for 35 years, Hungary has yet to produce a top-notch driver, with only Zsolt Baumgartner reaching F1, to perform poorly for Jordan in 2003 then Minardi in 2004.

Rising Hungarian star: The highest ranked Hungarian driver in 2021 was 21-year-old Laszlo Toth who brought up the rear of the field in the FIA Formula 3 Championship.

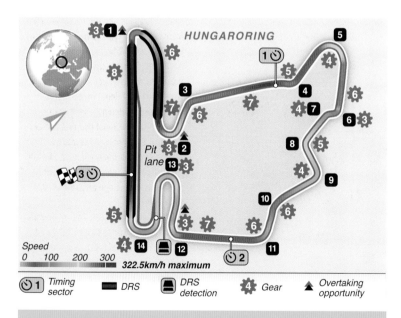

HUNGARORING

Pit lane

Speed
0   100   200   300
322.5km/h maximum

| ⏱1 | Timing sector | ▬ DRS | 🔲 DRS detection | ⚙4 Gear | ▲ Overtaking opportunity |

2021 POLE TIME: HAMILTON (MERCEDES), 1M15.419S, 129.940MPH/209.119KPH
2021 WINNER'S AVERAGE SPEED: 91.660MPH/147.512KPH
2021 FASTEST LAP: GASLY (ALPHATAURI), 1M18.394S, 125.009MPH/201.183KPH
LAP RECORD: HAMILTON (MERCEDES), 1M16.627S 127.892MPH/205.823KPH, 2020

SPA-FRANCORCHAMPS

Making the most of the sloping, tree-covered hills of the Ardennes, the Spa-Francorchamps circuit is a fabulous place for a circuit as it rises, twists and falls and always challenges.

The original circuit, opened on a ring of public roads in 1924, was a wonder. Starting down the slope from Francorchamps village, it climbed a long hill, descended into a neighbouring valley for a blast between the towns of Malmedy and Stavelot, then returned through a flat-out climb back from there. It was more than nine miles long.

The current circuit uses the first and last parts of that, linked in 1979 by a purpose-built loop from Les Combes to what is now Curve Paul Frere for a lap of 4.3 miles that retains the sort of magic that modern circuits simply can't achieve.

The lap begins with a really short blast to the La Source hairpin that can be a bit too much of a squeeze on the opening lap. Then it doubles back and plunges downhill past the old pits before kinking left, then right, at Eau Rouge and bucking even more sharply upwards through Raidillon. From here, there's a long climb up the Kemmel Straight to what is the most prolific place for passing, the Les Combes chicane. Then follows a downhill run all the way through the Rivage hairpin, the double rights at Pouhon before the slope eases off through Fagnes.

The uphill return starts at Curve Paul Frere, with Blanchimont a real eye-opener taken in seventh gear at just short of 200mph. The lap concludes with a really tight right-left chicane where drivers might fancy their chances of getting past a rival if they've collected a tow up the hill from Curve Paul Frere.

It is a truly challenging place to go racing, often affected by rainstorms, and the slopes and backdrop give the track a real identity.

INSIDE TRACK

BELGIAN GRAND PRIX

Date:	**28 August**
Circuit name:	**Spa-Francorchamps**
Circuit length:	**4.352 miles/7.004km**
Number of laps:	**44**
Email:	secretariat@spa-francorchamps.be
Website:	**www.spa-francorchamps.be**

PREVIOUS WINNERS

2012	**Jenson Button** McLAREN
2013	**Sebastian Vettel** RED BULL
2014	**Daniel Ricciardo** RED BULL
2015	**Lewis Hamilton** MERCEDES
2016	**Nico Rosberg** MERCEDES
2017	**Lewis Hamilton** MERCEDES
2018	**Sebastian Vettel** FERRARI
2019	**Charles Leclerc** FERRARI
2020	**Lewis Hamilton** MERCEDES
2021	**Max Verstappen** RED BULL

Location: Spa-Francorchamps is ten miles south of the resort town of Spa, just outside the village of Francorchamps from which it takes its name.

Its first grand prix: It first hosted a Belgian GP in 1925, before making its World Championship bow in the first year of the World Championship, 1950, when Juan Manuel Fangio won for Alfa Romeo.

A race to remember: Changeable weather is nothing new at Spa-Francorchamps, but it was indicative that Michael Schumacher read it best in 1992, one year after his F1 debut here. He was running behind Benetton team-mate Martin Brundle and noticed that his rain tyres were blistering and dived in to the pits for slicks. By continuing for a further lap, Brundle lost time and fell to fourth as Schumacher shone on a rare off day for Williams.

Greatest Belgian driver: Thierry Boutsen took three wins in 1989 and 1990, but Jacky Ickx came closer to a world title, in 1970, when he won three times for Ferrari but failed to overhaul the points tally of Jochen Rindt in the final three races that were held after the Austrian was killed in the Italian GP.

Rising Belgian star: Amaury Cordeel was racing in FIA F3 last year but failed to break into the top ten.

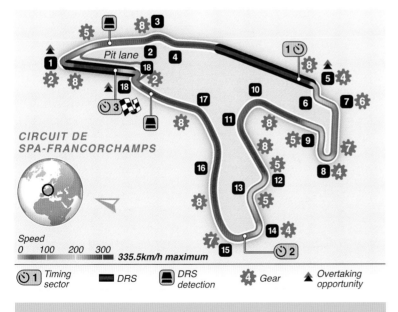

CIRCUIT DE SPA-FRANCORCHAMPS

Speed
0   100   200   300
335.5km/h maximum

🕒1 Timing sector   ▬ DRS   DRS detection   ⚙4 Gear   ▲ Overtaking opportunity

2021 POLE TIME: **VERSTAPPEN (RED BULL), 1M59.765S, 130.818MPH/210.532KPH**
2021 WINNER'S AVERAGE SPEED: **74.323MPH/119.611KPH**
2021 FASTEST LAP: **NOT APPLICABLE AS RUN BEHIND SAFETY CAR**
LAP RECORD: **BOTTAS (MERCEDES), 1M46.286S, 147.422MPH/237.290KPH, 2018**

⟫ ZANDVOORT

This historic Dutch circuit built extra grandstands last year to herald its F1 return and the atmosphere was electric as they came to cheer on their hero, Max Verstappen.

Anyone watching the sheer passion of the orange-clad fans urging Max Verstappen to victory last year will understand what F1 had been missing by Zandvoort's 35-year absence from the World Championship. It is a true gladiatorial setting, the circuit cupped by the dunes that not only keep the atmosphere in but the seaside breezes out.

Opened in 1948, it was the first masterpiece from circuit designer John Hugenholtz who would go on to design Suzuka. What made Zandvoort stand out was the lap's incredible flow up, over and around the dunes, thrilling with some really fast corners. This remained intact until the late 1980s when the second half of the lap was removed to make way for a holiday camp.

Fortunately, the run over the dunes to the plunging Scheivlak was restored in 1999 and a twisting return leg added. This, of course, was augmented in 2020 when the Hugenholtz Bocht behind the pits was made banked, as was the final corner of the lap, tilted by 18 degrees, this aimed to help slingshot the cars onto the start-finish straight. The idea behind this was to bring back the attacking and passing into the lap's first corner, the lightly-banked Tarzan, that had long been such a feature of this seaside circuit as the drivers wrestle their cars down from just under 200mph.

Certainly, Verstappen's title-winning potential brought the fans to Zandvoort in their droves, but their love of F1 was always strong, and their sheer delight in ending the country's long-running F1 drought was clear to see as they created an atmosphere that only countries with strong racing cultures can manage.

INSIDE TRACK

DUTCH GRAND PRIX

Date:	**4 September**
Circuit name:	**Zandvoort**
Circuit length:	**2.676miles/4.307km**
Number of laps:	**71**
Email:	**info@circuitzandvoort.nl**
Website:	**www.circuitzandvoort.nl**

PREVIOUS WINNERS

1977	**Niki Lauda** FERRARI
1978	**Mario Andretti** LOTUS
1979	**Alan Jones** WILLIAMS
1980	**Nelson Piquet** BRABHAM
1981	**Alain Prost** RENAULT
1982	**Didier Pironi** FERRARI
1983	**Rene Arnoux** FERRARI
1984	**Alain Prost** McLAREN
1985	**Niki Lauda** McLAREN
2021	**Max Verstappen** RED BULL

Location: The town of Zandvoort is on the North Sea coast a short train ride to the west of Amsterdam, with the circuit on its northern edge.

Its first grand prix: Formula 1 was in a state of flux in 1952. In fact, the World Championship was run to F2 regulations that year to ensure a decent grid of cars. Best of these were the Ferraris, and Alberto Ascari's was the pick of their pack, his win the fifth of a nine-race streak that stretched into 1953.

A race to remember: The Ford Cosworth DFV broke into F1 for the third race of 1967 with Lotus and rocked the establishment when Graham Hill qualified on pole before team-mate Jim Clark cantered clear to victory.

Greatest Dutch driver: Jan Lammers was the first to show promise in the late 1970s, but it was Jos Verstappen, father of Max, who was the first to reach the podium, doing this at the 1994 Hungarian GP when he raced as Michael Schumacher's team-mate at Benetton.

Rising Dutch star: Perhaps the brightest light is Rinus VeeKay – full name Rinus van Kalmthout – who became an Indycar winner this year at the age of 21 – while Richard Verschoor was a winner last year in his rookie year in F2.

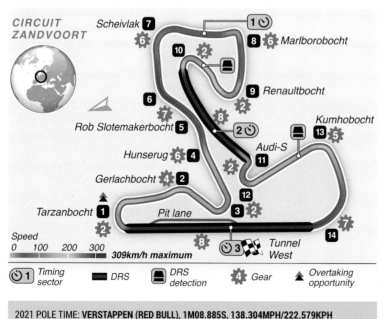

CIRCUIT ZANDVOORT

Scheivlak 7 · Marlborobocht · Renaultbocht · Kumhobocht · Audi-S · Rob Slotemakerbocht · Hunserug · Gerlachbocht · Tarzanbocht · Pit lane · Tunnel West

Speed
0 100 200 300
309km/h maximum

Timing sector · DRS · DRS detection · Gear · Overtaking opportunity

2021 POLE TIME: VERSTAPPEN (RED BULL), 1M08.885S, 138.304MPH/222.579KPH

2021 WINNER'S AVERAGE SPEED:126.876MPH/204.187KPH

2021 FASTEST LAP: HAMILTON (MERCEDES), 1M11.097S, 134.001MPH/215.654KPH

LAP RECORD: HAMILTON (MERCEDES), 1M11.097S 134.001MPH/215.654KPH, 2021

MONZA

It's one hundred years this year since Monza opened for racing, and this wonderful circuit can never escape its history. Indeed, nor should it, as it's a fabulous place packed with passionate fans.

At first glance, a lap of Monza looks incredibly simple, with only a handful of corners and its long straights punctuated only by a trio of chicanes. Drive the track, though, and its complexities are far more obvious. Add to that the fact that its chicanes can get more than a little busy when attacked by a pack of cars, and success at Monza can owe as much to defence as attack.

The lap starts with a blast to the first chicane, a right-left-right combination now, after a variety of formats were tested to slow the cars from the 1970s. The second part is tighter than the first and it's not rare to see contact there or drivers being slowed by running into the gravel at its exit.

The Curva Biassono then arcs right in seventh gear, taking the drivers up to the second chicane, this a gentler left-right combination. The two Lesmo corners that follow are both tricky right-handers, but they are far less fearsome than of old when the trees came very close to the edge of the circuit.

If a driver gets a good exit from sixth-gear Lesmo II, they can then carry that speed advantage all the way down towards the Ascari chicane, through the kink and under a bridge that carries the now defunct banked part of the circuit.

With drivers desperate to exit the corner as well as they can to carry as much speed as possible all the way down to the final corner, there can be collisions.

The entry to sixth-gear Parabolica is another place for passing, then it's back on the power as soon as a driver dares so that they might reach 220mph before braking for that first chicane.

INSIDE TRACK

ITALIAN GRAND PRIX

Date:	**11 September**
Circuit name:	**Autodromo Nazionale Monza**
Circuit length:	**3.600 miles/5.793km**
Number of laps:	**53**
Email:	**infoautodromo@monzanet.it**
Website:	**www.monzanet.it**

PREVIOUS WINNERS

2012	**Lewis Hamilton** McLAREN
2013	**Sebastian Vettel** RED BULL
2014	**Lewis Hamilton** MERCEDES
2015	**Lewis Hamilton** MERCEDES
2016	**Nico Rosberg** MERCEDES
2017	**Lewis Hamilton** MERCEDES
2018	**Lewis Hamilton** MERCEDES
2019	**Charles Leclerc** FERRARI
2020	**Pierre Gasly** ALPHATAURI
2021	**Daniel Ricciardo** McLAREN

Location: The town of Monza is 10 miles to the northwest of Milan and the circuit is located in a royal park there.

Its first grand prix: Monza's first World Championship round, in 1950, was won by Giuseppe Farina when Alberto Ascari had to take over his Ferrari team-mate Dorino Serafini's car when his own broke.

A race to remember: For the imagery of its first-time winner sitting on the podium after the ceremony was over, 2020's race stands out. This was Pierre Gasly, whose victory was made possible when Lewis Hamilton entered the pitlane when it was closed, earning a 10s stop-and-go penalty. He then had to hold off Carlos Sainz Jr., which he did, just.

Greatest Italian driver: Alberto Ascari put Ferrari on the map when he dominated in both 1952 and 1953 after Giuseppe Farina. Certainly, he made the most of having the most competitive car, but had already been runner-up in 1951. No other Italian driver has become World Champion since.

Rising Italian star: There used to be ranks of Italians in F1's feeder formulae, but it's currently hard to see Alessio Deledda or Matteo Nannini, stepping up to succeed Antonio Giovinazzi in F1 after mediocre F2 campaigns last year.

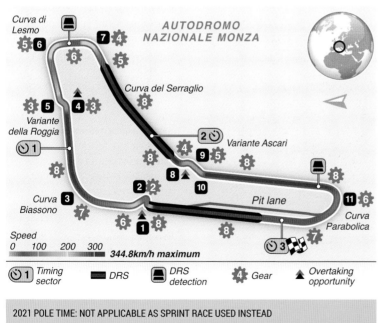

Curva di Lesmo

AUTODROMO NAZIONALE MONZA

Curva del Serraglio

Variante della Roggia

Variante Ascari

Curva Biassono

Pit lane

Curva Parabolica

Speed
0   100   200   300
344.8km/h maximum

🕐1 Timing sector	▬ DRS
💺 DRS detection	⚙4 Gear
▲ Overtaking opportunity	

2021 POLE TIME: NOT APPLICABLE AS SPRINT RACE USED INSTEAD
2021 WINNER'S AVERAGE SPEED: **139.613MPH/224.686KPH**
2021 FASTEST LAP: **RICCIARDO (McLAREN), 1M24.812S, 152.791MPH/245.894KPH**
LAP RECORD: **M SCHUMACHER (FERRARI), 1M21.046S 159.909MPH/257.349KPH, 2004**

» SOCHI

With plans afoot for the Russian GP to move to a new circuit nearer St Petersburg, this ought to be the last Russian GP held at this hybrid circuit on the Black Sea shore.

This street circuit produces incident rather than great racing action so, if this proves to be its last year of hosting the Russian GP, there won't be too many people who are put out by the race moving on.

The track's name – Sochi Autodrom – suggests a permanent racing facility, but it isn't; in reality it's a temporary street circuit that was laid out using land around several of the skating rinks used when the town hosted the Olympic Winter Games in 2014.

The first corner doesn't count for much, as it's just a right kink. Drivers have to get their braking right here if they fancy their easiest overtaking manoeuvre of the race: into the second corner. Turn 2 is a 90-degree right-hander approached at more than 200mph. Fortunately, there is plenty of width and generous run-off there,

as many a driver gets their braking wrong, year in, year out.

Then comes one of the strangest corners ever used in F1, as the track starts to arc left almost immediately after Turn 2 and keeps going in a parabola gentle enough for drivers to shift up to seventh gear as they run its 180-degree course. Then comes a 90-degree bend, then another, a kink, then another, in old school street circuit style.

It's only when the drivers reach Turn 10 that they see some open circuit, with a gently curving run on which they top 200mph on their way to another right-hander at Turn 13. A kink then four more right-angle bends bring the drivers back to the start-finish straight, where they know that a good exit might give them the chance to mount an attack into Turn 1.

INSIDE TRACK

RUSSIAN GRAND PRIX

Date:	**25 September**
Circuit name:	**Sochi Autodrom**
Circuit length:	**3.634 miles/5.848km**
Number of laps:	**53**
Email:	**info@sochiautodrom.ru**
Website:	**www.sochiautodrom.ru**

PREVIOUS WINNERS

2014	**Lewis Hamilton** MERCEDES
2015	**Lewis Hamilton** MERCEDES
2016	**Nico Rosberg** MERCEDES
2017	**Valtteri Bottas** MERCEDES
2018	**Lewis Hamilton** MERCEDES
2019	**Lewis Hamilton** MERCEDES
2020	**Valtteri Bottas** MERCEDES
2021	**Lewis Hamilton** MERCEDES

Location: Sochi is the jewel of the northern Black Sea shore, famed both as a summer resort favoured by Russia's leading politicians and as a winter sports resort, home to the 2014 Olympic Winter Games.

Its first grand prix: Lewis Hamilton had two blessings that helped him to win for Mercedes in 2014. The first was when team-mate Nico Rosberg lost the lead with a throttle problem. The second was when a problem with his rear wing came to nothing.

A race to remember: Hamilton had hoped to claim the 2020 title here but was penalized for making practice starts in the wrong place and this gave the race to Mercedes team-mate Valtteri Bottas.

Greatest Russian driver: Both Vitaly Petrov and Daniil Kvyat have visited an F1 podium. Petrov did it first, coming third in the 2011 Melbourne GP for Renault. Kvyat secured a surprise second at the Hungaroring for Scuderia Toro Rosso in 2015.

Rising Russian star: Robert Shwartzman has long been impressive. The 22-year-old was third in the World Kart series in 2013 and has shone at every level in car racing since then. He was FIA F3 champion in 2019 and a race winner in FIA F2 in both of the last two years for Prema Racing to rank fourth in 2020 and second in 2021.

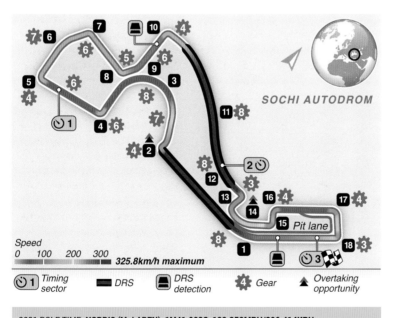

SOCHI AUTODROM

Speed
0 100 200 300
325.8km/h maximum

🕑1 Timing sector   ▬ DRS   ⬛ DRS detection   ⚙4 Gear   ▲ Overtaking opportunity

2021 POLE TIME: **NORRIS (McLAREN), 1M41.993S, 128.259MPH/206.414KPH**
2021 WINNER'S AVERAGE SPEED: **127.344MPH/204.940KPH**
2021 FASTEST LAP: **NORRIS (McLAREN), 1M37.423S, 134.276MPH/216.096MPH**
LAP RECORD: **HAMILTON (MERCEDES), 1M35.761S, 136.606MPH/219.847KPH. 2019**

MARINA BAY

Singapore's Marina Bay circuit is still the template of how a street circuit should be, with a wide variety of corners in a challenging layout and a brilliant cityscape as a backdrop.

Singapore has long stood for efficiency and clarity of purpose, so it came as little surprise when it accepted the challenge of putting on a grand prix on its streets and made a success of it.

Using some of the city's most prestigious streets, it provides a lap that mixes straights of a decent length with the inevitable 90-degree corners but also some sweeping ones too.

Starting with a chicane is a tricky option, especially as the second part feeds almost immediately into a sharp left at Turn 3. It's rare for all the cars to get through this sequence of turns unscathed on the opening lap. Turn 5 is a 90-degree right, but then the cars get to blast through a kink and keep accelerating until they hit 200mph before braking hard for third-gear Turn 7.

The next two corners are tight, but the backdrop changes as the track runs around the green spaces of the Singapore Cricket Club. The cars then cross the steel-framed Anderson Bridge before turning sharp left in front of the Fullerton Hotel and accelerate hard onto the welcome space of the Esplanade Bridge.

After dipping down at the far end of the bridge, the circuit turns right in front of the Esplanade Theater to start a run that takes in an esse at Turns 16 and 17, then a left-right-right-left combination in which the track disappears under a grandstand then re-emerges at its other end.

The double-apex final corner is taken in sixth gear and a good exit speed will help drivers reach close to 190mph before slowing and positioning their cars for the first corner.

INSIDE TRACK

SINGAPORE GRAND PRIX

Date:	**2 October**
Circuit name:	**Marina Bay Circuit**
Circuit length:	**3.152 miles/5.073km**
Number of laps:	**61**
Email:	**info@singaporegp.sg**
Website:	**www.singaporegp.sg**

PREVIOUS WINNERS

2010	**Fernando Alonso** FERRARI
2011	**Sebastian Vettel** RED BULL
2012	**Sebastian Vettel** RED BULL
2013	**Sebastian Vettel** RED BULL
2014	**Lewis Hamilton** MERCEDES
2015	**Sebastian Vettel** FERRARI
2016	**Daniel Ricciardo** RED BULL
2017	**Lewis Hamilton** MERCEDES
2018	**Lewis Hamilton** MERCEDES
2019	**Sebastian Vettel** FERRARI

Location: Street circuits are often hard to identify when the barriers, pit buildings and grandstands are removed. Singapore's circuit is in the heart of the city, running past the Supreme Court, City Hall and Singapore Flyer ferris wheel.

Its first grand prix: The circuit was considered a triumph when it made its debut in 2008. The race itself was notorious, though, as Renault pulled a fast one by apparently instructing Nelson Piquet Jr to spin into a wall to bring out the safety car just after Fernando Alonso had pitted, helping to vault up the order. Then others hit trouble and so Alonso completed his rise from 15th to win.

A race to remember: It didn't take long for the 2017 race to hit trouble, as Sebastian Vettel tried to recover from a poor start from pole. In trying to stop Max Verstappen from passing him, he clipped the Red Bull and fired it into his Ferrari team-mate Kimi Raikkonen who already had...

Rising Singaporean driver: Despite all the wealth generated in this south-eastern business hub, a grand prix host since 2008, Singaporean drivers have largely failed to make the grade. Its most promising newcomer is teenager Danial Frost who has been racing in the USA, in Indy Lights.

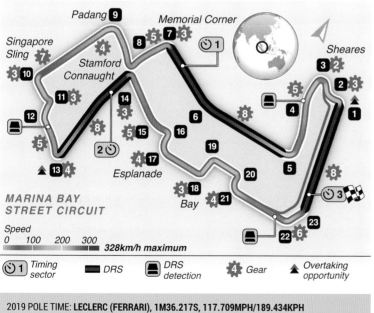

MARINA BAY STREET CIRCUIT

Speed
0   100   200   300
328km/h maximum

⏱1 Timing sector   ▬ DRS   ◰ DRS detection   ⚙ Gear   ▲ Overtaking opportunity

2019 POLE TIME: LECLERC (FERRARI), 1M36.217S, 117.709MPH/189.434KPH

2019 WINNER'S AVERAGE SPEED: 97.074MPH/156.226KPH

2019 FASTEST LAP: MAGNUSSEN (HAAS), 1M42.301S, 110.708MPH/178.168KPH

LAP RECORD: MAGNUSSEN (HAAS), 1M41.905S 109.900MPH/178.860KPH, 2018

» SUZUKA

Two years without Suzuka has been too long, but the world's emergence from the COVID pandemic has opened the circuit's doors again and the drivers are set to revel again in an old school venue.

The ever-increasing safety of F1 cars is a wonderful thing but, even this withstanding, Suzuka is still a circuit that makes the drivers think before looking to exceed track limits. It is undoubtedly a serious test, with a range of fabulously challenging corners and barriers that are close enough to the edge of the track to make them think twice before taking liberties, which is exactly how it should be.

The lap starts with a downhill sprint to a two-part opening corner, the first part of which is downhill going in and the second part, Turn 2, turning uphill on the exit. What follows is one of the best corners used in F1, the uphill esses, a four-corner sequence up the slope behind the paddock.

After a double left, the track levels out for a moment before the tricky Degner curves and then a rare design element that leads the track under its return leg.

A potential passing place follows next, where the track reaches a left-hand hairpin. Then there's a slight rise through a long right-hand arc that then rises to a lefthander and completes what is known as Spoon Curve as it drops the cars onto the lengthy return straight. In effect, it's a two-part straight, as the top-gear 130R curves two-thirds of the way along its course, taken at 190mph, it is now considered just a kink.

Drivers have to hit the anchors for the last section, jinking through a right-left chicane before getting the power down through the open final corner in the hope of getting a tow down the start-finish straight past the pits for a possible passing manoeuvre into Turn 1.

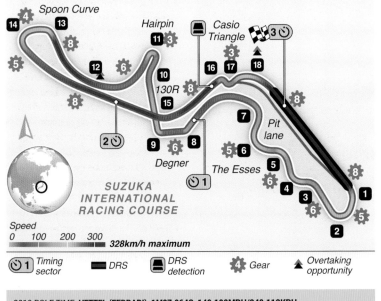

2019 POLE TIME: VETTEL (FERRARI), 1M27.064S, 149.199MPH/240.113KPH
2019 WINNER'S AVERAGE SPEED: 137.525MPH/221.325KPH
2019 FASTEST LAP: HAMILTON (MERCEDES), 1M30.983S, 142.772MPH/229.770KPH
LAP RECORD: HAMILTON (MERCEDES), 1M30.983S 142.772MPH/229.770KPH, 2019

INSIDE TRACK ●

JAPANESE GRAND PRIX

Date:	**9 October**
Circuit name:	**Suzuka Circuit**
Circuit length:	**3.608 miles/5.806km**
Number of laps:	**53**
Email:	**info@suzukacircuit.co.up**
Website:	**www.suzukacircuit.co.jp**

PREVIOUS WINNERS

2010	**Sebastian Vettel**	RED BULL
2011	**Jenson Button**	McLAREN
2012	**Sebastian Vettel**	RED BULL
2013	**Sebastian Vettel**	RED BULL
2014	**Lewis Hamilton**	MERCEDES
2015	**Lewis Hamilton**	MERCEDES
2016	**Nico Rosberg**	MERCEDES
2017	**Lewis Hamilton**	MERCEDES
2018	**Lewis Hamilton**	MERCEDES
2019	**Valtteri Bottas**	MERCEDES

Location: Situated 30 miles south west of the city of Nagoya, the circuit is a few miles inland, just where the land rises into gentle hills.

Its first grand prix: After two grands prix at Fuji Speedway in the 1970s, Suzuka got its turn in 1987. Gerhard Berger put his Ferrari on pole and won as the Italian team enjoyed an upswing in form as Williams stumbled, with Nigel Mansell pulling out after crashing in practice and Nelson Piquet, who would become champion, retiring from fourth.

A race to remember: One of the great drives came from Damon Hill when he mastered challenging conditions in his Williams to hold off Benetton's Michael Schumacher and keep the 1994 title battle open to the final round.

Greatest Japanese driver: Aguri Suzuki was a trailblazer for Japanese drivers with third place in the 1990 Japanese GP. This feat was matched by Takuma Sato in the 2004 United States GP, in a race boycotted by most of the teams.

Rising Japanese star: With Yuki Tsunoda having his maiden F1 season behind him, Japanese fans need to look to FIA F3 series race winner Ayumu Iwasa as their next in line as he is showing greater potential than F2 racer Marino Sato.

CIRCUIT OF THE AMERICAS

Building a circuit from scratch, as with this one in Texas, offers plenty of scope to build something special, and this track near Austin used a special ingredient, its steep topography.

INSIDE TRACK

UNITED STATES GRAND PRIX

Date:	**23 October**
Circuit name:	**Circuit of the Americas**
Circuit length:	**3.400 miles/5.472km**
Number of laps:	**56**
Email:	**info@circuitoftheamericas.com**
Website:	**www.circuitoftheamericas.com**

There's an incredibly long list of circuits in the USA, running from Sebring in 1959 to the Indianapolis Motor Speedway in 2000 with seven others in the intervening years.

Since 2012, though, the Circuit of the Americas has been the United States GP's home, and it's a popular one too, with this purpose-built circuit in Texas aping the best corners of the world's greatest circuits to good effect.

There's a steep climb from the grid to Turn 1, quite like at the Red Bull Ring. Then, plunging from this left-hand hairpin, the drivers arc right through Turn 2 as the track levels out again and enter a fabulous sequence of esses all the way through to Turn 9, mimicking the Esses at Suzuka, albeit on the level rather than on an incline as at the Japanese circuit.

After the Turn 11 hairpin, there's a long straight to Turn 12, with braking from 210mph at the circuit's fastest point into a key passing point, the 100-degree left at Turn 12.

The next three corners are tight. But then, rising gently on entry then falling from its apex comes the Turn 16–18 combination that forms a fabulously long right-hander. After a fifth gear Turn 19, the 20th and final corner of the lap is another 100-degree left, like Turn 12, but it's the exit from this one rather than the entry that counts. Drivers need to get hard onto the power as soon as they can to get close enough to a rival for a tow, and then carry their speed past the pits and up the steep slope to Turn 1 to try to line up a passing manoeuvre into that left-hand hairpin.

PREVIOUS WINNERS

2012	**Lewis Hamilton**	McLAREN
2013	**Sebastian Vettel**	RED BULL
2014	**Lewis Hamilton**	MERCEDES
2015	**Lewis Hamilton**	MERCEDES
2016	**Lewis Hamilton**	MERCEDES
2017	**Lewis Hamilton**	MERCEDES
2018	**Kimi Raikkonen**	FERRARI
2019	**Valtteri Bottas**	MERCEDES
2021	**Max Verstappen**	RED BULL

Location: The Texan state capital Austin lies largely on level ground, but the hills start to roll to the southeast, and COTA is found among these, some 10 miles from the city centre.

Its first grand prix: Lewis Hamilton has an astonishing hit rate at COTA and started from the first grand prix there in 2012 when he started second on the grid behind Sebastian Vettel's Red Bull and trailed him for much of the race before seizing a moment when Vettel was obstructed at tight Turn 12 by Narain Karthikeyan's HRT to dive past.

A race to remember: The 2018 United States GP was notable for a driver ending a 5½ year/111 grand prix winless streak. Kimi Raikkonen kept his tyres fresh on his Ferrari while Lewis Hamilton lost out by having to pit for a second time.

Greatest American driver: Mario Andretti holds this record. Phil Hill had been the USA's first world champion, in 1961, but Mario's title with Lotus in 1978 was far more impressive and was backed up by a stellar record in the Indycar Series across three decades.

Rising American star: The American junior single-seater scene is patchy, so its F1 hopefuls race elsewhere, with Logan Sargeant the best up-and-comer at the moment after shining in European F3 last year.

89

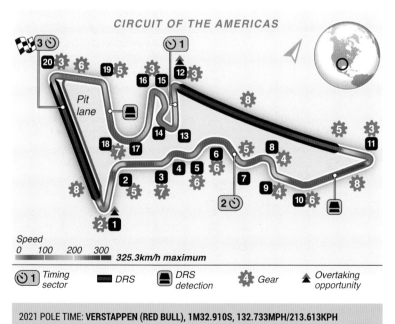

CIRCUIT OF THE AMERICAS

Speed
0   100   200   300
325.3km/h maximum

Timing sector | DRS | DRS detection | Gear | Overtaking opportunity

2021 POLE TIME: **VERSTAPPEN (RED BULL), 1M32.910S, 132.733MPH/213.613KPH**
2021 WINNER'S AVERAGE SPEED: **121.531MPH/195.586KPH**
2021 FASTEST LAP: **HAMILTON (MERCEDES), 1M38.485S, 125.219MPH/201.521KPH**
LAP RECORD: **LECLERC (FERRARI), 1M36.169S, 128.235MPH/206.374KPH, 2019**

⟫ MEXICO CITY

Long straights, an array of corners that produce passing opportunities and giant grandstands packed with enthusiastic fans make the home of Mexican motor racing a great place to hold a grand prix.

A long and wide start-finish straight is a great way to start a lap. Better still, the blast between the trees through this parkland setting is followed by a three-corner opening sequence that provides considerable scope for gaining a few places on the opening lap as the track turns right, then left, then right again, but also a similar amount of scope to fall back down the field.

This combination is followed by the lap's second longest straight down to a tight left, a tight right and then a hairpin at Turn 6. This is a turning point and the sequence of turns that follows is the best of the lap, with a double set of esses between Turns 7 and 10. To watch an F1 car being hard through there is a fabulous thing.

Carrying their speed through the kink at Turn 11, the drivers then brake hard to scrub it off before turning sharp right at Turn 12. What follows is an extraordinary stretch of track that snakes its way across what is normally a baseball stadium, with huge, lofty grandstands providing an amazing view of the action before the cars disappear through a cut between the grandstands and so turn onto the slight banking of the Peraltada, entering what had once been one of F1's most feared corners halfway around its long 180-degree course. In Nigel Mansell's days in 1992, this was taken in top gear, with bumps making it extra hazardous. Getting the power down early from third-gear Turn 16 gives drivers the best opportunity to catch a tow from a rival, touch 215mph by the end of the straight and then perhaps make a passing move on the wide turn in to Turn 1.

INSIDE TRACK 🇲🇽

MEXICAN GRAND PRIX

Date:	**30 October**
Circuit name:	**Autodromo Hermanos Rodriguez**
Circuit length:	**2.674 miles/4.303km**
Number of laps:	**71**
Email:	**Rosario@cie.com.mx**
Website:	www.autodromohermanosrodriguez.com.mx

PREVIOUS WINNERS

1989	**Ayrton Senna**	McLAREN
1990	**Alain Prost**	FERRARI
1991	**Riccardo Patrese**	WILLIAMS
1992	**Nigel Mansell**	WILLIAMS
2015	**Nico Rosberg**	MERCEDES
2016	**Lewis Hamilton**	MERCEDES
2017	**Max Verstappen**	RED BULL
2018	**Max Verstappen**	RED BULL
2019	**Lewis Hamilton**	MERCEDES
2021	**Max Verstappen**	RED BULL

Location: Mexico City is sprawling and chaotic, so the decision to lay out a circuit around the Magdalena Mixhuca park in its southeastern suburbs in 1962 was wise, as that space remains today while every other scrap of land is being built upon.

Its first grand prix: After a non-championship race in 1962, the World Championship paid its first visit in 1963 and Jim Clark dominated for Lotus, winning by 1m40s from Jack Brabham.

A race to remember: The 1964 title decider was between three British drivers. Clark was a lap from victory when his Lotus's engine failed. Graham Hill might have benefitted, but his BRM was struck by Lorenzo Bandini's Ferrari, and knocked out. Dan Gurney won, while second-placed John Surtees (Ferrari) took the title.

Greatest Mexican driver: In 2021, Sergio Perez matched Pedro Rodriguez's record for grand prix wins by a Mexican driver, two, though it was Pedro's younger brother Ricardo who showed the greater talent, but he died aged 20 in 1962 before he won an F1 race.

Rising Mexican star: With Raul Guzman having turned away from single-seaters to race Lamborghinis, Mexican fans will be hoping that Rafael Villagomez can find form in European F3.

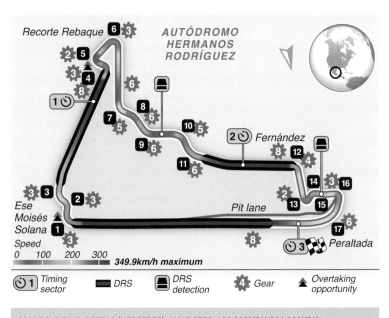

AUTÓDROMO HERMANOS RODRÍGUEZ

Recorte Rebaque

Fernández

Ese Moisés Solana

Speed
0   100   200   300
349.9km/h maximum

Pit lane

Peraltada

⟳1 Timing sector	▬ DRS
🅳 DRS detection	⚙4 Gear
▲ Overtaking opportunity	

2021 POLE TIME: **BOTTAS (MERCEDES), 1M15.875S, 126.889MPH/204.209KPH**

2021 WINNER'S AVERAGE SPEED: **115.398MPH/185.716KPH**

2021 FASTEST LAP: **BOTTAS (MERCEDES), 1M17.774S, 123.791MPH/199.223KPH**

LAP RECORD: **BOTTAS (MERCEDES), 1M17.774S, 123.791MPH/199.223KPH, 2021**

INTERLAGOS

Modern racing circuits are often accused of lacking character. When Interlagos is used as an example of an old school circuit, you can understand why. It's simply a magnificent venue.

It seems that all talk of the Brazilian GP being moved back to Rio de Janeiro for the first time since 1989 has been rescinded and, for that, F1 fans can rejoice, for Interlagos is a very special place.

Yes, its facilities are far below contemporary standards, but any driver who plunges out of the first corner will tell you that this big dipper is an amazing ride. Better still, any fan in the giant grandstands packed with vociferous Brazilian fans making the most of their day out and enjoying the incredible views will know that there are few better places to watch racing.

The first corner, Descida do Sol, has a blind exit as the track drops away and pretty much cradles the cars through a compression as it then arcs right through the Senna S. Then, accelerating hard, the drivers power all the way down the hill to Descida do Lago, hitting 195mph on the way. After a second left, the track climbs back up the slope to Ferradura (Turn 6) behind the paddock.

Then this pattern of dropping down the slope and coming back up continues, down to Pinheirinho (Turn 9), up to Cotovelo, down to Mergulho and on down a more gentle descent to Juncao (Turn 12). From here, although always arcing to the left, the track climbs, being contained after Subida dos Boxes (Turn 14) in a concrete channel between the high pit wall on one side and grandstands on the other. Drivers try to catch a tow to use in passing under heavy breaking into that first turn. Here there is a feeling of space dead ahead – it's where the original circuit used to carry on into a banked curve.

SAO PAOLO GRAND PRIX

Date:	**13 November**
Circuit name:	**Autodromo Jose Carlos Pace Interlagos**
Circuit length:	**2.667 miles/4.292km**
Number of laps:	**71**
Email:	**info@gpbrazil.com**
Website:	**www.gpbrazil.com**

PREVIOUS WINNERS

2011	**Mark Webber**	RED BULL
2012	**Jenson Button**	McLAREN
2013	**Sebastian Vettel**	RED BULL
2014	**Nico Rosberg**	MERCEDES
2015	**Nico Rosberg**	MERCEDES
2016	**Lewis Hamilton**	MERCEDES
2017	**Sebastian Vettel**	FERRARI
2018	**Lewis Hamilton**	MERCEDES
2019	**Max Verstappen**	RED BULL
2021	**Lewis Hamilton**	MERCEDES

Location: Sao Paulo's urban sprawl has almost consumed the circuit despite it being nine miles south of the city centre, whereas it was fully out in the countryside when built in 1940.

Its first grand prix: After hosting a non-championship race in 1972, Interlagos made its World Championship bow in 1973 and the crowd went wild as victory went to a driver born in Sao Paulo: Emerson Fittipaldi who led every lap in his Lotus.

A race to remember: Ayrton Senna had won 27 grands prix before he won at home in 1991. He led every lap, but an increasingly erratic gearbox forced him to do the last lap in sixth, pipping Williams' Riccardo Patrese by 3s. He was so exhausted that he had to be lifted from the car.

Greatest Brazilian driver: Fittipaldi laid down a marker, then Nelson Piquet moved it on in the 1980s. Then came Senna and he raced on towards three F1 titles with McLaren between 1988 and 1991.

Rising Brazilian star: Second place in the F2 race at Monaco marked Felipe Drugovich out to be the next Brazilian ready to tackle F1, moving ahead of Formula E racer Sergio Sette Camara in the reckoning.

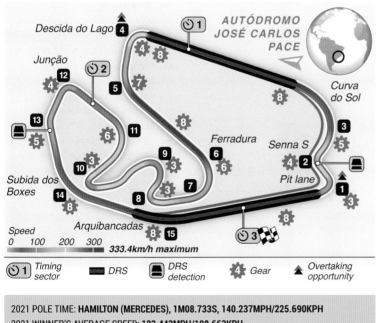

AUTÓDROMO JOSÉ CARLOS PACE

Descida do Lago · Junção · Curva do Sol · Ferradura · Senna S · Pit lane · Subida dos Boxes · Arquibancadas

Speed
0 100 200 300
333.4km/h maximum

Timing sector · DRS · DRS detection · Gear · Overtaking opportunity

2021 POLE TIME: **HAMILTON (MERCEDES), 1M08.733S, 140.237MPH/225.690KPH**
2021 WINNER'S AVERAGE SPEED: **123.443MPH/198.663KPH**
2021 FASTEST LAP: **PEREZ (RED BULL), 1M11.010S, 135.740MPH/218.453KPH**
LAP RECORD: **BOTTAS (MERCEDES), 1M10.540S, 136.645MPH/219.909KPH, 2018**

» YAS MARINA

It was hoped that the modifications to several points of the lap would improve the racing and thankfully it did, making the venue more suitable for hosting the final race of the season.

INSIDE TRACK

ABU DHABI GRAND PRIX

Date:	**20 November**
Circuit name:	**Yas Marina Circuit**
Circuit length:	**3.281 miles/5.281km**
Number of laps:	**58**
Email:	customerservice@yasmarinacircuit.com
Website:	**www.yasmarinacircuit.com**

When it opened in 2009, the teams were deeply impressed by the Yas Marina Circuit and the government had every reason to be proud that their investment had produced the most modern facility in the F1 racing world. It was bold, flash even, and incredibly well built, with top-notch facilities. And yet, over the years, it largely produced processions rather than races dotted with dicing. Changes of position tend to occur in the pits rather than on the track. Modification was long overdue.

Turn 1, a 90-degree left, can produce overtaking on the opening lap, but the first change came at Turn 5. It was changed with a left-right chicane being removed so that the drivers can pile straight into the left-hand hairpin, making it a definite passing place.

The lap's longest straight follows, feeding into a left-right chicane as before. It's at the end of the next straight that the drivers are faced with the second change. Instead of another chicane, Turn 9 is now a more open left-hander, and it's banked too, making it a place where passing is possible now.

One of the original design concepts was for the return leg from these long straights to echo the feel of Monaco, and it certainly does, as the track then runs past the marina and, like in the principality, is slower with corners coming thick and fast, but four of these have been opened out to provide better flow as the track runs under one of the circuit's trademarks, the short stretch where the track runs under an arch beneath the Yas Viceroy Hotel.

The track is now more suited to providing a stage for what we hope every year will be an action-packed championship finale.

PREVIOUS WINNERS

2012	**Kimi Raikkonen**	LOTUS
2013	**Sebastian Vettel**	RED BULL
2014	**Lewis Hamilton**	MERCEDES
2015	**Nico Rosberg**	MERCEDES
2016	**Lewis Hamilton**	MERCEDES
2017	**Valtteri Bottas**	MERCEDES
2018	**Lewis Hamilton**	MERCEDES
2019	**Lewis Hamilton**	MERCEDES
2020	**Max Verstappen**	RED BULL
2021	**Max Verstappen**	RED BULL

Location: The Yas Marina Circuit is located in a leisure complex centered on the marina. In addition to the yachts berthed there and the circuit, the complex includes the Ferrari World theme park, a golf course and hotels.

Its first grand prix: Abu Dhabi's first grand prix, in 2009, was a Red Bull Racing one-two, with Sebastian Vettel leading home Mark Webber in a race that Lewis Hamilton ought to have won but his McLaren suffered brake problems.

A race to remember: Until last year's dramatic finale, the 2010 grand prix was Yas Marina's best, but the 2020 edition, won by Max Verstappen was certainly exciting for McLaren. Their drivers Lando Norris and Carlos Sainz Jr. finished fifth and sixth to score enough points for the team to overhaul Racing Point to claim third place overall.

Greatest Abu Dhabian driver: World Endurance Championship racer Khaled Al Qubaisi remains the nation's most successful racer, but his daughters Amna and Hamda have been racing in Asian F3 and Italian F4 respectively, with younger sister Hamda looking the quicker.

Its toughest corner: This is now the re-profiled Turn 9 at the end of the second long straight, with its banking making it look extra spectacular.

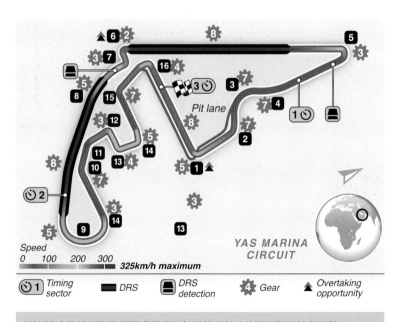

YAS MARINA CIRCUIT

Pit lane

Speed
0   100   200   300
325km/h maximum

⏱1 Timing sector	▬ DRS	🔲 DRS detection	⚙4 Gear	▲ Overtaking opportunity

2021 POLE TIME: **VERSTAPPEN (RED BULL), 1M22.109S, 143.873MPH/231.541KPH**
2021 WINNER'S AVERAGE SPEED: **126.429MPH/203.468KPH**
2021 FASTEST LAP: **VERSTAPPEN (RED BULL), 1M26.103S, 137.198MPH/220.800KPH**
LAP RECORD: **VERSTAPPEN (RED BULL), 1M26.103S, 137.198MPH/220.800KPH, 2021**

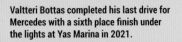
Valtteri Bottas completed his last drive for Mercedes with a sixth place finish under the lights at Yas Marina in 2021.

▶▶ REVIEW OF THE 2021 SEASON

Lewis Hamilton and Mercedes enjoyed a battle royale with Max Verstappen and Red Bull Racing. McLaren scored a win but were ranked fourth behind Ferrari. Alpine and AlphaTauri scrapped in the midfield, with the French team delighted with a win in Hungary. Aston Martin was erratic, while George Russell's second in the rain-obliterated Belgian GP helped Williams pass Alfa Romeo.

What could be better than a title battle between two teams and their lead drivers with the promise of one team being better than the other at different circuits across the season? Sadly the scrap between Hamilton and Verstappen grew increasingly tetchy and acrimonious, inflamed on social media, and resulted in contact with each other's cars.

After a clash at Silverstone, Verstappen's car ended up on top of Hamilton's at Monza and then the Dutchman appeared to guide the Briton off the track at Interlagos. There was angry contact on F1's first visit to Saudi Arabia, where an over-robust

Verstappen was penalised three times. Hamilton won the race so both drivers went into the final grand prix with 369.5 points.

Their respective team-mates Valtteri Bottas and Sergio Perez tried their hardest to play a role, but neither truly had the pace to be of a great deal of assistance. Thus, Mercedes won the constructors' championship for the eighth year in a row but lost out on the final lap of the last race as Max Verstappen landed the drivers' crown. Red Bull engine supplier Honda was delighted, as it gave them their first share of championship honours since Ayrton Senna won the title for McLaren in 1991.

McLaren set the initial pace among the admittedly distant chasers with Lando Norris leading the way as Daniel Ricciardo settled into his new team. This great team's finest day came at Monza, as Hamilton and Verstappen clashed and Ricciardo led Norris home in a one-two.

However, then came a step-leap from Ferrari, as Charles Leclerc, Carlos Sainz Jr and their engineers unlocked more performance from the SF21s – enough for them to end the team third overall.

Alpine was the only other team to take a win in 2021 and it was Esteban Ocon rather than returning double world champion Fernando Alonso who achieved this in Hungary. The renamed and reliveried team edged ahead of Red Bull's second team, AlphaTauri, for whom Pierre Gasly was mighty again, as shown by his third place on the streets of Baku and a pair of fourth place finishes, with rookie team-mate Yuki Tsunoda coming good to lead him home in a fouth/fifth double finish at the final round.

It wasn't just its understated green livery that made the Aston Martins seem anonymous in 2021; their ordinary form did little to make the TV directors seek them out. There were highlights, though, such as Sebastian Vettel's second place in Baku and

another in Hungary, although he was disqualified from that one.

Williams, in their first full year under new owners, moved forwards, especially after a stupendous qualifying lap at Spa on a wet but drying track put George Russell second on the grid. The race was run only behind the safety car and was soon abandoned with the British driver in second, but only half the points were awarded. It helped the team rank eighth overall.

The Sauber-run Alfa Romeo team spent most of the season vying with Aston Martin, with both teams often finding their drivers the ones just missing out on top-10 finishes and thus championship points. At the end of the year, Kimi Raikkonen stepped down into retirement as F1's most experienced driver, with Antonio Giovinazzi unceremoniously being shown the door to make way for a paying driver.

Haas F1 ended the season empty-handed, something that was down to two key factors. Firstly, its choice of running two F1 rookies in Mick Schumacher and Nikita Mazepin was clearly guided by financial considerations, as keeping on one of its 2020 veterans Romain Grosjean or Kevin Magnussen would surely have helped. Secondly, the Haas VF21 didn't seem to offer much performance.

BAHRAIN GP

The hoped for scenario of a real challenge to Lewis Hamilton and Mercedes came true when not only was Max Verstappen able to race with the seven-time world champion but looked set to beat him until one small mistake made him hand that victory back.

It was first blood to Red Bull Racing when Verstappen claimed pole, by 0.4s ahead of Hamilton, and Honda, pushing hard for its final shot, took a lot of credit for that.

The Dutchman duly led away, but there was almost immediately a safety car deployment as Haas rookie Nikita Mazepin spun out and his battered car needed to be recovered.

The racing began in earnest again after three laps and Verstappen and Hamilton pulled clear. Hamilton pitted after 13 laps, Verstappen after 17, and this gave Mercedes the lead. Valtteri Bottas, after falling behind Charles Leclerc's Ferrari, was soon closing in, but a problem removing the right front wheel in the pits took him out of the equation.

By staying out seven laps longer on his second set of tyres, Verstappen gained the upper hand and Hamilton realised that he had no choice but to nurse his tyres to the finish. Verstappen closed in and, got closer still when Hamilton locked up on lap 50, then pounced to go past at Turn 2 on lap 53, but all of his wheels had been over the white line and he had to give the place back, then couldn't get past in the last three laps.

Sergio Perez, who saved his F1 career when he won here in 2020 for Racing Point, had his Red Bull's electrics cut out fleetingly on the formation lap. After starting from the pitlane, his drive to fifth was perhaps more than he might have expected.

Back in F1, now with renamed Alpine, Fernando Alonso had to park his car with brake issues. The best rookie was Yuki Tsunoda who won plaudits for his handling of the second AlphaTauri as he diced with Kimi Raikkonen then Fernando Alonso and advanced after a poor start to finish ninth.

Aston Martin took a point on its F1 return when Lance Stroll finished tenth, while team-mate Sebastian Vettel had a troubled run from the rear of the grid.

SAKHIR ROUND 1

DATE: **28 MARCH 2021**

Laps: **56** • Distance: **188.167 miles/302.826km** • Weather: **Warm & dry**

Pos	Driver	Team	Result	Stops	Qualifying Time	Grid
1	**Lewis Hamilton**	Mercedes	1h32m03.897s	2	1m29.385s	2
2	**Max Verstappen**	Red Bull	1h32m04.642s	2	1m28.997s	1
3	**Valtteri Bottas**	Mercedes	1h32m41.280s	3	1m29.586s	3
4	**Lando Norris**	McLaren	1h32m50.363s	2	1m29.974s	7
5	**Sergio Perez ***	Red Bull	1h32m55.944s	3	1m30.659s	11
6	**Charles Leclerc**	Ferrari	1h33m02.987s	2	1m29.678s	4
7	**Daniel Ricciardo**	McLaren	1h33m09.901s	2	1m29.927s	6
8	**Carlos Sainz Jr.**	Ferrari	1h33m10.997s	2	1m30.215s	8
9	**Yuki Tsunoda**	AlphaTauri	1h33m29.589s	2	1m31.203s	13
10	**Lance Stroll**	Aston Martin	1h33m30.610s	2	1m30.601s	10
11	**Kimi Raikkonen**	Alfa Romeo	1h33m32.761s	2	1m31.238s	14
12	**Antonio Giovinazzi**	Alfa Romeo	55 laps	2	1m30.708s	12
13	**Esteban Ocon**	Alpine	55 laps	2	1m31.724s	16
14	**George Russell**	Williams	55 laps	2	1m33.430s	15
15	**Sebastian Vettel !,!!**	Aston Martin	55 laps	1	1m32.056s	20
16	**Mick Schumacher**	Haas	55 laps	2	1m32.449s	18
17	**Pierre Gasly**	AlphaTauri	52 laps/gearbox	3	1m29.809s	5
18	**Nicholas Latifi**	Williams	51 laps/boost leak	2	1m31.936s	17
R	**Fernando Alonso**	Alpine	32 laps/brakes	3	1m30.249s	9
R	**Nikita Mazepin**	Haas	0 laps/accident	0	1m33.273s	19

FASTEST LAP: BOTTAS, 1M32.090S, 131.461MPH/211.566KPH ON LAP 56 • RACE LEADERS: VERSTAPPEN 1-17 & 28-39, HAMILTON 18-27 & 40-56.
* STARTED FROM THE PITLANE • ! 5-PLACE GRID PENALTY FOR IGNORING YELLOW FLAGS • !! 10S PENALTY FOR CAUSING A COLLISION

Verstappen leads away at the start of the opening race, but Hamilton would go on to win it.

EMILIA ROMAGNA GP

Max Verstappen got the job done at Imola and so laid down a marker of his intent for 2021. Lewis Hamilton blew his chances with an error that dropped him to ninth before fighting back past Lando Norris to take second.

Qualifying wasn't just between Hamilton and Verstappen, as Norris looked set for pole, but his McLaren ran wide. Then, even with a slip-up at the end of his best lap, Sergio Perez landed second fastest time, demoting his team-mate to third.

There was drama before the start, as the breaks on both Aston Martins caught fire. Then, on a wet track, the field blasted away, struggling for grip on intermediate tyres. Verstappen made the best start and ran alongside Hamilton through the left-right chicane, emerging in front after the Mercedes ran over the kerbs in the second part of the corner, incurring minor wing damage.

Verstappen mastered the variable levels of grip around the circuit to rocket clear, but the safety car was deployed after Nicholas Latifi spun and collected Nikita Mazepin as he rejoined, scrapping this advantage.

Once released, Verstappen dropped his rivals again and thoughts turned to when the track might have dried enough to change to slicks. Verstappen came in on lap 27 and Hamilton next time around, their order remaining the same.

On lap 31, though, Hamilton slithered off when trying to pass George Russell's Williams at Tosa. He clipped the wall and had to pit for a new nose, rejoining ninth. The drama for Mercedes wasn't over, as Russell challenged Valtteri Bottas and got it wrong as there was only one dry line and he was on the wet one, causing a spectacular accident and bringing out the red flag.

Verstappen led away from the restart and Norris, who had been waved past team-mate Daniel Ricciardo in the first part of the race, got the jump on Charles Leclerc to take second. Bit by bit, Hamilton picked off those ahead and the last few laps were fierce as he tailed Norris, eventually getting by with three laps to go after a remarkable drive.

Verstappen was delighted with his first win of the year on a day when Hamilton slipped up.

IMOLA ROUND 2

DATE: 18 APRIL 2021

Laps: **63** · Distance: **192.034 miles/309.049km** · Weather: **Cool & damp**

Pos	Driver	Team	Result	Stops	Qualifying Time	Grid
1	**Max Verstappen**	Red Bull	2h02m34.598s	2	1m14.498s	3
2	**Lewis Hamilton**	Mercedes	2h02m56.598s	4	1m14.411s	1
3	**Lando Norris**	McLaren	2h02m58.300s	2	1m14.875s	7
4	**Charles Leclerc**	Ferrari	2h03m00.177s	2	1m14.740s	4
5	**Carlos Sainz Jr.**	Ferrari	2h03m01.634s	2	1m15.199s	11
6	**Daniel Ricciardo**	McLaren	2h03m25.818s	2	1m14.826s	6
7	**Pierre Gasly**	AlphaTauri	2h03m27.416s	4	1m14.790s	5
8	**Lance Stroll !**	Aston Martin	2h03m31.507s	3	no time	10
9	**Esteban Ocon**	Alpine	2h03m40.302s	5	1m15.210s	9
10	**Fernando Alonso**	Alpine	2h03m41.159s	3	1m15.593s	15
11	**Sergio Perez**	Red Bull	2h03m41.749s	2	1m14.446s	2
12	**Yuki Tsunoda *,!**	AlphaTauri	2h03m47.782s	3	no time	20
13	**Kimi Raikkonen !!**	Alfa Romeo	2h04m09.371s	3	1m15.974s	16
14	**Antonio Giovinazzi**	Alfa Romeo	62 laps	4	1m16.122s	17
15	**Sebastian Vettel ****	Aston Martin	61 laps	5	1m15.394s	13
16	**Mick Schumacher**	Haas	61 laps	4	1m16.279s	18
17	**Nikita Mazepin**	Haas	61 laps	4	1m16.797s	19
R	**Valtteri Bottas**	Mercedes	30 laps/collision	1	1m14.898s	8
R	**George Russell**	Williams	30 laps/collision	1	1m15.261s	12
R	**Nicholas Latifi**	Williams	0 laps/spun off	0	1m15.593s	14

FASTEST LAP: HAMILTON, 1M16.702S, 143.166MPH/230.403KPH ON LAP 60 · RACE LEADERS: VERSTAPPEN 1-26 & 29-63, HAMILTON 27-28.
* 5-PLACE GRID PENALTY FOR REPLACING THE GEARBOX · ** STARTED FROM THE PITLANE · ! 5S PENALTY FOR EXCEEDING TRACK LIMITS
!! 30S PENALTY FOR FAILING TO ENTER PITLANE FOR RESTART

» PORTUGUESE GP

Lewis Hamilton was pushed back to third place, but he didn't stay there for long, working his way to the front before putting his stamp on the race to pull clear by almost half a minute to record the 97th win of his F1 career.

Valtteri Bottas proved how determined he was not to be left behind by taking pole at the Autodromo Internacional do Algarve. The margin was only 0.007s over team-mate Hamilton but it reminded Mercedes that he isn't content to always have to be number two. With the Red Bulls a further 0.4s back on this tricky circuit, still slippery after being resurfaced in 2020, there was cause for optimism in the Mercedes camp.

The start was clean, but the end of the lap wasn't as Kimi Raikkonen was checking a setting on his steering wheel as the Alfa Romeos passed the pits and clipped team-mate Antonio Giovinazzi, ending his own race and leaving debris to clear.

After several laps behind the safety car, Max Verstappen got past Hamilton at the restart and they ran in this order until Hamilton regained second on lap 11, but Verstappen noted the Mercedes's tyre performance seemed to be falling away. Hamilton knew he had to make his move soon, and took the lead with a fabulous move around the outside of Bottas at the first corner on lap 20.

Verstappen knew though that second was possible and pitted a lap earlier than Bottas. He was gifted 1s by a slower Mercedes stop and then Bottas had a twitch at Turn 1 as he rejoined and this was enough for the Dutchman to get close enough to pounce a few corners later.

Sergio Perez showed improved form to take fourth for Red Bull after a scrap with McLaren's Lando Norris, while flashes of pace for Ferrari were not enough and Charles Leclerc was their better finisher, in sixth, but Carlos Sainz particularly disappointed after graining tyres dropped him to 11th, having running fourth early on.

Alpine took a double helping of points, with Esteban Ocon and Fernando Alonso seventh and eighth to make the most of chassis updates.

PORTIMAO ROUND 3 · DATE: **2 MAY 2021**

Laps: **66** · Distance: **190.652 miles/306.826km** · Weather: **Warm & sunny**

Pos	Driver	Team	Result	Stops	Qualifying Time	Grid
1	Lewis Hamilton	Mercedes	1h34m31.421s	1	1m18.355s	2
2	Max Verstappen	Red Bull	1h35m00.569s	2	1m18.746s	3
3	Valtteri Bottas	Mercedes	1h35m04.951s	2	1m18.348s	1
4	Sergio Perez	Red Bull	1h35m11.156s	1	1m18.890s	4
5	Lando Norris	McLaren	1h35m22.790s	1	1m19.116s	7
6	Charles Leclerc	Ferrari	1h35m27.202s	1	1m19.306s	8
7	Esteban Ocon	Alpine	1h35m35.170s	1	1m19.042s	6
8	Fernando Alonso	Alpine	1h35m36.229s	1	1m19.456s	13
9	Daniel Ricciardo	McLaren	1h35m46.790s	1	1m19.839s	16
10	Pierre Gasly	AlphaTauri	1h35m47.884s	1	1m19.475s	9
11	Carlos Sainz Jr.	Ferrari	1h35m50.376s	1	1m19.039s	5
12	Antonio Giovinazzi	Alfa Romeo	65 laps	1	1m19.216s	12
13	Sebastian Vettel	Aston Martin	65 laps	1	1m19.659s	10
14	Lance Stroll	Aston Martin	65 laps	1	1m19.913s	17
15	Yuki Tsunoda	AlphaTauri	65 laps	1	1m19.463s	14
16	George Russell	Williams	65 laps	1	1m19.109s	11
17	Mick Schumacher	Haas	64 laps	1	1m20.452s	19
18	Nicholas Latifi	Williams	64 laps	1	1m20.285s	18
19	Nikita Mazepin *	Haas	64 laps	2	1m20.912s	20
R	Kimi Raikkonen	Alfa Romeo	1 lap/collision	0	1m19.812s	15

FASTEST LAP: **BOTTAS, 1M19.865S, 130.325MPH/209.738KPH ON LAP 65** · RACE LEADERS: BOTTAS 1-19, HAMILTON 20-37 & 51-66, VERSTAPPEN 38-50 · * 5S PENALTY FOR IGNORING BLUE FLAGS

This was Hamilton at his best, fighting back from third then pulling away to win in style.

SPANISH GP

Lewis Hamilton queried a message to make a second pitstop when the team called him in at two-thirds distance, but Mercedes had done the sums and saved a set of tyres, and so reckoned one of his classic charges would topple Max Verstappen. And so it did.

The pace of Hamilton and Verstappen was all but identical in qualifying, with the Mercedes driver ahead by just 0.036s for his 100th pole, and this set up an enthralling race between the pair. Bottas, as ever, was the only other driver in touch, with Charles Leclerc's Ferrari a further two-thirds of a second behind.

Verstappen made the better start, tucked into Hamilton's slipstream and then dived up the inside. It was a ballsy move, but it worked as Hamilton had no choice but to cede. Sadly for Mercedes, Valtteri Bottas also had to lift in avoidance and this enabled Leclerc to grab third for Ferrari. Thus, instead of battling with the lead duo, as his qualifying pace suggested, the Finn was trapped, losing ground.

On lap 6 Yuki Tsunoda's AlphaTauri stopped and the safety car had to be deployed, closing all the gaps. Verstappen continued in the lead, then surprised Red Bull by pitting on lap 24, with the stop, understandably, not being as slick as usual. Although Hamilton remained in second after his stop, Bottas did get past Leclerc.

Hamilton caught Verstappen and was surprised to be told to pit, but Mercedes had saved a second set of medium compound tyres. All Hamilton had to do on rejoining was pass Bottas and make up 23s on Verstappen.

Red Bull was unable to respond, as Verstappen had no further set of mediums. All he could do was wait for the attack. And it came his way, albeit delayed by Bottas being obstructive with 14 laps to go. Hamilton got past, but time had been lost, making the chase harder. Yet he kept at his task and slipstreamed past on lap 60 of 66.

With enough of a gap to Bottas, Verstappen made a late pitstop for fresh rubber and so took the extra point for fastest lap, but knew that Mercedes had outthought Red Bull.

The Mercedes strategist knew best and Hamilton did the rest to overtake Verstappen and win.

BARCELONA ROUND 4 DATE: 9 MAY 2021
Laps: 66 · Distance: 190.825 miles/307.104km · Weather: Hot & sunny

Pos	Driver	Team	Result	Stops	Qualifying Time	Grid
1	Lewis Hamilton	Mercedes	1h33m07.680s	2	1m16.741s	1
2	Max Verstappen	Red Bull	1h33m23.521s	2	1m16.777s	2
3	Valtteri Bottas	Mercedes	1h33m34.290s	2	1m16.873s	3
4	Charles Leclerc	Ferrari	1h34m02.296s	2	1m17.510s	4
5	Sergio Perez	Red Bull	1h34m11.351s	2	1m17.701s	8
6	Daniel Ricciardo	McLaren	1h34m21.448s	2	1m17.622s	7
7	Carlos Sainz Jr.	Ferrari	1h34m22.350s	2	1m17.620s	6
8	Lando Norris	McLaren	65 laps	2	1m18.010s	9
9	Esteban Ocon	Alpine	65 laps	1	1m17.580s	5
10	Pierre Gasly	AlphaTauri	65 laps	2	1m17.982s	12
11	Lance Stroll	Aston Martin	65 laps	2	1m17.974s	11
12	Kimi Raikkonen	Alfa Romeo	65 laps	1	1m18.917s	17
13	Sebastian Vettel	Aston Martin	65 laps	2	1m18.079s	13
14	George Russell	Williams	65 laps	2	1m19.154s	15
15	Antonio Giovinazzi	Alfa Romeo	65 laps	2	1m18.356s	14
16	Nicholas Latifi	Williams	65 laps	3	1m19.219s	19
17	Fernando Alonso	Alpine	65 laps	2	1m18.147s	10
18	Mick Schumacher	Haas	64 laps	2	1m19.117s	18
19	Nikita Mazepin *	Haas	64 laps	2	1m19.807s	20
R	Yuki Tsunoda	AlphaTauri	6 laps/fuel pressure	0	1m18.556s	16

FASTEST LAP: **VERSTAPPEN, 1M18.149S, 133.816MPH/215.357KPH ON LAP 62** · RACE LEADERS: VERSTAPPEN 1-23 & 29-59, HAMILTON 24-28 & 60-66 · * 3-PLACE GRID PENALTY FOR IMPEDING ANOTHER DRIVER

» MONACO GP

Max Verstappen controlled this one from the start and took the championship lead when Lewis Hamilton struggled and could finish only seventh after qualifying badly, while Mercedes' lead challenger Valtteri Bottas's chances were wrecked in the pits.

The first task for any driver with a competitive car at Monaco is to try to secure pole position. So, Mercedes and Red Bull fancied their chances. Yet, it was to be a Ferrari that took top spot, with Charles Leclerc then bringing out the red flags when he crashed next time around on the exit of Piscine. This meant that no one else could improve, as happened in a more deliberate way when Michael Schumacher blocked the track at Rascasse in 2006 and so prevented any of his rivals from going faster.

The main concern for Leclerc was the extent of the damage to the rear of his Ferrari. Rather than risk a five-place grid penalty for fitting a new gearbox, the team checked it over and were confident that all was fine. Sadly, as Leclerc set off on his out lap for the race, it was clear that they had overlooked something. He limped back to the garage, they checked things over, then he got out. There would be no start for Leclerc for his home grand prix.

This meant that Verstappen became the effective pole sitter and he took full advantage to lead into Sainte Devote, but only after cutting across the nose of Bottas, with Carlos Sainz Jr. and Lando Norris the next two. Hamilton, having qualified only seventh on the grid, was sixth behind Pierre Gasly.

By opening out a 5s gap, Verstappen controlled the race and his advantage was stretched when Mercedes made a mess of Bottas's pitstop, with his front right wheel refusing to come off. Sainz Jr. accepted second place gladly.

The McLarens ran in the famed pale blue and orange colours of Gulf, and Norris rewarded the change by taking third, with team-mate Daniel Ricciardo 12th.

Hamilton was frustrated that Mercedes' decision to bring him in early didn't result in an undercut and he not only remained behind Gasly, but was jumped by Vettel.

MONTE CARLO ROUND 5   DATE: 23 MAY 2021
Laps: 78 · Distance: **161.734 miles/260.286km** · Weather: **Warm & sunny**

Pos	Driver	Team	Result	Stops	Qualifying Time	Grid
1	**Max Verstappen**	Red Bull	1h38m56.820s	1	1m10.576s	2
2	**Carlos Sainz Jr.**	Ferrari	1h39m05.788s	1	1m10.611s	4
3	**Lando Norris**	McLaren	1h39m16.247s	1	1m10.620s	5
4	**Sergio Perez**	Red Bull	1h39m17.310s	1	1m11.573s	9
5	**Sebastian Vettel**	Aston Martin	1h39m49.411s	1	1m11.419s	8
6	**Pierre Gasly**	AlphaTauri	1h39m50.716s	1	1m10.900s	6
7	**Lewis Hamilton**	Mercedes	1h40m05.051s	2	1m11.095s	7
8	**Lance Stroll**	Aston Martin	77 laps	1	1m11.600s	13
9	**Esteban Ocon**	Alpine	77 laps	1	1m11.486s	11
10	**Antonio Giovinazzi**	Alfa Romeo	77 laps	1	1m11.779s	10
11	**Kimi Raikkonen**	Alfa Romeo	77 laps	1	1m11.642s	14
12	**Daniel Ricciardo**	McLaren	77 laps	1	1m11.598s	12
13	**Fernando Alonso**	Alpine	77 laps	1	1m12.205s	17
14	**George Russell**	Williams	77 laps	1	1m11.830s	15
15	**Nicholas Latifi**	Williams	77 laps	1	1m12.366s	18
16	**Yuki Tsunoda**	AlphaTauri	77 laps	1	1m12.096s	16
17	**Nikita Mazepin**	Haas	75 laps	1	1m12.958s	19
18	**Mick Schumacher ***	Haas	75 laps	1	no time	20
R	**Valtteri Bottas**	Mercedes	29 laps/wheel nut	1	1m10.601s	3
NS	**Charles Leclerc**	Ferrari	0 laps/gearbox	0	1m10.346s	1

FASTEST LAP: HAMILTON, 1M12.909S, 102.383MPH/164.769KPH ON LAP 69 · RACE LEADER: VERSTAPPEN 1-78.
* 5-PLACE GRID PENALTY FOR REPLACING GEARBOX

The first driver into Ste Devote usually wins at Monaco and this was the case for Verstappen.

AZERBAIJAN GP

Sergio Perez was smiling broadly at the end of this grand prix, having secured the second win of his F1 career while championship protagonists Max Verstappen and Lewis Hamilton came away with nothing, the Dutchman being especially unlucky with tyre failure when leading.

Bouncing back from not starting in Monaco, Ferrari's Charles Leclerc took a second consecutive pole, in a final session again brought to a premature end. This time, it was his team-mate Carlos Sainz Jr. and Yuki Tsunoda who crashed to bring out the red flags. With Mercedes having been struggling to get heat into their Pirellis, Hamilton was pleased to end up second fastest ahead of Verstappen and Pierre Gasly.

Leclerc managed to start this time, but led only the first lap before Hamilton put his Mercedes into the lead at Turn 15 when the Monegasque driver made an error. After five laps of trying, Verstappen also moved past the Ferrari.

Perez, who had gained two places on the opening lap demoted Leclerc the next time around. Verstappen was given a gift when Hamilton was held back as he tried to leave his pitstop by the arrival of Gasly's AlphaTauri. Verstappen duly made his pitstop next time around and came out ahead, as did Perez, just, the lap after that.

Verstappen was in control when Lance Stroll suffered a left rear blowout and on the main straight on lap 30, his Aston Martin snapped sideways, slamming the wall. The Canadian was shaken but alright, but the clean-up of the debris meant a long safety car period.

When the safety car withdrew, there were 15 laps to go and Verstappen pulled away as he pleased, but then, on lap 46 of 51, the race changed in a huge way as Verstappen had his left rear tyre blow as he came onto the pit straight. He was out on the spot as Perez flashed by, with the race being halted soon afterwards.

Perez was challenged by Hamilton at the restart, but the Mercedes driver braked too late and skated past, rejoining last as Perez resumed the lead and won as he pleased.

Sergio Perez inherited the second win of his F1 career when Verstappen had a blow-out.

BAKU ROUND 6
DATE: **6 JUNE 2021**
Laps: **51** · Distance: **190.170 miles/306.049km** · Weather: **Hot & sunny**

Pos	Driver	Team	Result	Stops	Qualifying Time	Grid
1	**Sergio Perez**	Red Bull	2h13m36.410s	3	1m41.917s	6
2	**Sebastian Vettel**	Aston Martin	2h13m37.795s	3	1m42.224s	11
3	**Pierre Gasly**	AlphaTauri	2h13m39.172s	3	1m41.565s	4
4	**Charles Leclerc**	Ferrari	2h13m40.238s	3	1m41.218s	1
5	**Lando Norris !**	McLaren	2h13m41.164s	3	1m41.747s	9
6	**Fernando Alonso**	Alpine	2h13m42.792s	4	1m42.327s	8
7	**Yuki Tsunoda**	AlphaTauri	2h13m43.034s	3	1m42.211s	7
8	**Carlos Sainz Jr.**	Ferrari	2h13m44.119s	3	1m41.576s	5
9	**Daniel Ricciardo**	McLaren	2h13m45.284s	3	1m42.558s	13
10	**Kimi Raikkonen**	Alfa Romeo	2h13m45.986s	3	1m42.587s	14
11	**Antonio Giovinazzi**	Alfa Romeo	2h13m46.664s	4	no time	20
12	**Valtteri Bottas**	Mercedes	2h13m47.674s	3	1m42.659s	10
13	**Mick Schumacher**	Haas	2h13m50.651s	5	1m44.158s	17
14	**Nikita Mazepin**	Haas	2h13m50.725s	6	1m44.238s	18
15	**Lewis Hamilton**	Mercedes	2h13m54.078s	3	1m41.450s	2
16	**Nicholas Latifi ***	Williams	2h14m18.789s	2	1m43.128s	16
17	**George Russell**	Williams	48 laps/gearbox	4	1m42.758s	15
18	**Max Verstappen**	Red Bull	45 laps/tyre	1	1m41.563s	3
R	**Lance Stroll**	Aston Martin	29 laps/tyre	0	no time	19
R	**Esteban Ocon**	Alpine	3 laps/power unit	1	1m42.273s	12

FASTEST LAP: VERSTAPPEN, 1M44.481S, 128.524MPH/206.839KPH ON LAP 44 · RACE LEADERS: LECLERC 1, HAMILTON 2-10, VERSTAPPEN 11 & 18-45, PEREZ 12-13 & 46-51, VETTEL 14-17 · ! 3-PLACE GRID PENALTY FOR FAILING TO HEED RED FLAG
* 30S PENALTY FOR NOT USING PITLANE

FRENCH GP

A win is worth 25 points, but victory for Max Verstappen at Paul Ricard felt far more valuable than that, as Red Bull Racing outthought Mercedes and he outraced Lewis Hamilton to open out a 12-point championship lead, suggesting a change of momentum in his favour.

Pole didn't result in the lead for Verstappen for long, as he ran wide at the first corner and so ceded the advantage to Hamilton. Yet, after he pitted from second for new tyres after 18 laps, Mercedes kept Hamilton out a lap longer and were surprised when this resulted in his Mercedes coming out alongside the Dutchman rather than ahead, with Verstappen then flying past into Turn 1.

So far so good for Red Bull, but the team then elected to bring Verstappen in again and his second pitstop on lap 32 dropped him from first to fourth. Yet the gamble paid off as his fresher tyres gave him such superior performance that he took third when team-mate Sergio Perez let him by and then found it easy to pass Bottas at Signes. The final target was of course Hamilton.

Questions were asked about whether Hamilton should have pitted for fresh tyres too, but this would still have brought him out behind Verstappen thus offering no advantage, so he had no choice but to resist on his tiring rubber.

The seven-time World Champion was caught with two laps to go and simply didn't have the tyre life left to hold out, with Verstappen getting by easily.

Hamilton's former team-mate Nico Rosberg raised his hackles by saying that Lewis's defence of the lead had been "soft", but Lewis said that robust defence would have been pointless as Verstappen's tyres were so much fresher.

There was a feeling, following Red Bull's third straight win with a better car, that Mercedes was saving some of its capped budget to develop its 2022 car rather than spending it on improving the W12.

With both Mercedes struggling for grip late on, and Bottas angry with the team for not considering a two-stopper, Perez motored past the Finn to finish third.

PAUL RICARD ROUND 7

DATE: **20 JUNE 2021**

Laps: 53 • **Distance: 192.432 miles/309.690km** • Weather: **Hot & sunny**

Pos	Driver	Team	Result	Stops	Qualifying Time	Grid
1	**Max Verstappen**	Red Bull	1h27m25.770s	2	1m29.990s	1
2	**Lewis Hamilton**	Mercedes	1h27m28.674s	1	1m30.248s	2
3	**Sergio Perez**	Red Bull	1h27m34.581s	1	1m30.445s	4
4	**Valtteri Bottas**	Mercedes	1h2740.388s	1	1m30.376s	3
5	**Lando Norris**	McLaren	1h28m29.802s	1	1m31.252s	8
6	**Daniel Ricciardo**	McLaren	1h28m41.627s	1	1m31.382s	10
7	**Pierre Gasly**	AlphaTauri	1h28m42.366s	1	1m30.868s	6
8	**Fernando Alonso**	Alpine	1h28m43.465s	1	1m31.340s	9
9	**Sebastian Vettel**	Aston Martin	1h28m45.436s	1	1m31.767s	12
10	**Lance Stroll**	Aston Martin	1h28m57.716s	1	2m12.584s	19
11	**Carlos Sainz Jr.**	Ferrari	1h29m05.107s	1	1m30.840s	5
12	**George Russell**	Williams	52 laps	1	1m32.065s	14
13	**Yuki Tsunoda ***	AlphaTauri	52 laps	1	no time	20
14	**Esteban Ocon**	Alpine	52 laps	1	1m31.736s	11
15	**Antonio Giovinazzi**	Alfa Romeo	52 laps	1	1m31.813s	13
16	**Charles Leclerc**	Ferrari	52 laps	2	1m30.987s	7
17	**Kimi Raikkonen**	Alfa Romeo	52 laps	1	1m33.354s	17
18	**Nicholas Latifi**	Williams	52 laps	1	1m33.062s	16
19	**Mick Schumacher**	Haas	52 laps	1	no time	15
20	**Nikita Mazepin**	Haas	52 laps	1	1m33.554s	18

FASTEST LAP: VERSTAPPEN, 1M36.404S, 135.556MPH/218.156KPH ON LAP 35 • RACE LEADERS: HAMILTON 1-18 & 32-51, PEREZ 19-23, VERSTAPPEN 24-31 & 52-53 • * 5-PLACE GRID PENALTY FOR REPLACING THE GEARBOX

A two-stop strategy worked perfectly for Verstappen as he raced to his third win of 2021.

STYRIAN GP

Red Bull Racing extended its winning streak to four grands prix in a row as Max Verstappen powered away from the front of the grid and stayed there. For Lewis Hamilton, it was a depressing result, as he wasn't even close to challenging the Dutchman.

Verstappen laid down the gauntlet for the first of two visits in two weekends to the Red Bull Ring by taking pole by 0.026s from Hamilton after Valtteri Bottas, second fastest on track, was hit with a three-place grid penalty for a pitstop misdemeanour. The qualifying result itself was enough to delight team chairman Dietrich Mateschitz, a Red Bull pole at the Red Bull Ring. What followed on Sunday would make Mateschitz smile even more.

Verstappen blasted up the sharp rise to the first corner with his RB16 easily in front of Hamilton's Mercedes. And, to Red Bull's delight, he would lead every single lap from there. It was all too clear that even if Mercedes moved him to a two-stop strategy that Verstappen had the pace to counter that. As it was, Hamilton did come in for a third set of tyres, but that was right at the end when he was sufficiently clear of the car in third place to grab a set of soft tyres and then use them to take the point for setting the race's fastest lap. Not having the fastest car at the show was beginning to be less of a novelty.

Lando Norris started from third on the grid and stayed there despite an attack by Sergio Perez in the second Red Bull. The Mexican kept the pressure up but took 10 laps to get past, with Valtteri Bottas going by too.

After the pitstops, the order changed only in that Perez's stop was slow, and so Bottas moved into third place. In the closing laps, however, he struggled lapping slower cars and Perez closed right in, but Bottas resisted the attack around the final lap to take the final place on the podium.

Norris had gone easy early on to preserve tyre life and this worked well. Indeed, McLaren might have taken sixth place as well, but Daniel Ricciardo's engine suddenly lost power early on and so he fell back.

Hamilton chases after Verstappen, but it was to be a chase in vain as Red Bull won again.

RED BULL RING ROUND 8

DATE: 27 JUNE 2021

Laps: **71** · Distance: **190.172 miles/306.452km** · Weather: **Hot & sunny**

Pos	Driver	Team	Result	Stops	Qualifying Time	Grid
1	Max Verstappen	Red Bull	1h22m18.925s	1	1m03.841s	1
2	Lewis Hamilton	Mercedes	1h22m54.668s	2	1m04.067s	2
3	Valtteri Bottas !	Mercedes	1h23m05.832s	1	1m04.035s	5
4	Sergio Perez	Red Bull	1h23n06.359s	2	1m04.168s	4
5	Lando Norris	McLaren	70 laps	1	1m04.120s	3
6	Carlos Sainz Jr.	Ferrari	70 laps	1	1m04.800s	12
7	Charles Leclerc	Ferrari	70 laps	2	1m04.472s	7
8	Lance Stroll	Aston Martin	70 laps	1	1m04.708s	9
9	Fernando Alonso	Alpine	70 laps	1	1m04.574s	8
10	Yuki Tsunoda !!	AlphaTauri	70 laps	1	1m04.514s	11
11	Kimi Raikkonen	Alfa Romeo	70 laps	1	1m05.429s	18
12	Sebastian Vettel	Aston Martin	70 laps	1	1m04.875s	14
13	Daniel Ricciardo	McLaren	70 laps	1	1m04.808s	13
14	Esteban Ocon	Alpine	70 laps	1	1m05.217s	17
15	Antonio Giovinazzi	Alfa Romeo	70 laps	1	1m04.913s	15
16	Mick Schumacher	Haas	69 laps	1	1m06.041s	19
17	Nicholas Latifi	Williams	68 laps	1	1m05.175s	16
18	Nikita Mazepin	Haas	68 laps	1	1m06.192s	20
R	George Russell	Williams	36 laps/power unit	2	1m04.671s	10
R	Pierre Gasly	AlphaTauri	1 lap/collision	0	1m04.236s	6

FASTEST LAP: HAMILTON, 1M07.058S, 144.040MPH/231.811KPH ON LAP 71 · RACE LEADER: VERSTAPPEN 1-71.
! 3-PLACE GRID PENALTY FOR DANGEROUS DRIVING IN THE PITLANE · !! 3-PLACE GRID PENALTY FOR IMPEDING ANOTHER DRIVER

Lewis Hamilton was all smiles when he announced that he had signed for a further two years with Mercedes, but was less happy at the prospect of being beaten by Max Verstappen at the same circuit for a second weekend in a row. And this is precisely what happened and he failed even to make the podium.

It must have felt like groundhog day for the teams to return to the Red Bull Ring, albeit this time for the Austrian GP. Red Bull Racing was happy as its cars were great here and Mercedes was not as it wasn't expecting to close a sizeable lap advantage to their multi-coloured rivals.

Max Verstappen duly took pole again, but the surprise was that he didn't do so ahead of team-mate Sergio Perez or either of the Mercedes drivers, but by the smallest of margins from McLaren's Lando Norris who achieved a career best qualifying position. Fourth and fifth places for Hamilton and Valtteri Bottas showed how Mercedes had struggled.

Verstappen led away, easily clear of Norris, and led for all 71 laps. He won by 18s, despite a spell when the field was bunched by the safety car after Esteban Ocon's Alpine was caught between Antonio Giovanizzi's Alfa Romeo and Mick Schumacher's Haas early on the opening lap making a second pitstop.

Norris was pressured at the restart by Perez trying to go around the outside into Schlossgold but getting it wrong and falling to tenth as Hamilton took third from Bottas. Then Hamilton set about Norris, but was helped when the McLaren was harshly hit with a 5s penalty for allowing Perez no space. This dropped him behind Bottas, but he soon started catching the Finn, who was chasing Hamilton. The world champion was struggling and both passed him. Perez later got two 5s penalties and ended sixth.

For the thousands of Verstappen fans, Max's win was what they came for, with the added bonus of Mercedes being even further off the pace than the previous race.

George Russell had had a remarkable run to qualify ninth, eighth when Sebastian Vettel was put back three positions, but he finished in 11th, beaten to the last point by Fernando Alonso.

RED BULL RING ROUND 9

DATE: **4 JULY 2021**

Laps: **71** · Distance: **190.172 miles/306.452km** · Weather: **Warm & sunny**

Pos	Driver	Team	Result	Stops	Qualifying Time	Grid
1	**Max Verstappen**	Red Bull	1h23m54.543s	2	1m03.720s	1
2	**Valtteri Bottas**	Mercedes	1h24m12.516s	1	1m04.049s	5
3	**Lando Norris**	McLaren	1h24m14.562s	1	1m03.768s	2
4	**Lewis Hamilton**	Mercedes	1h24m40.995s	2	1m04.014s	4
5	**Carlos Sainz Jr.**	Ferrari	1h24m51.687s	1	1m04.559s	10
6	**Sergio Perez !!**	Red Bull	1h24m52.458s	1	1m03.990s	3
7	**Daniel Ricciardo**	McLaren	1h24m54.938s	1	1m04.719s	13
8	**Charles Leclerc**	Ferrari	1h24m55.738s	1	1m04.600s	12
9	**Pierre Gasly**	AlphaTauri	1h24m56.387s	2	1m04.107s	6
10	**Fernando Alonso**	Alpine	70 laps	1	1m04.856s	14
11	**George Russell**	Williams	70 laps	1	1m04.591s	8
12	**Yuki Tsunoda !**	AlphaTauri	70 laps	2	1m04.273s	7
13	**Lance Stroll !**	Aston Martin	70 laps	2	1m04.618s	9
14	**Antonio Giovinazzi**	Alfa Romeo	70 laps	2	1m05.083s	15
15	**Kimi Raikkonen !!!**	Alfa Romeo	70 laps	1	1m05.009s	16
16	**Nicholas Latifi !!!!**	Williams	70 laps	1	1m05.195s	18
17	**Sebastian Vettel ***	Aston Martin	69 laps	3	1m04.570s	11
18	**Mick Schumacher**	Haas	69 laps	1	1m05.427s	19
19	**Nikita Mazepin !!!!**	Haas	69 laps	2	1m05.951s	20
R	**Esteban Ocon**	Alpine	0 laps/collision	0	1m05.051s	17

FASTEST LAP: VERSTAPPEN, 1M06.200S, 145.907MPH/234.815KPH ON LAP 62 · RACE LEADER: VERSTAPPEN 1-71
* 3-PLACE GRID PENALTY FOR IMPEDING ANOTHER DRIVER · ! 5S PENALTY FOR PIT LANE OFFENCES · !! 10S PENALTY FOR FORCING ANOTHER DRIVER OFF THE TRACK · !!! 20S PENALTY FOR CAUSING A COLLISION · !!!! 30S PENALTY FOR FAILING TO HEED DOUBLE YELLOW FLAGS

The McLaren crew celebrate Lando Norris being on form as he flashes by to finish third.

Arriving for his home grand prix 32 points behind Max Verstappen, Lewis Hamilton knew that he needed to rediscover winning ways. And this he did, to the delight of the first near-capacity crowd of the season, but only after a clash with Verstappen on the opening lap that left Red Bull Racing livid.

The first novelty about the British GP was that the World Championship was allowed for the first time in the 2021 season to have a near-capacity crowd and, although uneasy about the possibility of triggering a surge in infection, everyone involved was delighted to have the fans back.

The second novelty was that the grid for the grand prix was decided by the finishing order in a 17-lap sprint race held on the Saturday. Hamilton took pole for this, but his one-lap pace was better than his race pace and so when Verstappen went past him after a superior getaway, he had no answers and ended second after a remarkably uneventful sprint race.

So, on Sunday, to the start proper and Hamilton was first away, with Verstappen back in front as they turned out of the Loop but with the Mercedes driver coming back at him into Luffield. It was feisty stuff, and then came Copse, with Hamilton diving up the inside and not backing out of it as the Dutchman turned across his bows. In a flash, the Red Bull's rear right suspension collapsed and the car was fired off into the tyrewall on the outside of the seventh-gear corner. Verstappen was winded and furious.

Hamilton was able to continue, passed by Charles Leclerc, but the red flags flew and it was a while before the debris was cleared. Leclerc got past Hamilton again at the restart and edged clear until his Ferrari's engine stuttered and the Mercedes closed in. Hamilton was told that he had received a 10s penalty for his role in the collision with Verstappen and so emerged from his pitstop fourth behind Leclerc, Valtteri Bottas and Lando Norris.

Then Hamilton went hunting and grabbed the lead with two laps to go, diving up that same inside line at Copse he had used on Verstappen, but this time being left enough space to do the job, delighting the crowd.

Hamilton versus Verstappen, just what could go wrong? Peace lasted only until Copse...

SILVERSTONE ROUND 10

DATE: **18 JULY 202**

Laps: 52 · Distance: **190.262 miles/306.198km** · Weather: **Hot & sunny**

Pos	Driver	Team	Result	Stops	Qualifying Time	Grid
1	**Lewis Hamilton**	Mercedes	1h58m23.284s	2	-	2
2	**Charles Leclerc**	Ferrari	1h58m27.155s	2	-	4
3	**Valtteri Bottas**	Mercedes	1h58m34.409s	2	-	3
4	**Lando Norris**	McLaren	1h58m51.857s	2	-	5
5	**Daniel Ricciardo**	McLaren	1h59m05.908s	2	-	6
6	**Carlos Sainz Jr.**	Ferrari	1h59m06.738s	2	-	10
7	**Fernando Alonso**	Alpine	1h59m35.377s	2	-	7
8	**Lance Stroll**	Aston Martin	1h59m37.573s	2	-	14
9	**Esteban Ocon**	Alpine	1h59m39.446s	2	-	9
10	**Yuki Tsunoda**	AlphaTauri	1h59m45.349s	2	-	16
11	**Pierre Gasly**	AlphaTauri	1h59m48.611s	3	-	11
12	**George Russell**	Williams	51 laps	2	-	12
13	**Antonio Giovinazzi**	Alfa Romeo	51 laps	2	-	15
14	**Nicholas Latifi**	Williams	51 laps	2	-	17
15	**Kimi Raikkonen**	Alfa Romeo	51 laps	2	-	13
16	**Sergio Perez !**	Red Bull	51 laps	4	-	20
17	**Nikita Mazepin**	Haas	51 laps	2	-	19
18	**Mick Schumacher**	Haas	51 laps	2	-	18
R	**Sebastian Vettel**	Aston Martin	40 laps/lost power	2	-	8
R	**Max Verstappen**	Red Bull	0 laps/collision	0	-	1

FASTEST LAP: PEREZ, 1M28.617S, 148.704MPH/239.317KPH ON LAP 50 · RACE LEADERS: LECLERC 1-49, HAMILTON 50-52.
! REQUIRED TO START FROM THE PIT LANE AS CAR WAS MODIFIED UNDER PARC FERME CONDITIONS.
NB. GRID DETERMINED BY FINISHING ORDER IN SPRINT RACE

⟫ HUNGARIAN GP

This one was different. After a massed shunt at the first corner, there was a restart. Bizarrely, only one car set off from the grid as the rest opted to start from the pits after changing tyres and Alpine's Esteban Ocon raced away to take his first F1 win.

The first corner at the Hungaroring has seen many an opening lap clash over the decades, but 2021's brawl was a notably all-encompassing one. It was triggered when Valtteri Bottas left his braking too late and his Mercedes clattered into Lando Norris's McLaren, which then snapped sideways and smashed into Max Verstappen, while Bottas's momentum took him on into the rear of the other Red Bull, Sergio Perez's. With Charles Leclerc and Lance Stroll also caught up, the race had to be stopped.

Then came one of the most extraordinary images in F1 history as only one of the 16 cars still running formed up on the grid for the restart. This was Lewis Hamilton, his Mercedes still on intermediate tyres. The other nine teams decided the track was drying enough to change to dries. The cars entered the pits to change tyres and restart from the pitlane.

The writing was on the wall, as the cars leaving the pits had way more grip than Hamilton, so he pitted at the end of the lap and came out in last place. This was a massive blunder by Mercedes.

Ocon made the most of this opportunity and raced clear to win, with team-mate Fernando Alonso defending resolutely to keep the recovering Hamilton back in fourth place for long enough to ensure that he could advance no higher than third behind Aston Martin's Sebastian Vettel. Afterwards, Hamilton reported he had been feeling dizzy and suspected he had long Covid.

Not long after the race, news filtered through that Vettel had been disqualified, as there hadn't been sufficient fuel left in his tank for the post-race sample to be taken. So, Hamilton's third became second and Verstappen's tenth became ninth, meaning that the Dutchman gained an extra point, but the Englishman gained an extra three, thus stretching his new championship lead to eight points.

HUNGARORING ROUND 11

DATE: **1 AUGUST 2021**

Laps: **70** · Distance: **190.531 miles/306.630km** · Weather: **Hot & wet/dry**

Pos	Driver	Team	Result	Stops	Qualifying Time	Grid
1	Esteban Ocon	Alpine	2h04m43.199s	3	1m16.653s	8
2	Lewis Hamilton	Mercedes	2h04m45.935s	4	1m15.419s	1
3	Carlos Sainz Jr.	Ferrari	2h04m58.217s	3	no time	15
4	Fernando Alonso	Alpine	2h04m58.850s	3	1m16.715s	9
5	Pierre Gasly	AlphaTauri	2h05m46.813s	4	1m16.483s	5
6	Yuki Tsunoda	AlphaTauri	2h05m59.002s	3	1m17.919s	16
7	Nicholas Latifi	Williams	2h06m01.109s	3	1m18.036s	18
8	George Russell	Williams	2h06m02.293s	3	1m17.944s	17
9	Max Verstappen	Red Bull	2h06m03.443s	5	1m15.840s	3
10	Kimi Raikkonen	Alfa Romeo	69 laps	4	1m17.564s	13
11	Daniel Ricciardo	McLaren	69 laps	3	1m16.871s	11
12	Mick Schumacher !	Haas	69 laps	3	no time	20
13	Antonio Giovinazzi !!	Alfa Romeo	69 laps	5	1m17.583s	14
DQ	Sebastian Vettel	Aston Martin	2h04m45.058s	3	1m16.750s	10
R	Nikita Mazepin	Haas	3 laps/collision	2	1m18.922s	19
R	Lando Norris	McLaren	2 laps/collision	1	1m16.489s	6
R	Valtteri Bottas	Mercedes	0 laps/collision	0	1m15.734s	2
R	Sergio Perez	Red Bull	0 laps/collision	0	1m16.421s	4
R	Charles Leclerc	Ferrari	0 laps/collision	0	1m16.496s	7
R	Lance Stroll	Aston Martin	0 laps/collision	0	1m16.893s	12

FASTEST LAP: **GASLY, 1M18.394S, 125.009MPH/201.183KPH ON LAP 70** · RACE LEADERS: **HAMILTON 1-2, OCON 3-37 & 40-70, ALONSO 38-39.**
· **!** 5-PLACE GRID PENALTY · **!!** STARTED FROM THE PITLANE

Bottas gets it all wrong into the first corner and takes Sergio Perez's Red Bull off with him.

BELGIAN GP

When is a grand prix not a grand prix? When it's a washout. There has often been rain at Spa-Francorchamps in the past, but this was excessive and so the race was abandoned after one lap, handing victory to Max Verstappen and a surprise second to George Russell.

When Lando Norris crashed his McLaren at Eau Rouge in qualifying, he had already been fastest in the first and second qualifying and was heading off for another lap at the start of the third session. If that lap had been good enough for pole, it would have translated into a win on raceday.

Naturally, all he could think of at the time was his wasted opportunity, his one lap good only for tenth in session and, when augmented by a five-place grid penalty for fitting a replacement gearbox, it was disaster enough. Sebastian Vettel had already called for the session to be halted as cars had been aquaplaning before Norris crashed and he probably felt validated. Nevertheless, drivers will naturally push until told not to and they hadn't been told not to...

As it happened, Max Verstappen's Red Bull ended up quickest in qualifying, going back out more than 40 minutes after Norris caused the session to be halted, with conditions gradually improving. What was remarkable, though, was the identity of the driver who lapped second fastest, as it was George Russell for Williams. He alone elected to wait as long as possible before going out on intermediate tyres, risking all, and his silky smooth lap put him at the top of the timesheets, only to be beaten by Verstappen at the death. For Williams, in its first year owned by Dorilton Capital, it was a massive moment in the rebuilding of the team.

With a considerable amount of standing water, the start was delayed and delayed. Eventually, 25 minutes later than planned, the field was led around by a safety car for two laps. They returned to the pits, waited another three hours and tried again. This time they pitted after three laps and a result was declared, making polesitter Verstappen the winner and a delighted Russell an ecstatic second.

Verstappen splashes around, with Russell sitting in his wake, as they follow the safety car.

SPA-FRANCORCHAMPS ROUND 12 DATE: 29 AUGUST 2021
Laps: 1 · Distance: **4.275 miles/6.880km** · Weather: **Extremely wet & cool**

Pos	Driver	Team	Result	Stops	Qualifying Time	Grid
1	**Max Verstappen**	Red Bull	3m27.071s	0	1m59.765s	1
2	**George Russell**	Williams	3m29.066s	0	2m00.086s	2
3	**Lewis Hamilton**	Mercedes	3m29.672s	0	2m00.099s	3
4	**Daniel Ricciardo**	McLaren	3m31.567s	0	2m00.864s	4
5	**Sebastian Vettel**	Aston Martin	3m34.550s	0	2m00.935s	5
6	**Pierre Gasly**	AlphaTauri	3m37.248s	0	2m01.164s	6
7	**Esteban Ocon**	Alpine	3m38.650s	0	2m03.513s	8
8	**Charles Leclerc**	Ferrari	3m39.679s	0	1m57.721s	9
9	**Nicholas Latifi**	Williams	3m42.555s	0	1m58.056s	10
10	**Carlos Sainz Jr.**	Ferrari	3m43.237s	0	1m58.137s	11
11	**Fernando Alonso**	Alpine	3m47.661s	0	1m58.295s	12
12	**Valtteri Bottas !!**	Mercedes	3m49.485s	0	2m02.502s	13
13	**Antonio Giovinazzi**	Alfa Romeo	3m51.233s	0	2m02.306s	14
14	**Lando Norris ***	McLaren	3m54.180s	0	1m56.025s	15
15	**Yuki Tsunoda**	AlphaTauri	3m55.400s	0	2m02.413s	16
16	**Mick Schumacher**	Haas	3m56.578s	0	2m03.973s	17
17	**Nikita Mazepin**	Haas	3m59.064s	0	2m04.939s	18
18	**Kimi Raikkonen !**	Alfa Romeo	4m03.125s	0	2m04.452s	20
19	**Sergio Perez**	Red Bull	4m05.276s	0	2m02.112s	7
20	**Lance Stroll !!!**	Aston Martin	4m11.179s	0	1m58.231s	19

FASTEST LAP: MAZEPIN, 3M18.016S, 77.721MPH/125.081KPH ON LAP 1 · RACE LEADER: VERSTAPPEN 1.
* 5-PLACE GRID PENALTY FOR CAUSING A CRASH IN QUALIFYING · ! STARTED FROM THE PITLANE · !! 5-PLACE GRID PENALTY FOR CAUSING A COLLISION · !!! 10S PENALTY FOR MODIFYING CAR DURING RACE STOPPAGE

The Dutch fans could not have wished for a better outcome for their first grand prix since 1985 when Max Verstappen ruled proceedings to achieve a dominant win for Red Bull Racing ahead of his title rival Lewis Hamilton, sending the place wild with delight.

F1's return to the Netherlands had been scheduled for 2020, but the COVID pandemic scuppered that. It was a blow at the time but, had it happened, Hamilton would probably have won. By being held back until last year, Verstappen and Red Bull had moved up a level and so the orange army of Max fans got their wish of a home win.

Despite the tweaks to the circuit layout with banked corners added at Hugenholtzbocht and the final corner, Arie Luyendijk Bocht, it became apparent from the moment that the cars hit the track that overtaking was going to be far from commonplace. So this put extra emphasis on qualifying and Verstappen produced a lap time that Hamilton narrowly failed to beat, triggering wild applause.

At the start of the race, Verstappen delighted the fans again when he took a clear lead before they reached Tarzan. With Verstappen edging clear, Mercedes had to find a way back into the race. They brought Hamilton in after 20 laps and Verstappen came in next time around to counter.

At this point, it seemed that Valtteri Bottas might have a role to play in helping team-mate Hamilton by holding back Verstappen, but the Dutchman got past him before the Finn came in for his first pitstop.

Towards the end of the race, after a second change of tyres, Hamilton's rubber became less effective and Verstappen edged clear towards victory. Then Bottas accidentally set fastest lap and, with it being clear that he couldn't catch Max, Lewis pitted again for the fresh rubber that would help him to net the point for fastest lap while still safe in second place.

The final place on the podium went to Bottas, the only other driver on the lead lap, but the screaming fans only had eyes for one driver up there, their hero Max Verstappen.

ZANDVOORT ROUND 13   DATE: **5 SEPTEMBER 2021**
Laps: **72** • Distance: **190.504 miles/306.587km** • Weather: **Warm & sunny**

Pos	Driver	Team	Result	Stops	Qualifying Time	Grid
1	Max Verstappen	Red Bull	1h30m05.395s	2	1m08.885s	1
2	Lewis Hamilton	Mercedes	1h30m26.327s	3	1m08.923s	2
3	Valtteri Bottas	Mercedes	1h31m01.855s	2	1m09.222s	3
4	Pierre Gasly	AlphaTauri	71 laps	1	1m09.478s	4
5	Charles Leclerc	Ferrari	71 laps	1	1m09.527s	5
6	Fernando Alonso	Alpine	71 laps	1	1m09.956s	9
7	Carlos Sainz Jr.	Ferrari	71 laps	1	1m09.537s	6
8	Sergio Perez !	Red Bull	71 laps	2	1m10.530s	20
9	Esteban Ocon	Alpine	71 laps	1	1m09.933s	8
10	Lando Norris	McLaren	71 laps	1	1m10.406s	13
11	Daniel Ricciardo	McLaren	71 laps	1	1m10.166s	10
12	Lance Stroll	Aston Martin	70 laps	1	1m10.367s	12
13	Sebastian Vettel	Aston Martin	70 laps	2	1m10.731s	15
14	Antonio Giovinazzi	Alfa Romeo	70 laps	2	1m09.590s	7
15	Robert Kubica	Alfa Romeo	70 laps	1	1m11.301s	16
16	Nicholas Latifi *	Williams	70 laps	1	1m11.161s	19
17	George Russell	Williams	69 laps	2	1m10.332s	11
18	Mick Schumacher	Haas	69 laps	2	1m11.387s	17
R	Yuki Tsunoda	AlphaTauri	48 laps/transmission	1	1m11.314s	14
R	Nikita Mazepin	Haas	41 laps/hydraulics	1	1m11.875s	18

FASTEST LAP: HAMILTON, 1M11.097S, 134.001MPH/215.654KPH ON LAP 72 • RACE LEADERS: VERSTAPPEN 1-21 & 30-72, BOTTAS 22-29.
* 5-PLACE GRID PENALTY FOR REPLACING GEARBOX • ! REQUIRED TO START FROM BACK OF GRID FOR USING ADDITIONAL POWER UNIT ELEMENTS

The orange army had its wishes met with F1's return to Zandvoort, then a win for Verstappen.

ITALIAN GP

Some will remember the 2021 Italian GP for the clash between Max Verstappen and Lewis Hamilton, but perhaps it should be remembered more for the fact that this was the race at which McLaren started winning again and, better still, took a deserved one-two result.

One thing that needs to be cleared up immediately is that McLaren did not fluke their first win since the 2012 Brazilian GP. And this is what made team chief Zak Brown's delight all the more intense, as their win after a 170-race drought, their one-two finish, came on merit at Monza.

As at the British GP, a sprint race set the grid for the main event, and this was won by Valtteri Bottas ahead of Verstappen, but the luckless Finn had a penalty that meant he would start the race from the back of the grid. Verstappen was elevated to pole, something that did nothing to cheer Hamilton who only finished fifth in the sprint, behind the ever-improving McLarens.

Daniel Ricciardo had been playing second fiddle to Lando Norris since joining McLaren, with a best result of fourth to the young Briton's three third places, but he seemed to find his MCL35M's sweet spot at Monza and made a demon start to pass Verstappen into the first chicane. Behind them, Hamilton resisted Norris and then tried a move on Verstappen that was rebuffed and Norris grabbed the opportunity to take third.

Verstappen had a terrible first pitstop and came out tenth, yet this wasn't to help Hamilton, as his pitstop was also slow, meaning they were side-by-side when the Mercedes driver rejoined. On reaching the first chicane, Verstappen was on the outside, Hamilton the inside, then Verstappen on top of Hamilton. Only the once unpopular halo saved Lewis from serious injury or worse. The safety car was deployed.

Ricciardo resumed in the lead when it withdrew and Norris wrested second place back from Charles Leclerc, much to the *tifosi*'s disappointment. He was then demoted further by Bottas who worked his way forward from the back of the grid to third, after Sergio Perez was hit with a five-second penalty.

With neither driver ceding into the first chicane, Verstappen ends up on top of Hamilton.

MONZA ROUND 14

DATE: 12 SEPTEMBER 2021

Laps: **53** · Distance: **190.587 miles/306.720km** · Weather: **Hot & sunny**

Pos	Driver	Team	Result	Stops	Qualifying Time	Grid
1	**Daniel Ricciardo**	McLaren	1h21m54.365s	1	-	2
2	**Lando Norris**	McLaren	1h21m56.112s	1	-	3
3	**Valtteri Bottas ***	Mercedes	1h21m59.286s	1	-	20
4	**Charles Leclerc**	Ferrari	1h22m01.674s	1	-	5
5	**Sergio Perez !!**	Red Bull	1h22m03.088s	1	-	8
6	**Carlos Sainz Jr.**	Ferrari	1h22m04.900s	1	-	6
7	**Lance Stroll**	Aston Martin	1h22m10.169s	1	-	9
8	**Fernando Alonso**	Alpine	1h22m11.566s	1	-	10
9	**George Russell**	Williams	1h22m14.107s	1	-	14
10	**Esteban Ocon**	Alpine	1h22m15.233s	1	-	12
11	**Nicholas Latifi**	Williams	1h22m18.108s	1	-	13
12	**Sebastian Vettel**	Aston Martin	1h22m18.986s	2	-	11
13	**Antonio Giovinazzi**	Alfa Romeo	1h22m21.581s	2	-	7
14	**Robert Kubica**	Alfa Romeo	1h22m24.134s	1	-	17
15	**Mick Schumacher**	Haas	1h22m45.453s	1	-	18
R	**Nikita Mazepin**	Haas	41 laps/power unit	3	-	16
R	**Max Verstappen**	Red Bull	25 laps/collision	0	-	1
R	**Lewis Hamilton**	Mercedes	25 laps/collision	0	-	4
R	**Pierre Gasly !**	AlphaTauri	3 laps/suspension	1	-	19
NS	**Yuki Tsunoda**	AlphaTauri	0 laps/brakes	0	-	15

FASTEST LAP: RICCIARDO, 1M24.812S, 152.791MPH/245.894KPH ON LAP 53 · RACE LEADERS: RICCIARDO 1-21 & 27-53, VERSTAPPEN 22, NORRIS 23, HAMILTON 24-25, LECLERC 26 · * MADE TO START AT BACK OF GRID FOR USING ADDITIONAL POWER UNIT ELEMENTS ! 5-PLACE GRID PENALTY FOR REPLACING GEARBOX · !! 5-PLACE RACE PENALTY FOR GAINING AN ADVANTAGE BY LEAVING THE TRACK. NB. GRID DETERMINED BY FINISHING ORDER IN SPRINT RACE

RUSSIAN GP

This was the one that got away from McLaren's Lando Norris when the rain fell late in the race. Yet, while he rued missing out on taking his first grand prix win, Lewis Hamilton nipped through to achieve a staggering feat in landing his 100th...

Buoyed by their one-two at Monza, McLaren had high hopes for the Russian GP and Lando Norris delivered by claiming pole. The 21-year-old was beaten away at the start by Ferrari's Carlos Sainz Jr. and had to trail around behind the Spaniard for a dozen laps before getting by.

With Max Verstappen having to start at the rear of the grid because of an engine change (as well as his three-place grid penalty collected at the Italian GP) this was a great opportunity for Hamilton to regain the championship lead, as he was starting fourth. Yet he was slow away and got demoted to seventh, running behind George Russell who had qualified an outstanding third, Lance Stroll, Daniel Ricciardo and Fernando Alonso.

Worse still for Hamilton, Verstappen moved rapidly up the order and was up to sixth by half-distance.

It looked as though Norris had everything in hand, as he was 10s clear of Hamilton going into the closing laps. Then, when rain began to fall with five laps to go, it was light at first, allowing Norris to press on. With little to lose, Verstappen came in for rain tyres, as he was seventh with little chance of making up ground to Hamilton who was running second if he didn't. Hamilton was brought in a lap later.

This is when Norris made a decision he would rue, electing to stay out on slick tyres, as the rain intensified and he was duly overhauled within a few corners by Hamilton and so lost his shot at victory. Worse than that, it was so wet that by the time he had pitted and rejoined with two laps to go, he was seventh, allowing Verstappen to come through to second and so minimise his loss to Hamilton.

Another driver who lost out was Charles Leclerc who, like Norris, stayed out too long and he tumbled all the way to 15th place.

SOCHI ROUND 15

DATE: **26 SEPTEMBER 2021**

Laps: **53** · Distance: **192.466 miles/309.745km** · Weather: **Warm & dry, then wet**

Pos	Driver	Team	Result	Stops	Qualifying Time	Grid
1	Lewis Hamilton	Mercedes	1h30m41.001s	2	1m44.050s	4
2	Max Verstappen !!!	Red Bull	1h31m34.272s	2	no time	20
3	Carlos Sainz Jr.	Ferrari	1h31m43.476s	2	1m42.510s	2
4	Daniel Ricciardo	McLaren	1h31m46.608s	2	1m44.156s	5
5	Valtteri Bottas !!	Mercedes	1h31m48.534s	2	1m44.710s	16
6	Fernando Alonso	Alpine	1h32m02.322s	2	1m44.204s	6
7	Lando Norris	McLaren	1h32m08.225s	2	1m41.993s	1
8	Kimi Raikkonen	Alfa Romeo	1h32m09.956s	2	1m49.586s	13
9	Sergio Perez	Red Bull	1h32m11.077s	2	1m45.337s	8
10	George Russell	Williams	1h32m21.552s	2	1m42.983s	3
11	Lance Stroll *	Aston Martin	1h32m37.199s	2	1m44.956s	7
12	Sebastian Vettel	Aston Martin	52 laps	2	1m46.573s	10
13	Pierre Gasly	AlphaTauri	52 laps	2	1m46.641s	11
14	Esteban Ocon	Alpine	52 laps	2	1m1m45.865s	9
15	Charles Leclerc !!!	Ferrari	52 laps	2	no time	19
16	Antonio Giovinazzi !	Alfa Romeo	52 laps	2	1m51.023s	17
17	Yuki Tsunoda	AlphaTauri	52 laps	3	1m46.751s	12
18	Nikita Mazepin	Haas	51 laps	2	1m53.764s	15
19	Nicholas Latifi !!!	Williams	47 laps/crash damage	2	no time	18
R	Mick Schumacher	Haas	32 laps/hydraulics	2	1m49.830s	14

FASTEST LAP: NORRIS, 1M37.423S, 134.276MPH/216.096KPH ON LAP 39 · RACE LEADERS: SAINZ JR. 1-12, NORRIS 13-28 & 37-50, PEREZ 29-36, HAMILTON 51-53 · * 10S PENALTY FOR CAUSING A COLLISION · ! 5-PLACE GRID PENALTY FOR REPLACING THE GEARBOX · !! 15-PLACE GRID PENALTY FOR USING ADDITIONAL POWER UNIT ELEMENTS · !!! MADE TO START FROM BACK OF THE GRID FOR USING ADDITIONAL POWER UNIT ELEMENTS

If 10 grand prix wins is great, Lewis ponders what adjective fits being the first driver to 100.

TURKISH GP

Valtteri Bottas was smiling after taking his first win of the year, but team-mate Lewis Hamilton certainly wasn't as he felt that his charge up the order had been spiked by his strategist bringing him in for a tyre change last in the race, leaving him to finish fifth.

Hamilton had been fastest in qualifying, but pole position went to Bottas instead because Hamilton's car had exceeded the permitted limit of extra power unit parts through the season. This meant that he was hit with a ten-place grid penalty. It would be the same for anyone, and it was introduced in an attempt to keep costs in check, but it's not the most popular rule from the fans' point-of-view either.

Bottas made the most of pole and led the field away on a wet track, pleased to be at the head of the ball of spray. Fernando Alonso was clipped at the first turn by Pierre Gasly when they went three abreast with Sergio Perez. It was clear that Mercedes had a performance advantage on this flowing circuit and the Finn was able to use it well to lead the field home easily, with Max Verstappen fully 14s behind at the chequered flag.

All Hamilton could do was pick off those ahead of him, which he did, reaching fifth place by lap 20. Just after mid-distance, he found a hard nut to crack in Perez. The Mexican was stout in defence, even when it looked as though the Mercedes driver had got ahead, and Red Bull Racing had to be pleased with his performance.

Hamilton was asked to come in for a fresh set of intermediate tyres on lap 42 but elected to stay out, perhaps enticed by the fact that he had closed to within 5s of Verstappen after Perez had pitted.

Eight laps later, strategist Pete Bonnington radioed Hamilton again and this time he came in, dropping from third to fifth when he emerged. Then, when he couldn't get his new tyres to work as he wanted them to, Hamilton became livid, being in danger of being caught by AlphaTauri's Gasly. He was able to remain in fifth but, with Verstappen taking 18 points for second, he left Turkey six points behind his Red Bull Racing rival.

Bottas improved a mediocre season by racing to victory after leading from pole in the wet.

111

ISTANBUL PARK ROUND 16

DATE: **10 OCTOBER 2021**

Laps: **58** • Distance: **192.249 miles/309.396km** • Weather: **Warm but drizzling**

Pos	Driver	Team	Result	Stops	Qualifying Time	Grid
1	**Valtteri Bottas**	Mercedes	1h31m04.103s	1	1m22.998s	1
2	**Max Verstappen**	Red Bull	1h31m18.687s	1	1m23.196s	2
3	**Sergio Perez**	Red Bull	1h31m37.574s	1	1m23.706s	6
4	**Charles Leclerc**	Ferrari	1h31m41.917s	1	1m23.265s	3
5	**Lewis Hamilton !**	Mercedes	1h31m45.915s	1	1m22.828s	11
6	**Pierre Gasly**	AlphaTauri	1h31m48.395s	1	1m23.326s	4
7	**Lando Norris**	McLaren	1h31m51.316s	1	1m23.954s	7
8	**Carlos Sainz Jr. !!**	Ferrari	1h31m55.629s	1	no time	19
9	**Lance Stroll**	Aston Martin	1h32m26.121s	1	1m24.305s	8
10	**Esteban Ocon**	Alpine	57 laps	0	1m24.842s	12
11	**Antonio Giovinazzi**	Alfa Romeo	57 laps	1	1m26.430s	16
12	**Kimi Raikkonen**	Alfa Romeo	57 laps	1	1m27.525s	17
13	**Daniel Ricciardo !!**	McLaren	57 laps	1	no time	20
14	**Yuki Tsunoda**	AlphaTauri	57 laps	1	1m24.368s	9
15	**George Russell**	Williams	57 laps	1	1m25.007s	13
16	**Fernando Alonso**	Alpine	57 laps	1	1m23.477s	5
17	**Nicholas Latifi**	Williams	57 laps	1	1m26.086s	15
18	**Sebastian Vettel**	Aston Martin	57 laps	2	1m24.795s	10
19	**Mick Schumacher**	Haas	56 laps	1	1m25.200s	14
20	**Nikita Mazepin**	Haas	56 laps	1	1m28.449s	18

FASTEST LAP: BOTTAS, 1M30.432S, 132.041MPH/212.500KPH ON LAP 58 • RACE LEADERS: BOTTAS 1-37 & 47-58, LECLERC 38-46 • ! 10-PLACE GRID PENALTY FOR USING ADDITIONAL POWER UNIT ELEMENTS • !! REQUIRED TO START FROM BACK OF GRID FOR USING ADDITIONAL POWER UNIT ELEMENTS

» UNITED STATES GP

This was an intense game of chess as fast-starting Lewis Hamilton took the upper hand, only to be outthought by the fast-reacting Red Bull Racing, which got Max Verstappen out of the pits ahead where, on shot tyres, he hung on to win.

It was tight into the first corner on lap 1, but Hamilton did just enough to be sure of diving up the inside to pass pole starter Verstappen for the lead. The Dutchman attached himself to the Mercedes driver's tail. But then, after just 10 laps, he dived into the pits to make the first of his two planned stops. This seemed early in a 56-lap race, but the tactician's consideration was to prove correct as, when Hamilton made his first stop three laps later, he came back out behind.

Now it was Mercedes' time to try to outthink Red Bull, but they couldn't as the tyre-hungry COTA surface reduced their options. The maths of making an early second pitstop then adding a third simply didn't add up. So, with his rear tyres going off, Verstappen was caught but not passed and hung on to win by 1.333s to extend his championship lead to 12 points.

Sergio Perez finished third and it was only then that fans discovered his drinks bottle had failed at the start and he was fading with dehydration as he hung on to finish third, a result that moved him into fourth in the rankings ahead of Lando Norris.

Charles Leclerc finished a further 10s back in fourth after dropping Daniel Ricciardo, while Ferrari team-mate Carlos Sainz Jr ended up seventh, upset at having been told early on to hand a place back to Lando Norris. He ended up one place down on Valtteri Bottas who didn't do the best job of coming forward from a five-place grid penalty.

For Alpine, it was a disaster, as both of its drivers dropped out of the running. First, Esteban Ocon had to pit for a new nose after clashing with Antonio Giovinazzi's Alfa Romeo. Then he exited with a collapsed rear end a few laps before Fernando Alonso quit, his rear wing giving way, blaming bumps in the circuit.

CIRCUIT OF THE AMERICAS ROUND 17 DATE: 24 OCTOBER 2021

Laps: 56 • Distance: 191.634 miles/308.405km • Weather: Hot & sunny

Pos	Driver	Team	Result	Stops	Qualifying Time	Grid
1	Max Verstappen	Red Bull	1h34m36.552s	2	1m32.910s	1
2	Lewis Hamilton	Mercedes	1h34m37.885s	2	1m33.119s	2
3	Sergio Perez	Red Bull	1h35m18.775s	2	1m33.134s	3
4	Charles Leclerc	Ferrari	1h35m28.798s	2	1m33.606s	4
5	Daniel Ricciardo	McLaren	1h35m53.406s	2	1m33.808s	6
6	Valtteri Bottas !	Mercedes	1h35m56.680s	2	1m33.475s	9
7	Carlos Sainz Jr	Ferrari	1h36m00.097s	2	1m33.792s	5
8	Lando Norris	McLaren	1h36m00.947s	2	1m33.887s	7
9	Yuki Tsunoda	AlphaTauri	55 laps	2	1m34.918s	10
10	Sebastian Vettel !!	Aston Martin	55 laps	2	1m35.500s	18
11	Antonio Giovinazzi	Alfa Romeo	55 laps	2	1m35.794s	12
12	Lance Stroll	Aston Martin	55 laps	2	1m35.983s	13
13	Kimi Raikkonen	Alfa Romeo	55 laps	2	1m36.311s	15
14	George Russell !!	Williams	55 laps	2	no time	20
15	Nicholas Latifi	Williams	55 laps	2	1m35.995s	14
16	Mick Schumacher	Haas	54 laps	2	1m36.499s	16
17	Nikita Mazepin	Haas	54 laps	3	1m36.796s	17
R	Fernando Alonso !!	Alpine	49 laps/wing	3	1m44.549s	19
R	Esteban Ocon	Alpine	40 laps/rear end	2	1m35.377s	11
R	Pierre Gasly	AlphaTauri	14 laps/suspension	1	1m34.118s	8

FASTEST LAP: HAMILTON, 1M38.485S, 125.219MPH/201.521KPH ON LAP 41 • RACE LEADERS: HAMILTON 1-13 & 30-37, VERSTAPPEN 14-29 & 38-56 • ! 5-PLACE GRID PENALTY FOR USING AN ADDITIONAL POWER UNIT ELEMENT • !! REQUIRED TO START FROM BACK OF GRID FOR USING ADDITIONAL POWER UNIT ELEMENTS

Hamilton led at COTA, but Red Bull Racing helped Verstappen emerge in front and stay there.

MEXICAN GP

Red Bull Racing was expected to have a performance advantage at altitude, but somehow didn't fill the front row, as Mercedes did. No matter, Max Verstappen went around the outside into Turn 1. And that was that, with nothing Lewis Hamilton could do to defeat him.

The technicalities of whether Mercedes or Red Bull ought to have been better in the thin air of Mexico were much discussed. Reckoning that Red Bull's high-rake design would give it an advantage, people were shocked when the Mercedes outqualified them, Valtteri Bottas taking pole ahead of Hamilton.

Then came the start and Bottas made a bad one. This allowed Verstappen to get into his tow, use that and then pull alongside on the run to the first corner, making it three abreast. He then simply drove around the outside of Bottas, who was then thumped from behind by a locked-up Daniel Ricciardo, sending his McLaren to the pits for a replacement nose. Bottas came in as well as both opted to take the moment for a set of hard compound tyres. Mercedes team principal Toto Wolff was less than happy that Bottas had stayed in the middle of the track rather than heading to the lefthand side to block Verstappen on the long drag to Turn 1.

In the avoiding action behind, Esteban Ocon was lucky to get away with being squeezed by Yuki Tusnoda and Mick Schumacher, both of whom retired.

Verstappen simply controlled the race from there. Hamilton soon realised he had no hope of matching the Red Bull driver's pace. In fact, the story of what then turned into a processional race was whether Sergio Perez could pass Hamilton. His home crowd urged him on, but he came up just short.

With McLaren's hopes dented by Ricciardo having to pit for a new nose and Lando Norris having to start from 18th on the grid, Ferrari stole an advantage with updates to its hybrid system and moved up to third in the points table as Charles Leclerc and Carlos Sainz Jr finished fifth and sixth.

Max Verstappen leads as Valtteri Bottas is spun around on the first lap of the Mexican GP.

MEXICO CITY ROUND 18

DATE: 7 NOVEMBER 2021

Laps: **71** • Distance: **189.738 miles/305.354km** • Weather: **Sunny & warm**

Pos	Driver	Team	Result	Stops	Qualifying Time	Grid
1	**Max Verstappen**	Red Bull	1h38m39.086s	1	1m16.225s	3
2	**Lewis Hamilton**	Mercedes	1h38m55.641s	1	1m16.020s	2
3	**Sergio Perez**	Red Bull	1h38m56.838s	1	1m16.342s	4
4	**Pierre Gasly**	AlphaTauri	1h39m42.931s	1	1m16.456s	5
5	**Charles Leclerc**	Ferrari	1h40m00.123s	1	1m16.837s	8
6	**Carlos Sainz Jr**	Ferrari	70 laps	1	1m16.761s	6
7	**Sebastian Vettel**	Aston Martin	70 laps	1	1m17.746s	9
8	**Kimi Raikkonen**	Alfa Romeo	70 laps	1	1m17.958s	10
9	**Fernando Alonso**	Alpine	70 laps	1	1m18.452s	12
10	**Lando Norris !**	McLaren	70 laps	1	1m36.830s	18
11	**Antonio Giovinazzi**	Alfa Romeo	70 laps	1	1m18.290s	11
12	**Daniel Ricciardo**	McLaren	70 laps	2	1m16.763s	7
13	**Esteban Ocon !**	Alpine	70 laps	1	1m18.405s	19
14	**Lance Stroll *!**	Aston Martin	69 laps	2	1m20.873s	20
15	**Valtteri Bottas**	Mercedes	69 laps	4	1m15.875s	1
16	**George Russell ***	Williams	69 laps	1	1m18.172s	16
17	**Nicholas Latifi**	Williams	69 laps	2	1m18.756s	13
18	**Nikita Mazepin**	Haas	68 laps	2	1m19.303s	15
R	**Mick Schumacher**	Haas	0 laps/collision	0	1m18.858s	14
R	**Yuki Tsunoda !**	AlphaTauri	0 laps/collision	0	1m17.158s	17

FASTEST LAP: BOTTAS, 1M17.774S, 123.791MPH/199.223KPH ON LAP 69 • RACE LEADERS: VERSTAPPEN 1-33 & 40-71, PEREZ 34-39
* 5-PLACE GRID PENALTY FOR REPLACING THE GEARBOX • ! REQUIRED TO START FROM BACK OF GRID FOR USING ADDITIONAL POWER UNIT ELEMENTS

» SAO PAULO GP

Lewis Hamilton reckoned that this win was better than any of the hundred that went before it. Indeed, he has never had to eradicate the equivalent of a 25-place grid penalty before. Catching and passing Max Verstappen in a real scrap made it all the sweeter.

Consider the facts: Hamilton's Mercedes was found to have a rear wing that exceeded the permissible limits of its DRS operation, so he was disqualified after qualifying and put to the back of the grid. Fortunately, there was a sprint race, not just a regular grand prix.

Driving like a man possessed, he picked off car after car to climb to fifth. Then, with additional power unit elements required, he was put back five places, meaning that he would start the main race from tenth on the grid, with Verstappen starting second behind Valtteri Bottas.

Pole didn't convert into the lead for the Finn, though, as Verstappen passed him at the start. Hamilton made even greater progress by passing four rivals on the opening lap. And he kept advancing from there, being waved past by Bottas then having to fight to pass Sergio Perez. That left just Verstappen and it was clear that Hamilton's new engine gave him a considerable straight-line advantage.

The gap between them came down until Hamilton nosed in front coming out of the Curva do Sol on lap 48 of 71. He had the outside line into the Descida do Lago lefthander at the foot of the hill and when Verstappen either braked too late or simply didn't steer enough into the corner, both cars went off onto the painted area beyond the kerbing, before rejoining. Mercedes' principal Toto Wolff sought punishment for Verstappen, but the stewards declined.

Yet, Hamilton's speed was too much for Verstappen and he soon passed before pulling away not just to take win number 101 by more than 10s in a drive heralded as one of the all-time greats, but to reduce his points deficit to the Dutch racer to just 14 with three races remaining. Had he not won, then the margin would have multiplied to twice that.

INTERLAGOS ROUND 19

DATE: 14 NOVEMBER 2021

Laps: **71** · Distance: **190.064 miles/305.879km** · Weather: **Hot & sunny**

Pos	Driver	Team	Result	Stops	Qualifying Time	Grid
1	**Lewis Hamilton !**	Mercedes	1h32m22.851s	2	-	10
2	**Max Verstappen**	Red Bull	1h32m33.347s	2	-	2
3	**Valtteri Bottas**	Mercedes	1h32m36.427s	2	-	1
4	**Sergio Perez**	Red Bull	1h33m02.791s	3	-	4
5	**Charles Leclerc**	Ferrari	1h33m12.368s	2	-	6
6	**Carlos Sainz Jr.**	Ferrari	1h33m14.671s	2	-	3
7	**Pierre Gasly**	AlphaTauri	70 laps	2	-	7
8	**Esteban Ocon**	Alpine	70 laps	1	-	8
9	**Fernando Alonso**	Alpine	70 laps	1	-	12
10	**Lando Norris**	McLaren	70 laps	2	-	5
11	**Sebastian Vettel**	Aston Martin	70 laps	2	-	9
12	**Kimi Raikkonen !!**	Alfa Romeo	70 laps	2	-	20
13	**George Russell**	Williams	70 laps	2	-	17
14	**Antonio Giovinazzi**	Alfa Romeo	70 laps	2	-	13
15	**Yuki Tsunoda**	AlphaTauri	70 laps	2	-	15
16	**Nicholas Latifi**	Williams	70 laps	2	-	16
17	**Nikita Mazepin**	Haas	69 laps	1	-	19
18	**Mick Schumacher**	Haas	69 laps	3	-	18
R	**Daniel Ricciardo**	McLaren	49 laps/power unit	1	-	11
R	**Lance Stroll**	Aston Martin	47 laps/crash damage	1	-	14

FASTEST LAP: PEREZ, 1M11.010S, 135.740MPH/218.453PH ON LAP 71 · RACE LEADERS: VERSTAPPEN 1-27, 31-39 & 44-58, BOTTAS 28-30, HAMILTON 40-43 & 59-71 · ! 5-PLACE GRID PENALTY FOR USING ADDITIONAL POWER UNIT ELEMENTS · !! MADE TO START AT BACK OF GRID FOR CAR BEING MODIFIED IN PARC FERME

Max Verstappen forces Lewis Hamilton wide at Descida do Lago as they fight for the lead.

QATAR GP

Lewis Hamilton made it two wins in a row to close the gap to championship leader Max Verstappen after leading every lap from pole for Mercedes. Alpine's Fernando Alonso followed them home in third place for his first podium finish since 2014.

As the teams turned up at Losail for their third grand prix in three weekends, tension continued to simmer between Mercedes and Red Bull Racing, with principals Toto Wolff and Christian Horner enacting a battle of soundbites. However, the first time Qatar hosted a round of the World Championship will be remembered for several other matters.

One was the way that Hamilton dominated qualifying and the race. Another will be the way that Verstappen had to fight back to second place after a five-place penalty made him start seventh on the grid. The third will be how Horner blamed a "rogue" marshal for waving a double yellow flag that didn't show up on Verstappen's steering wheel warning system or on trackside warning panels. He thus ignored it and was punished with his grid penalty. The final thing will be the punctures that shaped the outcome of this race as they struck three of the cars, most dramatically leading to Valtteri Bottas's retirement from car damage suffered as he returned to the pits.

The story of the race is a simple one, as it was Hamilton all the way. Verstappen knew that he had to gain places quickly and he did, making up places away from the start and passing Pierre Gasly's AlphaTauri for second on lap 5. After that, no one else was in with a shout, such was this pair's dominance. Their speed also gave them the option of pitting twice without fear of being passed by the best of the one-stoppers.

While Hamilton always had the measure of Verstappen, the chief interest was over who would finish third and, at the end, it was Alonso who had to hold off Sergio Perez in the second Red Bull in the closing laps as the two-stopping Mexican came at him. Contributing to a great day for Alpine in its quest to usurp AlphaTauri, Esteban Ocon was fifth to the finish.

Lewis Hamilton blasts into the lead at the start of the inaugural Qatar GP at Losail.

LOSAIL ROUND 20

DATE: 21 NOVEMBER 2021

Laps: 57 • Distance: **190.549 miles/306.660km** • Weather: **Warm & dry**

Pos	Driver	Team	Result	Stops	Qualifying Time	Grid
1	Lewis Hamilton	Mercedes	1h24m28.471s	2	1m20.827s	1
2	Max Verstappen !!	Red Bull	1h24m54.214s	3	1m21.424s	7
3	Fernando Alonso	Alpine	1h25m27.928s	1	1m21.670s	3
4	Sergio Perez	Red Bull	1h25m30.777s	2	1m22.346s	11
5	Esteban Ocon	Alpine	1h25m49.041s	1	1m22.028s	9
6	Lance Stroll	Aston Martin	1h25m49.745s	1	1m22.460s	12
7	Carlos Sainz Jr	Ferrari	1h25m50.382s	1	1m21.840s	5
8	Charles Leclerc	Ferrari	1h25m51.597s	1	1m22.463s	13
9	Lando Norris	McLaren	56 laps	2	1m21.731s	4
10	Sebastian Vettel	Aston Martin	56 laps	1	1m22.785s	10
11	Pierre Gasly	AlphaTauri	56 laps	2	1m21.640s	2
12	Daniel Ricciardo	McLaren	56 laps	1	1m22.597s	14
13	Yuki Tsunoda	AlphaTauri	56 laps	2	1m21.881s	8
14	Kimi Raikkonen	Alfa Romeo	56 laps	2	1m23.156s	16
15	Antonio Giovinazzi	Alfa Romeo	56 laps	2	1m23.262s	18
16	Mick Schumacher	Haas	56 laps	1	1m23.407s	19
17	George Russell	Williams	55 laps	2	1m22.756s	15
18	Nikita Mazepin	Haas	55 laps	1	1m25.859s	20
R	Nicholas Latifi	Williams	50 laps/puncture	1	1m23.213s	17
R	Valtteri Bottas !	Mercedes	48 laps/car damage	2	1m21.478s	6

FASTEST LAP: VERSTAPPEN, 1M23.196S, 144.654MPH/232.799KPH ON LAP 57 • RACE LEADERS: HAMILTON 1-57
! 3-PLACE GRID PENALTY FOR NOT HEEDING YELLOW FLAG • !! 5-PLACE GRID PENALTY FOR NOT HEEDING DOUBLE YELLOW FLAG

SAUDI ARABIAN GP

This was gloves off fighting between Lewis Hamilton and Max Verstappen in a play of three parts, after two early red flags at the Jeddah Corniche circuit changed the order one way and then the other. Eventually, Hamilton won to set the stage for the final round.

This was a year's worth of soap opera crammed into one event. First, there was Verstappen's brilliant qualifying lap that stumbled coming out of the final corner. So, Hamilton took pole and his rival started third behind Valtteri Bottas.

The start was clean but the safety car came out early on after Mick Schumacher clipped a wall. Most pitted, but Verstappen, running third, did not. Then out came the red flags and that move suddenly looked inspired, as he could change to the harder tyres and retain the lead for the restart. Hamilton was livid, not sure that the stoppage was merited.

At the restart, Hamilton got inside Verstappen, the Dutchman was forced wide, but came back on in front by Turn 2. Behind them, Bottas triggered a chain reaction, with Sergio Perez spun by Charles Leclerc and George Russell hit by Nikita Mazepin. Red flag two.

Then came the decision about Verstappen having to hand back a place for gaining it by going off the track. This promoted Esteban Ocon to pole for the second restart, with Hamilton second. When the lights went green, Verstappen used his medium compound tyres to pass Hamilton and Ocon. Hamilton quickly took second and set off after Verstappen.

After a virtual safety car, triggered by Yuki Tsunoda, Hamilton went for the lead. He and Verstappen touched, the latter went wide and was then told to hand the place back. When he slowed, however, Hamilton had not yet been told and hit the Red Bull up the rear.

Verstappen then gave the place back and immediately passed Hamilton again. But Hamilton used the DRS two laps later to retake the lead. Extraordinary. Finally, Verstappen told the team his tyres were gone and accepted second, with Bottas passing Ocon on the final straight for third.

JEDDAH ROUND 21

DATE: **5 DECEMBER 2021**

Laps: **50** · Distance: **191.817 miles/308.700km** · Weather: **Warm & dry**

Pos	Driver	Team	Result	Stops	Qualifying Time	Grid
1	Lewis Hamilton	Mercedes	2h06m15.118s	3	1m27.511s	1
2	Max Verstappen * !!	Red Bull	2h06m36.943s	2	1m27.653s	3
3	Valtteri Bottas	Mercedes	2h06m42.649s	3	1m27.622s	2
4	Esteban Ocon	Alpine	2h06m42.751s	2	1m28.647s	9
5	Daniel Ricciardo	McLaren	2h06m55.239s	2	1m28.668s	11
6	Pierre Gasly	AlphaTauri	2h06m56.731s	2	1m28.125s	6
7	Charles Leclerc	Ferrari	2h06m59.593s	3	1m28.054s	4
8	Carlos Sainz Jr	Ferrari	2h07m01.724s	2	1m53.652s	15
9	Antonio Giovinazzi	Alfa Romeo	2h07m13.623s	2	1m28.754s	10
10	Lando Norris	McLaren	2h07m16.476s	3	1m28.180s	7
11	Lance Stroll	Aston Martin	2h07m32.330s	3	1m29.368s	18
12	Nicholas Latifi	Williams	2h07m38.367s	3	1m29.177s	16
13	Fernando Alonso	Alpine	49 laps	4	1m28.920s	13
14	Yuki Tsunoda !	AlphaTauri	49 laps	3	1m28.442s	8
15	Kimi Raikkonen	Alfa Romeo	49 laps	3	1m28.885s	12
R	Sebastian Vettel	Aston Martin	44 laps/crash damage	0	1m29.198s	17
R	Sergio Perez	Red Bull	14 laps/accident	0	1m28.123s	5
R	George Russell	Williams	14 laps/accident	2	1m29.054s	14
R	Nikita Mazepin	Haas	14 laps/accident	0	1m30.473s	20
R	Mick Schumacher	Haas	8 laps/accident	0	1m29.464s	19

FASTEST LAP: HAMILTON, 1M30.734S, 152.212MPH/244.962KPH ON LAP 47 · RACE LEADERS: HAMILTON 1-10 & 43-50, VERSTAPPEN 11-15 & 17-42, OCON 16 · * 5-SECOND PENALTY FOR LEAVING TRACK AND GAINING AN ADVANTAGE · ! 5-SECOND PENALTY FOR CAUSING A COLLISION · !! 10-SECOND PENALTY FOR CAUSING A COLLISION

Verstappen dives up the inside of Hamilton and Esteban Ocon at the second restart.

ABU DHABI GP

People were worried that there would be a clash between Max Verstappen and Lewis Hamilton on the opening lap, but there was none. However, what happened in the lead-up to the final lap decided both the race and title in the Dutchman's favour.

Mercedes arrived with momentum on their side, but Verstappen produced a wondrous qualifying lap to take pole by 0.3s. He wasted this by getting wheelspin at the start and Hamilton shot into the lead. Verstappen fought back and dived inside him cleanly at Turn 7. Hamilton went wide and came back on in the lead and was allowed to keep it, upsetting Red Bull Racing.

Having started on soft tyres, Verstappen pitted first, on lap 13. Hamilton followed suit a lap later and resumed in a lead that he extended at will, emphasising how Mercedes had re-established its upper hand for the final three races.

By not pitting, Sergio Perez took over the lead and delayed Hamilton, lopping his advantage over the Dutchman from 7s to just 1s in two laps. Verstappen was back in the mix, but then the gap opened again so he queried whether he would pit for more fresh tyres. The team did the maths and said there was no decision, yet.

Having waited for Bottas to pit, Verstappen was brought in on lap 37 and emerged still second but now some 17s down with 20 laps to go. At first the gap came down, then the rate of gain fell away. Hamilton had this in the bag and Red Bull had no answers. Indeed, with 10 laps to go, team principal Christian Horner admitted that a miracle was needed.

Horner got his wish when Nicholas Latifi crashed on lap 51 and the safety car was scrambled. Then came confusion about whether or not the lapped cars would be waved past. They were, but not all of them, with race director Michael Masi hurrying things to be sure that they got one final racing lap. Verstappen started this on Hamilton's tail and made the most of the gift to dive by at Turn 5. And that was that, with protests from Mercedes eventually rejected.

Lewis Hamilton congratulates Max Verstappen after a stunning finish to the Abu Dhabi GP.

YAS MARINA ROUND 22

DATE: 12 DECEMBER 2021

Laps: 58 · Distance: **190.324 miles/306.298km** · Weather: **Warm & dry**

Pos	Driver	Team	Result	Stops	Qualifying Time	Grid
1	**Max Verstappen**	Red Bull	1h30m17.345s	3	1m22.109s	1
2	**Lewis Hamilton**	Mercedes	1h30m19.601s	1	1m22.480s	2
3	**Carlos Sainz Jr**	Ferrari	1h30m22.518s	1	1m22.992s	5
4	**Yuki Tsunoda**	AlphaTauri	1h30m23.037s	2	1m23.220s	8
5	**Pierre Gasly**	AlphaTauri	1h30m23.876s	2	1m24.043s	12
6	**Valtteri Bottas**	Mercedes	1h30m24.808s	1	1m23.036s	6
7	**Lando Norris**	McLaren	1h31m16.545s	2	1m22.931s	3
8	**Fernando Alonso**	Alpine	1h31m19.053s	1	1m23.460s	11
9	**Esteban Ocon**	Alpine	1h31m21.371s	1	1m23.389s	9
10	**Charles Leclerc**	Ferrari	1h31m23.402s	2	1m23.122s	7
11	**Sebastian Vettel**	Aston Martin	1h31m24.872s	1	1m24.305s	15
12	**Daniel Ricciardo**	McLaren	57 laps	2	1m23.409s	10
13	**Lance Stroll**	Aston Martin	57 laps	2	1m24.066s	13
14	**Mick Schumacher**	Haas	57 laps	2	1m24.906s	19
15	**Sergio Perez**	Red Bull	55 laps/mechanical	3	1m22.947s	4
R	**Nicholas Latifi**	Williams	50 laps/accident	1	1m24.338s	16
R	**Antonio Giovinazzi**	Alfa Romeo	33 laps/gearbox	0	1m24.251s	14
R	**George Russell**	Williams	26 laps/gearbox	1	1m24.423s	17
R	**Kimi Raikkonen**	Alfa Romeo	25 laps/brakes	1	1m24.779s	18
NS	**Nikita Mazepin**	Haas	0 laps/COVID	0	1m25.685s	20

FASTEST LAP: **VERSTAPPEN, 1M26.103S, 137.198MPH/220.800KPH ON LAP 39** · RACE LEADERS: HAMILTON 1-14 & 21-57, PEREZ 15-20, VERSTAPPEN 58

⟫ FINAL RESULTS 2021

POS	DRIVER	NAT	CAR-ENGINE	R1	R2	R3	R4	R5	R6
1	MAX VERSTAPPEN	NED	RED BULL-HONDA RB16B	2P	1	2	2F	1	18
2	LEWIS HAMILTON	GBR	MERCEDES F1 W12	1	2PF	1	1P	7F	15
2	VALTTERI BOTTAS	FIN	MERCEDES F1 W12	3F	R	3PF	3	R	12
4	SERGIO PEREZ	MEX	RED BULL-HONDA RB16B	5	11	4	5	4	1
5	CARLOS SAINZ JR	ESP	FERRARI SF21	8	5	11	7	2	8
6	LANDO NORRIS	GBR	McLAREN-MERCEDES MCL35M	4	3	5	8	3	5
7	CHARLES LECLERC	MON	FERRARI SF21	6	4	6	4	NSP	4F
8	DANIEL RICCIARDO	AUS	McLAREN-MERCEDES MCL35M	7	6	9	6	12	9
9	PIERRE GASLY	FRA	ALPHATAURI-HONDA AT02	17	7	10	10	6	3
10	FERNANDO ALONSO	ESP	ALPINE-RENAULT A521	R	10	8	17	13	6
11	ESTEBAN OCON	FRA	ALPINE-RENAULT A521	13	9	7	9	9	9
12	SEBASTIAN VETTEL	GER	ASTON MARTIN-MERCEDES AMR21	15	15	13	13	5	2
13	LANCE STROLL	CDN	ASTON MARTIN-MERCEDES AMR21	10	8	14	11	8	R
14	YUKI TSUNODA	JAP	ALPHATAURI-HONDA AT02	9	12	15	R	16	7
15	GEORGE RUSSELL	GBR	WILLIAMS-MERCEDES FW43B	14	R	16	14	14	17
16	KIMI RAIKKONEN	FIN	ALFA ROMEO-FERRARI C41	11	13	R	12	11	10
17	NICHOLAS LATIFI	CDN	WILLIAMS-MERCEDES FW43B	18	R	18	16	15	16
18	ANTONIO GIOVINAZZI	ITA	ALFA ROMEO-FERRARI C41	12	14	12	15	10	11
19	MICK SCHUMACHER	GER	HAAS-FERRARI VF-21	16	16	17	18	18	13
20	ROBERT KUBICA	POL	ALFA ROMEO-FERRARI C41	-	-	-	-	-	
21	NIKITA MAZEPIN	RUS	HAAS-FERRARI VF-21	R	17	19	19	17	

GP SCORING

1st	25 points	1st	3 points
2nd	18 points	2nd	2 points
3rd	15 points	3rd	1 points
4th	12 points		
5th	10 points		
6th	8 points		
7th	6 points		
8th	4 points		
9th	2 points		
10th	1 point		

(SPRINT columns: 1st 3 points, 2nd 2 points, 3rd 1 points)

Fastest lap 1 point (only applied to top-10 finishes)

POS	TEAM-ENGINE	R1	R2	R3	R4	R5	R6
1	MERCEDES (+10 F, +9 S#)	1/3	2/R	1/3	1/3	7/R	12/
2	RED BULL-HONDA (+8 F, +7 S#)	2/5	1/11	2/4	2/5	1/4	1/1
3	FERRARI (+1 S#)	6/8	4/5	6/11	4/7	2/NS	4/
4	McLAREN-MERCEDES (+2 F, +1 S#)	4/7	3/6	5/9	6/8	3/12	5/
5	ALPINE-RENAULT	13/R	9/10	7/8	9/17	9/13	6/
6	ALPHATAURI-HONDA (+1 F)	9/17	7/12	10/15	10/R	6/16	3/
7	ASTON MARTIN-MERCEDES	10/15	8/15	13/14	11/13	5/8	2/
8	WILLIAMS-MERCEDES	14/18	R/R	16/18	14/16	14/15	16/
9	ALFA ROMEO-FERRARI	11/12	13/14	12/R	12/15	10/11	10/
10	HAAS-FERRARI	16/R	16/17	17/19	18/19	17/18	13/

SYMBOLS AND GRAND PRIX KEY

ROUND 1	BAHRAIN GP	ROUND 7	FRENCH GP	ROUND 13	DUTCH GP	ROUND 19	SAO PAOLO GP
ROUND 2	EMILIA ROMAGNA GP	ROUND 8	STYRIAN GP	ROUND 14	ITALIAN GP	ROUND 20	QATAR GP
ROUND 3	PORTUGUESE GP	ROUND 9	AUSTRIAN GP	ROUND 15	RUSSIAN GP	ROUND 21	SAUDI ARABIAN GP
ROUND 4	SPANISH GP	ROUND 10	BRITISH GP	ROUND 16	TURKISH GP	ROUND 22	ABU DHABI GP
ROUND 5	MONACO GP	ROUND 11	HUNGARIAN GP	ROUND 17	UNITED STATES GP		
ROUND 6	AZERBAIJAN GP	ROUND 12	BELGIAN GP	ROUND 18	MEXICAN GP		

DQ DISQUALIFIED **F** FASTEST LAP **NC** NOT CLASSIFIED **NS** NON-STARTER **P** POLE POSITION **R** RETIRED **S**[#] SPRINT **W** WITHDRAWN

R7	R8	R9	R10	R11	R12	R13	R14	R15	R16	R17	R18	R19	R20	R21	R22	TOTAL
1PF	1P	1PF	RPS[1]	9	1P	1	RS[2]	2	2	1P	1	2S[2]	2F	2	1PF	395.5
2	2F	4	1S[2]	2P	3	2F	R	1	5	2F	2	1	1P	1PF	2	387.5
4	3	2	3S[3]	R	12	3	3S[1]	5	1PF	6	15PF	3PS[1]	R	3	6	226
3	4	6	16F	R	19	8	5	9	3	3	3	4F	4	R	15	190
11	6	5	6	3	10	7	6	3	8	7	6	6S[3]	7	8	3	164.5
5	5	3	4	R	14	10	2	7PF	7	8	10	10	9	10	7	160
16	7	8	2	R	8	5	4	15	4	4	5	5	8	7	10	159
6	13	7	5	11	4	11	1PFS[3]	4	13	5	12	R	12	5	12	115
7	R	9	11	5F	6	4	R	13	6	R	4	7	11	6	5	110
8	9	10	7	4	11	6	8	6	16	R	9	9	3	13	8	81
14	14	R	9	1	7	9	10	14	10	R	13	8	5	4	9	74
9	12	17	R	DQ2	5	13	12	12	18	10	7	11	10	R	11	43
10	8	13	8	R	20	12	7	11	9	12	14	R	6	11	13	34
13	10	12	10	6	15	R	NS	17	14	9	R	15	13	14	4	32
12	R	11	12	8	2	17	9	10	15	14	16	13	R	R	R	16
17	11	15	15	10	18	-	-	8	12	13	8	12	14	15	R	10
18	17	16	14	7	9	16	11	19	17	15	17	16	R	12	R	7
15	15	14	13	13	13	14	13	16	11	11	11	14	15	9	R	3
19	16	18	18	12	16	18	15	R	19	16	R	18	16	R	14	0
-	-	-	-	-	15	14	-	-	-	-	-	-	-	-	-	0
20	18	19	17	R	17F	R	R	18	20	17	18	17	18	R	NS	0

R7	R8	R9	R10	R11	R12	R13	R14	R15	R16	R17	R18	R19	R20	R21	R22	TOTAL
2/4	2/3	2/4	1/3	2/R	3/12	2/3	3/R	1/5	1/5	2/6	2/15	1/3	1/R	1/3	2/6	613.5
1/3	1/4	1/6	16/R	9/R	1/19	1/8	5/R	2/9	2/3	1/3	1/3	2/4	2/4	2/R	1/15	585.5
11/16	6/7	5/8	2/6	3/R	8/10	5/7	4/6	3/15	4/8	4/7	5/6	5/6	7/8	7/8	3/10	323.5
5/6	5/13	3/7	4/5	11/R	4/14	10/11	1/2	4/7	7/13	5/8	10/12	10/R	9/12	5/10	7/12	275
8/14	9/14	10/R	7/9	1/4	7/11	6/9	8/10	6/14	10/16	R/R	9/13	8/9	3/5	4/13	8/9	155
7/13	10/R	9/12	10/11	5/6	6/15	4/R	R/NS	13/17	6/14	9/R	4/R	7/15	11/13	6/14	4/5	142
9/10	8/12	13/17	8/R	DQ/R	5/20	12/13	7/12	11/12	9/18	10/12	7/14	11/R	6/10	11/R	11/13	77
12/18	17/R	11/16	12/14	7/8	2/9	16/R	9/11	10/19	15/17	14/15	16/17	17/18	16/18	12/R	R/R	23
15/17	11/15	14/15	13/15	10/13	13/18	14/15	13/14	8/16	11/12	11/13	8/11	12/14	14/15	9/15	R/R	13
19/20	16/18	18/19	17/18	12/R	16/17	18/R	15/R	18/R	19/20	16/17	18/R	17/18	16/18	R/R	14/NS	0

⟩⟩ FORMULA ONE RECORDS

STARTS

DRIVERS

349	Kimi Raikkonen	(FIN)	181	Romain Grosjean	(FRA)	128	Mario Andretti	(USA)
336	Fernando Alonso	(SPA)	180	Ralf Schumacher	(GER)		Adrian Sutil	(GER)
325	Rubens Barrichello	(BRA)	178	Valtteri Bottas	(FIN)	126	Jack Brabham	(AUS)
308	Michael Schumacher	(GER)	176	Graham Hill	(GBR)	123	Ronnie Peterson	(SWE)
307	Jenson Button	(GBR)	175	Jacques Laffite	(FRA)	120	Kevin Magnussen	(DEN)
288	Lewis Hamilton	(GBR)	171	Niki Lauda	(AUT)	119	Pierluigi Martini	(ITA)
280	Sebastian Vettel	(GER)	165	Jacques Villeneuve	(CDN)	116	Damon Hill	(GBR)
270	Felipe Massa	(BRA)	163	Thierry Boutsen	(BEL)		Jacky Ickx	(BEL)
256	Riccardo Patrese	(ITA)	162	Mika Hakkinen	(FIN)		Alan Jones	(AUS)
	Jarno Trulli	(ITA)		Johnny Herbert	(GBR)	114	Keke Rosberg	(FIN)
247	David Coulthard	(GBR)	161	Ayrton Senna	(BRA)		Patrick Tambay	(FRA)
230	Giancarlo Fisichella	(ITA)	159	Heinz-Harald Frentzen	(GER)	112	Denny Hulme	(NZL)
216	Mark Webber	(AUS)	158	Martin Brundle	(GBR)		Daniil Kvyat	(RUS)
213	Sergio Perez	(MEX)		Olivier Panis	(FRA)		Jody Scheckter	(RSA)
210	Gerhard Berger	(AUT)	152	John Watson	(GBR)	111	Heikki Kovalainen	(FIN)
	Daniel Ricciardo	(AUS)	149	Rene Arnoux	(FRA)		John Surtees	(GBR)
208	Andrea de Cesaris	(ITA)	147	Eddie Irvine	(GBR)	109	Philippe Alliot	(FRA)
206	Nico Rosberg	(GER)		Derek Warwick	(GBR)		Mika Salo	(FIN)
204	Nelson Piquet	(BRA)	146	Carlos Reutemann	(ARG)	108	Elio de Angelis	(ITA)
201	Jean Alesi	(FRA)	144	Emerson Fittipaldi	(BRA)	106	Jos Verstappen	(NED)
199	Alain Prost	(FRA)	141	Carlos Sainz Jr	(SPA)	104	Jo Bonnier	(SWE)
194	Michele Alboreto	(ITA)		Max Verstappen	(NED)		Pedro de la Rosa	(SPA)
190	Jacques Laffite	(FRA)	135	Jean-Pierre Jarier	(FRA)		Jochen Mass	(GER)
187	Nigel Mansell	(GBR)	132	Eddie Cheever	(USA)	100	Bruce McLaren	(NZL)
182	Nico Hulkenberg	(GER)		Clay Regazzoni	(SWI)		Lance Stroll	(CDN)

CONSTRUCTORS

1,030	Ferrari	524	Alfa Romeo II (*nee* Sauber	230	March
903	McLaren		including BMW Sauber)	197	BRM
822	Williams	492	Lotus	132	Osella
694	Alpine (*nee* Toleman then	460	Red Bull (*nee* Stewart	129	Renault
	Benetton then Renault II, Lotus II		then Jaguar Racing)	122	Haas
	& Renault III)	425	Mercedes GP (*nee* BAR then		
648	AlphaTauri (*nee* Minardi then		Honda Racing then Brawn GP)		
	Toro Rosso)	418	Tyrrell		
557	Aston Martin II (*nee* Jordan then	409	Prost (*nee* Ligier)		
	Midland then Spyker then Force	394	Brabham		
	India then Racing Point)	383	Arrows		

DRIVERS

103	Lewis Hamilton	(GBR)		Max Verstappen	(NED)		James Hunt	(GBR)
91	Michael Schumacher	(GER)	16	Stirling Moss	(GBR)		Ronnie Peterson	(SWE)
53	Sebastian Vettel	(GER)	15	Jenson Button	(GBR)		Jody Scheckter	(RSA)
51	Alain Prost	(FRA)	14	Jack Brabham	(AUS)	9	Mark Webber	(AUS)
41	Ayrton Senna	(BRA)		Emerson Fittipaldi	(BRA)	8	Denny Hulme	(NZL)
32	Fernando Alonso	(SPA)		Graham Hill	(GBR)		Jacky Ickx	(BEL)
31	Nigel Mansell	(GBR)	13	Alberto Ascari	(ITA)		Daniel Ricciardo	(AUS)
27	Jackie Stewart	(GBR)		David Coulthard	(GBR)	7	Rene Arnoux	(FRA)
25	Jim Clark	(GBR)	12	Mario Andretti	(USA)		Juan Pablo Montoya	(COL)
	Niki Lauda	(AUT)		Alan Jones	(AUS)	6	Tony Brooks	(GBR)
24	Juan Manuel Fangio	(ARG)		Carlos Reutemann	(ARG)		Jacques Laffite	(FRA)
23	Nelson Piquet	(BRA)	11	Rubens Barrichello	(BRA)		Riccardo Patrese	(ITA)
	Nico Rosberg	(GER)		Felipe Massa	(BRA)		Jochen Rindt	(AUT)
22	Damon Hill	(GBR)		Jacques Villeneuve	(CDN)		Ralf Schumacher	(GER)
21	Kimi Raikkonen	(FIN)	10	Gerhard Berger	(AUT)		John Surtees	(GBR)
20	Mika Hakkinen	(FIN)		Valtteri Bottas	(FIN)		Gilles Villeneuve	(CDN)

CONSTRUCTORS

237	Ferrari	17	BRM	4	Jordan	
182	McLaren	16	Cooper	3	March	
124	Mercedes GP (including Honda Racing, Brawn GP)	15	Renault		Wolf	
114	Williams	10	Alfa Romeo	2	AlphaTauri (including Toro Rosso)	
79	Lotus	9	Ligier		Honda	
75	Red Bull (including Stewart)		Maserati	1	BMW Sauber	
49	Alpine (including Benetton, Renault II, Lotus II & Renault III)		Matra		Eagle	
			Mercedes		Hesketh	
35	Brabham		Vanwall		Penske	
23	Tyrrell	5	Aston Martin (including Jordan & Racing Point)		Porsche	
					Shadow	

The recently retired Kimi Raikkonen in action for Ferrari at the Brazilian Grand Prix, in his World Championship-winning season in 2007.

DRIVERS

13	Michael Schumacher	2004		Michael Schumacher	2000		Jacques Villeneuve	1997
	Sebastian Vettel	2013		Michael Schumacher	2001	6	Mario Andretti	1978
11	Lewis Hamilton	2014	8	Mika Hakkinen	1998		Alberto Ascari	1952
	Lewis Hamilton	2018		Lewis Hamilton	2021		Jim Clark	1965
	Lewis Hamilton	2019		Damon Hill	1996		Juan Manuel Fangio	1954
	Lewis Hamilton	2020		Michael Schumacher	1994		Damon Hill	1994
	Michael Schumacher	2002		Ayrton Senna	1988		James Hunt	1976
	Sebastian Vettel	2011	7	Fernando Alonso	2005		Nigel Mansell	1987
10	Lewis Hamilton	2015		Fernando Alonso	2006		Kimi Raikkonen	2007
	Lewis Hamilton	2016		Jim Clark	1963		Nico Rosberg	2015
	Max Verstappen	2021		Alain Prost	1984		Michael Schumacher	1998
9	Lewis Hamilton	2017		Alain Prost	1988		Michael Schumacher	2003
	Nigel Mansell	1992		Alain Prost	1993		Michael Schumacher	2006
	Nico Rosberg	2016		Kimi Raikkonen	2005		Ayrton Senna	1989
	Michael Schumacher	1995		Ayrton Senna	1991		Ayrton Senna	1990

CONSTRUCTORS

19	Mercedes GP	2016		McLaren	2005		McLaren	1991
16	Mercedes GP	2014		McLaren	1989		McLaren	2007
	Mercedes GP	2015		Williams	1992		Renault	2005
15	Ferrari	2002		Williams	1993		Renault	2006
	Ferrari	2004	9	Ferrari	2001		Williams	1997
	McLaren	1988		Ferrari	2006	7	Ferrari	1952
	Mercedes GP	2019		Ferrari	2007		Ferrari	1953
13	Mercedes GP	2020		McLaren	1998		Ferrari	2008
12	McLaren	1984		Mercedes GP	2021		Lotus	1963
	Mercedes GP	2017		Red Bull	2010		Lotus	1973
	Red Bull	2011		Williams	1986		McLaren	1999
	Williams	1996		Williams	1987		McLaren	2000
11	Benetton	1995	8	Benetton	1994		McLaren	2012
	Red Bull	2021		Brawn GP	2009		Red Bull	2012
	Mercedes GP	2018		Ferrari	2003		Tyrrell	1971
10	Ferrari	2000		Lotus	1978		Williams	1991 & 1994

MOST POLE POSITIONS

DRIVERS

103	Lewis Hamilton	(GBR)	22	Fernando Alonso	(SPA)		Ronnie Peterson	(SWE)
68	Michael Schumacher	(GER)	20	Valtteri Bottas	(FIN)	13	Jack Brabham	(AUS)
65	Ayrton Senna	(BRA)		Damon Hill	(GBR)		Graham Hill	(GBR)
57	Sebastian Vettel	(GER)	18	Mario Andretti	(USA)		Jacky Ickx	(BEL)
33	Jim Clark	(GBR)		Rene Arnoux	(FRA)		Juan Pablo Montoya	(COL)
	Alain Prost	(FRA)		Kimi Raikkonen	(FIN)		Jacques Villeneuve	(CDN)
32	Nigel Mansell	(GBR)	17	Jackie Stewart	(GBR)	12	Gerhard Berger	(AUT)
30	Nico Rosberg	(GER)	16	Felipe Massa	(BRA)		David Coulthard	(GBR)
29	Juan Manuel Fangio	(ARG)		Stirling Moss	(GBR)	11	Max Verstappen	(NED)
26	Mika Hakkinen	(FIN)	14	Alberto Ascari	(ITA)		Mark Webber	(AUS)
24	Niki Lauda	(AUT)		Rubens Barrichello	(BRA)	10	Jochen Rindt	(AUT)
	Nelson Piquet	(BRA)		James Hunt	(GBR)			

CONSTRUCTORS

230	Ferrari	14	Tyrrell		Matra	
156	McLaren	12	Alfa Romeo	3	Shadow	
135	Mercedes GP (including Brawn GP, Honda Racing, BAR)	11	BRM		Toyota	
			Cooper	2	Lancia	
128	Williams	10	Maserati	1	BMW Sauber	
107	Lotus	9	Ligier		Scuderia Toro Rosso	
72	Red Bull Racing	8	Mercedes			
39	Brabham	7	Vanwall			
34	Alpine (including Toleman, Benetton, Renault II, Lotus II & Renault III)	5	March			
31	Renault	4	Aston Martin (including Jordan, Force India & Racing Point)			

Above: Jim Clark was champion for Lotus twice in the 1960s.

Opposite: Michael Schumacher, shown in 2004, won five titles in a row for Ferrari.

Lewis Hamilton celebrates landing his the first of his seven F1 titles in 2008 after a thrilling finale in Brazil.

MOST FASTEST LAPS

DRIVERS

76	Michael Schumacher	(GER)	21	Gerhard Berger	(AUT)	15	Clay Regazzoni	(SWI)
59	Lewis Hamilton	(GBR)	20	Nico Rosberg	(GER)		Jackie Stewart	(GBR)
46	Kimi Raikkonen	(FIN)	19	Valtteri Bottas	(FIN)	14	Jacky Ickx	(BEL)
41	Alain Prost	(FRA)		Damon Hill	(GBR)	13	Alberto Ascari	(ITA)
38	Sebastian Vettel	(GER)		Stirling Moss	(GBR)		Alan Jones	(AUS)
30	Nigel Mansell	(GBR)		Ayrton Senna	(BRA)		Riccardo Patrese	(ITA)
28	Jim Clark	(GBR)		Mark Webber	(AUS)	12	Rene Arnoux	(FRA)
25	Mika Hakkinen	(FIN)	18	David Coulthard	(GBR)		Jack Brabham	(AUS)
24	Niki Lauda	(AUT)	17	Rubens Barrichello	(BRA)		Juan Pablo Montoya	(COL)
23	Juan Manuel Fangio	(ARG)	16	Felipe Massa	(BRA)	11	John Surtees	(GBR)
	Nelson Piquet	(BRA)		Daniel Ricciardo	(AUS)	10	Mario Andretti	(USA)
22	Fernando Alonso	(SPA)		Max Verstappen	(NED)		Graham Hill	(GBR)

CONSTRUCTORS

253	Ferrari	56	Alpine (including Toleman, Benetton, Renault, Lotus II & Renault III)	14	Alfa Romeo
159	McLaren			13	Cooper
133	Williams	40	Brabham	12	Matra
94	Mercedes GP (including BAR, Honda Racing & Brawn GP)	22	Tyrrell	11	Prost (including Ligier)
		18	Renault	9	Mercedes
76	Red Bull Racing	15	BRM	7	March
71	Lotus		Maserati	6	Vanwall

MOST POINTS (this figure is gross tally, ie. including scores that were later dropped)

DRIVERS

Points	Driver		Points	Driver		Points	Driver	
4,165.5	Lewis Hamilton	(GBR)	614	Ayrton Senna	(BRA)	309	Pierre Gasly	(FRA)
3,061	Sebastian Vettel	(GER)	560	Charles Leclerc	(MON)	307	Juan Pablo Montoya	(COL)
1,980	Fernando Alonso	(SPA)	536.5	Carlos Sainz Jr	(SPA)	306	Lando Norris	(GBR)
1,873	Kimi Raikkonen	(FIN)	535	David Coulthard	(GBR)	289	Graham Hill	(GBR)
1,738	Valtteri Bottas	(FIN)	521	Nico Hulkenberg	(GER)	281	Emerson Fittipaldi	(BRA)
1,594.5	Nico Rosberg	(GER)	485.5	Nelson Piquet	(BRA)		Riccardo Patrese	(ITA)
1,566	Michael Schumacher	(GER)	482	Nigel Mansell	(GBR)	277.5	Juan Manuel Fangio	(ARG)
1,557.5	Max Verstappen	(NED)	420.5	Niki Lauda	(AUT)	275	Giancarlo Fisichella	(ITA)
1,274	Daniel Ricciardo	(AUS)	420	Mika Hakkinen	(FIN)	274	Jim Clark	(GBR)
1,235	Jenson Button	(GBR)	391	Romain Grosjean	(FRA)		Robert Kubica	(POL)
1,167	Felipe Massa	(BRA)	385	Gerhard Berger	(AUT)	272	Esteban Ocon	(FRA)
1,047.5	Mark Webber	(AUS)	360	Damon Hill	(GBR)	261	Jack Brabham	(AUS)
896	Sergio Perez	(MEX)		Jackie Stewart	(GBR)	259	Nick Heidfeld	(GER)
798.5	Alain Prost	(FRA)	329	Ralf Schumacher	(GER)	255	Jody Scheckter	(RSA)
658	Rubens Barrichello	(BRA)	310	Carlos Reutemann	(ARG)	248	Denny Hulme	(NZL)

CONSTRUCTORS

Points	Constructor	Points	Constructor	Points	Constructor
8,694	Ferrari	1,636	Aston Martin (including Jordan, Midland, Spyker, Force India & Racing Point)	424	Prost (including Ligier)
6,800.5	Mercedes GP (including BAR, Honda Racing, Brawn GP)			333	Cooper
				312	Renault
5,807.5	McLaren	1,514	Lotus	278.5	Toyota
5,717	Red Bull Racing (including Stewart, Jaguar Racing)	928	Alfa Romeo II (including Sauber)	200	Haas
		854	Brabham	171.5	March
3,590	Williams	785	AlphaTauri (including Minardi & Toro Rosso)	167	Arrows
3159.5	Alpine (including Toleman, Benetton, Renault II, Lotus II & Renault III)			155	Matra
		617	Tyrrell		
		439	BRM		

CHAMPIONSHIP TITLES

DRIVERS

Titles	Driver			Driver	
7	Lewis Hamilton	(GBR)		Jenson Button	(GBR)
	Michael Schumacher	(GER)		Giuseppe Farina	(ITA)
5	Juan Manuel Fangio	(ARG)		Mike Hawthorn	(GBR)
4	Alain Prost	(FRA)		Damon Hill	(GBR)
	Sebastian Vettel	(GER)		Phil Hill	(USA)
3	Jack Brabham	(AUS)		Denis Hulme	(NZL)
	Niki Lauda	(AUT)		James Hunt	(GBR)
	Nelson Piquet	(BRA)		Alan Jones	(AUS)
	Ayrton Senna	(BRA)		Nigel Mansell	(GBR)
	Jackie Stewart	(GBR)		Kimi Raikkonen	(FIN)
2	Fernando Alonso	(SPA)		Jochen Rindt	(AUT)
	Alberto Ascari	(ITA)		Keke Rosberg	(FIN)
	Jim Clark	(GBR)		Nico Rosberg	(GER)
	Emerson Fittipaldi	(BRA)		Jody Scheckter	(RSA)
	Mika Hakkinen	(FIN)		John Surtees	(GBR)
	Graham Hill	(GBR)		Max Verstappen	(NED)
1	Mario Andretti	(USA)		Jacques Villeneuve	(CDN)

CONSTRUCTORS

Titles	Constructor	Titles	Constructor
16	Ferrari		Renault
9	Williams	1	Benetton
8	McLaren		Brawn
	Mercedes GP		BRM
7	Lotus		Matra
4	Red Bull		Tyrrell
2	Brabham		Vanwall
	Cooper		

NB. The Lotus stats listed are based on the team that ran from 1958-1994, whereas those listed as Lotus II are for the team that ran from 2012-2015. Those marked as Alpine are for the team based at Enstone that started as Toleman in 1981, became Benetton in 1986, then Renault II in 2002, Lotus II in 2012 and Renault III in 2016. The Renault listings are for the team that ran from 1977 to 1985, the stats for Red Bull Racing include those of the Stewart Grand Prix and Jaguar Racing teams from which it evolved, and those for Mercedes GP for the team that started as BAR in 1999, ran as Honda GP from 2006 and then as Brawn GP in 2009. Aston Martin II's stats include those of Jordan, Midland, Spyker, Force India and Racing Point, while Scuderia AlphaTauri's include those of its forerunner Minardi and Scuderia Toro Rosso. Alfa Romeo II's figures are for the team created in 2019 from Sauber, with no connection to the two iterations of the works team that ran from 1950-1951 and 1979-1985.

⟫ 2022 SEASON FILL-IN CHART

DRIVER	TEAM	Round 1 – 20 March BAHRAIN GP	Round 2 – 27 March SAUDI ARABIAN GP	Round 3 – 10 April AUSTRALIAN GP	Round 4 – 24 April EMILIA ROMAGNA GP	Round 5 – 8 May MIAMI GP	Round 6 – 22 May SPANISH GP	Round 7 – 29 May MONACO GP	Round 8 – 12 June AZERBAIJAN GP	Round 9 – 19 June CANADIAN GP	Round 10 – 3 July BRITISH GP
LEWIS HAMILTON	Mercedes										
GEORGE RUSSELL	Mercedes										
MAX VERSTAPPEN	Red Bull										
SERGIO PEREZ	Red Bull										
CARLOS SAINZ JR	Ferrari										
CHARLES LECLERC	Ferrari										
LANDO NORRIS	McLaren										
DANIEL RICCIARDO	McLaren										
FERNANDO ALONSO	Alpine										
ESTEBAN OCON	Alpine										
PIERRE GASLY	AlphaTauri										
YUKI TSUNODA	AlphaTauri										
SEBASTIAN VETTEL	Aston Martin										
LANCE STROLL	Aston Martin										
NICHOLAS LATIFI	Williams										
ALEX ALBON	Williams										
VALTTERI BOTTAS	Alfa Romeo										
GUANYOU ZHOU	Alfa Romeo										
MICK SCHUMACHER	Haas F1										
NIKITA MAZEPIN	Haas F1										

SCORING SYSTEM: 25, 18, 15, 12, 10, 8, 6, 4, 2, 1 POINTS FOR THE FIRST 10 FINISHERS IN EACH GRAND PRIX
& 1 POINT FOR FASTEST LAP SET BY A DRIVER FINISHING IN TOP 10

Round 11 – 10 July AUSTRIAN GP	Round 12 – 24 July FRENCH GP	Round 13 – 31 July HUNGARIAN GP	Round 14 – 28 Aug BELGIAN GP	Round 15 - 4 Sept DUTCH GP	Round 16 – 11 Sept ITALIAN GP	Round 17 – 25 Sept RUSSIAN GP	Round 18 – 2 Oct SINGAPORE GP	Round 19 – 9 Oct JAPANESE GP	Round 20 – 23 Oct UNITED STATES GP	Round 21 – 30 Oct MEXICAN GP	Round 22 – 13 Nov SAO PAOLO GP	Round 23 – 20 Nov ABU DHABI GP	POINTS TOTAL

The publishers would like to thank the following sources for their kind permission to reproduce the pictures in this book.

Max Verstappen's pulling power for the orange army was huge. This is the greeting his fans put on when he won in Austria.

ALAMY STOCK PHOTO: /XPB/PA Images: 114

GRAPHIC NEWS: 11T, 12R, 13R, 15T, 16R, 17R, 21T, 22R, 23R, 25T, 26R, 27R, 31T, 32R, 33R, 35T, 36R, 37R, 41T, 42R, 43R, 45T, 46R, 47R, 51T, 52R, 53R, 55T, 56R, 57R, 68, 69, 70, 71, 72, 73, 76, 77, 78, 79, 80, 81, 82, 83, 84, 85, 86, 87, 88, 89, 90, 91, 92

MOTORSPORT IMAGES: 25B, 42L, 43L, 45B, 51B, 63T, 121, 122, 123, 124; /Jerry Andre: 74-75, 107, 109; /Sam Bloxham: 103; / Charles Coates: 23L, 30, 32L, 33L, 34, 41B, 59C, 59B, 61TR, 98; / Ercole Colombo: 21B, 61C; /Glenn Dunbar: 63BL, 102, 104, 108; /Steve Etherington: 11B, 12L, 52L, 66-67, 110; /FIA: 16L, 17L, 63C, 105; /Andrew Ferraro: 15B, 35B; /Drew Gibson: 20; /Manuel Goria: 55B; /Andy Hone: 10, 18-19, 37L, 53L, 59TL, 94-95, 100, 101, 112, 128; /JEP: 8-9; /Zak Mauger: 47L, 54, 56L, 93, 115; / Rainer Schlegelmilch: 31B; /Mark Sutton: 2, 14, 24, 38-39, 40, 44, 50, 57L, 59TR, 61TL, 63BR, 64-65, 96, 106, 111, 113, 116; / Steven Tee: 5, 6-7, 13L, 22L, 26L, 27L, 28-29, 36L, 48-49, 97, 99, 117; /Alexander Trienitz: 46L

SHUTTERSTOCK: /YES Market Media: 61B

Every effort has been made to acknowledge correctly and contact the source and/or copyright holder of each picture. Any unintentional errors or omissions will be corrected in future editions of this book.